The Limits of Hope

The Limits of

Hope

An Adoptive
Mother's Story

Ann Kimble Loux

University Press of Virginia

Charlottesville and London

The University Press of Virginia
© 1997 by the Rector and Visitors of the University of Virginia
All rights reserved
Printed in the United States of America

First published 1997

The paper used in this publication meets the minimum requirements of the
American National Standard for Information Sciences—Permanence of Paper for
Printed Library Materials, ANSI Z39.48-1984.

Library of Congress Cataloging-in-Publication Data
Loux, Ann Kimble.
The limits of hope: an adoptive mother's story / Ann Kimble Loux.
p. cm.
ISBN 0-8139-1710-7 (cloth : alk. paper)
1. Older child adoption—United States. 2. Special needs adoption—
United States. 3. Loux, Ann Kimble. 4. Adoptive parents—
United States—Biography. I. Title.
HV875.55.L68 1997
362.73'4'092—dc21
[B]   96-46372
CIP

To Sandy and Julie
with respect

Contents

Foreword

When it is legally determined that parental abuse or neglect is severe enough to impair a child's development, the court has the power to sever all parental custody rights. When this authority is exercised, it is assumed that the best interests of the child are always served by placement in the "right" adoptive family. The recognition of a child's need for a permanent home undergirds all current adoptive practices regarding children at risk: hence national advertising campaigns telling us that "children grow best in families" and that "every child deserves a family."

Taken as a group, child welfare specialists evince the unshakable belief that unconditionally loving environments provided by "good" adoptive families will eventually neutralize the legacy of past abuse and neglect. This "love conquers all" hypothesis has as its corollary the notion that the abundant nurturance found in well-functioning families may also alter biological templates for temperament, personality development, and learning styles. These assumptions suggest that children are endlessly resilient and will escape the effects of early trauma and biological histories if raised in the "right" home. This is the outlook proffered to parents who decide to adopt high-risk children. But does this hopeful perspective square with the realities experienced by substantial numbers of adoptive parents attempting to raise their high-risk children?

Ann Loux's thoughtful and caring account of the struggle to raise two psychologically damaged and biologically constrained daughters will help shatter the myth that adoptive children, regardless of their histories, invariably thrive in genuinely loving families. The truth of her experience, similar to that of thousands of other adoptive parents, is something with which policymakers will eventually have to come to grips—financial implications notwithstanding. In the not too distant future, we will have to recognize that children can be and are permanently damaged by toxic parenting. The gradual emergence of a scientific database will force us to acknowledge that if these children are to be adopted, adoptive families will have to be protected. This protection will be found only in ready access to specialized educational programming, expert clinical services, and an array of social service resources throughout the adoptive child's passage into adulthood. This will be more expensive than persuading parents to adopt special-needs children and then leaving them to fend for themselves, or responding to their appeals for professional help by pointing out their inadequacies as parents.

Dr. Hugh M. Leichtman
Director, Wediko Children's Services

Preface

Why have I written a book that gave pain in the process, a book that will deliver shock and dismay to readers, a book many who love me advised, "Write it if you must; just don't ever publish it."

I undertook this book in the fervent hope that most of its readers would respond as one of my friends has, "What I really appreciated was the release these stories brought me. As a teacher of desperate adolescents, I always wonder if I should bring them home with me, if I should choose one and dedicate my life to improving her life. I'm often ashamed of my anger and my frustration. Your stories made me feel as if I am doing what I can."

This book is for those who have extended a helping hand to children, but who have been exhausted and frustrated and angered by their lack of success. This book is for parents and teachers, psychologists and social workers who feel that they struggle in isolation.

This book is for those who have discovered that many of the consolations in life will not arise from what we accomplish or from what our children accomplish, but from coming gradually to understand what we cannot change. This book insists that we will somehow understand our children when, for example, they become drug addicts and prostitutes—when they do everything we would have them not do, but refuse to stop searching for acceptance. This book is for those whose children and students and clients have taught them ways of living outside of their experience, who have persuaded them of an inevitability behind many paths they never expected to understand.

This book will frustrate those who believe that love and a sound environment can change everything, that they themselves and their children are always subject to the powers of human will. This book will also challenge those who believe that freedom to choose is the primary condition of human life.

Most of all this book is for parents, for mothers—for biological mothers, for adoptive mothers, especially for adoptive mothers of abused and neglected children—for all mothers who have felt uncertainty and guilt after their best efforts. The frustrations encountered in this narrative are familiar to all parents, to a greater or lesser degree. As parents we struggle on, never certain of the appropriate goals for a particular child or of our progress. I hope that as they turn the pages, the adoptive parents of abused and neglected children will decide:

Yes, I made a thousand mistakes. Of course I might have done two thousand things differently. But I was never traveling alone. And I did what I could, given all the circumstances.

In our sorrows, as a friend told me, we are fortunate. Although Margey and Dawn may have been my sorrows, they taught me to include whole other worlds in my judgments. They brought the gift of a complicated life.

To protect privacy, many names—of both places and people—have been changed. The letters quoted and referred to here are from a collection I've kept since the children first began to write. The source for Margey's monologues, presented as direct quotations, is fifty-plus pages of single-spaced monologues that I took down immediately after those conversations took place. A counselor friend recommended writing the material down as a method to help me gain distance and perspective on all my daughter was trying to tell me. During the period when I kept that journal, I was also afraid that Margey would not live very long; I wanted something of her to keep.

Acknowledgments

To Nancy Traer who traveled the same path.

To Dorothy Manier who would have helped more had she lived longer.

To Laurie, Joe, Chris, Sandy, Julie, and Mike, who lived the story.

To my family, especially my mother, Doris Brown Kimble, my sister, Melanie Kimble Ray, and my mother-in-law, Magdaline Klug Loux, all of whom always understood.

To Julie Jensen for boosting me into writing.

To Sabrina Tingley for her help with Julie.

To my brother Ray, who saw so many sides.

To Becky Stoddart, who inspired confidence.

To Richard Holway for wisdom.

To Dennis Marshall and Deborah A. Oliver for eagle eyes and endless patience.

To Gail Mandell, Jeanne Rodes, Penny Jameson, and Linnea Vacca for making me get it right.

To Cara Sandberg, who knew both sides.

To Sonia Gernes, Nancy Hansen, Janet McCann, Brian Mize, Margaret Whitt, and Julie White for writing back.

To Carol Bradley, Sue Farrer, Gabrielle Robinson, and Elaine Hemley, who edited and applauded.

To William O'Rourke for many kindnesses.

To Courtney Jamieson, Kiley Moran, Laura Steibl O'Brien, Michael Manier, and Tricia O'Connor, who cheered.

The Limits of Hope

Decision

Mark and I decided to have children right after we got married in 1966. The Vietnam War was escalating and Mark needed a draft deferment. We wanted children anyway, so we decided not to wait. Kate and Sam were born eighteen months apart in 1967 and 1968 and Mark got his deferment. Jack followed in 1970. None of the three babies ever gave us serious worry. For the most part they cried only when they were hungry or sleepy, and they were high-spirited, full of curiosity, and extremely active. Once while all three were exploring her office, I asked the pediatrician if it was normal for children to be so active. Dr. Hanley looked at me steadily and asked how I would be feeling if I were asking the opposite question.

One evening when I was visibly pregnant with Jack, some friends from Carlton College came for dinner. Dan probably presumed we were follow-the-pope Catholics, given the pace of our production line. At any rate, he asked us straight out how many children we intended to have, suggesting that we were already well into one child more than our share, particularly if we intended to take seriously the enlightened concept of zero population growth. "If you want children so bad, you should think about adopting," he said.

His words hit hard, perhaps because we had never thought about one's fair share of children. Folks raised in heavily Roman Catholic communities like Saint Paul, Minnesota, didn't tend to come upon such values by themselves. After we'd gotten over being annoyed with Dan's preaching, Mark and I began to consider his ideas seriously. Both because of Dan's persuasiveness on global population control and because I was worn out after three births in quick succession, we decided not to have the anticipated fourth child right away.

As young adults in the late 1960s, we took seriously the Kennedy maxim: Ask what you can do for your country. Neither of us had served in the Peace Corps or the Papal Volunteers. We had, however, been lucky in our experience as parents, so we figured we could take in a child who needed a home. We weren't even fussy about getting an infant, because we'd had a massive dose of that phase of child rearing.

Kate was seven, Sam five and a half, and Jack four, old enough for us to ask their opinions about the adoption of a sister. The boys thought a brother might be preferable, but they could see the beauty of two and two. Kate was going to get her fondest wish. She'd always felt a bit excluded from the natural camaraderie between Sam and Jack.

As Mark and I were both ardent supporters of the civil rights movement, our first plan was to adopt a cross-racial child. But when I mentioned the idea to my father, born and bred in Mississippi, he said straight out, "Well if you do, just don't bring it down here." At first I refused to be threatened, but the more I considered it, the sillier it seemed to leave one family behind to get another.

At that time, in 1974, many U.S. families were adopting Korean and Vietnamese babies; Mark and I considered that next. But as it turned out, my father was prejudiced against Asians as well as African Americans. He wanted to know why we had to go to the far ends of the earth, when there were all kinds of children who needed homes in our own backyards. He had a point, and we were in basic agreement with him about the need to take care of one's own house before taking up housekeeping elsewhere. Mark and I thought and thought, talked and talked. Eventually, we decided that I should go down to Catholic Social Services and talk with a woman who had arranged many infant adoptions in the Twin Cities—Maureen O'Brien.

Maureen invited us to visit her office to look through several books with pictures of children from all over the country who were available for adoption. The faces of all these children looked out at us, and the short summaries of their lives beside the pictures touched Mark and me deeply.

At Maureen O'Brien's suggestion, Mark and I visited a family who had adopted older children, a brother and sister, four years earlier; the children were then eight and nine. The Crosbys had always wanted more children, and when their three biological children were teenagers, they'd decided to adopt a four- and a five-year-old.

We asked about their experience. They said the adopted children had a lot of problems. The little boy was hard to discipline; the little girl was removed from everything. Both children were frequently involved in hassles at school; neither of them seemed to be able to make friends; they didn't spend much time with one another. Both Claire's and Tom's voices were low; they showed virtually no affect when they answered our questions. They never volunteered a response if they weren't asked a direct question. Finally, Mark asked the Crosbys if they would do it again. They'd thought we might ask that question, they said, but they didn't really want to discuss it. It had been really hard—nothing like they'd expected.

Mark and I felt a little sorry for the Crosbys; they did not seem happy. We thought they were naturally introverted and somewhat un-communicative. We even wondered if they were the best parents to adopt. We certainly did not identify with them.

When I spoke with the pediatri-cian, Dr. Hanley, about what we were planning, her face stood still. She mused about how difficult this adoption was likely to be because we would be dealing with great differences in intelligence between the adopted children and our biological children. A considerable problem, she thought. I assured her that both Mark and I came from families with a wide range of intelligences. Dr. Hanley said she didn't know about that, she had seen people struggle with the difficulties of bring-ing together children who were so different. She shook her head. We had no idea what we were in for, she said.

No problem, not to worry, I told her. Again I felt sorry for all the families Dr. Hanley was describing, but did not feel any kinship with them. Mark had spent his summers working in a settlement-house summer camp; I was the oldest of eight, six of whom were wild and woolly brothers. It didn't occur to us that there was such a thing as a child we'd have difficulty accepting. Eventually we decided to try adoption of an older child, because they were more difficult to place.

Maureen checked out all the particulars of the family: Did we make enough money? Was the house large enough? Mark's salary as a young college professor was adequate, she decided, but she had questions about my continuing to work part-time, though she could see how the money might be helpful. I told Maureen that I wanted to continue working: I was a good teacher and enjoyed the outside stimulation, and of course the money was important for anything beyond a carefully budgeted lifestyle. Maureen acquiesced to my teaching part-time. She found the house pleasant and welcoming—a children's kingdom. There was enough room, three bedrooms upstairs and a finished base-ment downstairs, and—perhaps the biggest plus for children—the corner lot was large and filled with tall oak trees, a swing set, sandbox, ropeswing, and a magical "trolley" that attracted the neighborhood children.

Mark and I told Maureen O'Brien we were ready to adopt, to look for a little girl. A week later, Maureen wanted to know if we could take two little girls instead of one. We thought it over, talked about it with Kate, Sam, and Jack, and decided, why not? All three children were delighted with the idea of two new siblings; another addition made their party grander.

The sisters were available for adoption immediately. They had been taken away from their mother because of abuse and neglect, and some months earlier had been placed in a foster home. Legally everything was clear and free, which was frequently not the case in older adoptions. Parents sometimes cling to their rights for months, even years. Maureen showed us pictures and gave a few background details. The mother was Polish and the father Italian; she was blonde and fair, he darker. Both parents seemed to be of average intelligence. The mother had tried hard to keep her daughters after she began having trouble with the Welfare Department. For example, she took them to a speech therapist as she was required to do, because both were way behind in their speech development. She had also attempted to keep their doctors' appointments. But when she failed repeatedly to have them immunized properly and could not maintain suitable housing, the Welfare Department decided to terminate her rights. She appeared in court and begged that the children be allowed to return to her. She loved them, of course. But for various reasons (both she and the man drank a good deal) she wasn't able to give them the care they needed.

Maureen arranged for Mark and me to meet the girls at Como Park Zoo one Sunday afternoon. At the gate, Maureen introduced a little blonde girl named Margey, who was almost four, and another even smaller child, a dark-haired girl named Dawn, who wasn't quite three. Then Maureen left so we could get to know one another.

Margey's hair curled in the back. She had long, thin legs and she moved very fast, jerking from one point to another. Her hair was thick and dense like mine and Sam's, and her eyes were as blue as Mark's mother's and Jack's. She was shy, delicate, thin—she and Jack looked equally scrawny. She cocked her head and looked at us sideways as if to size us up. Dawn's hair was short and dark, even a little reddish, like Mark's, and cut in a pixie. Actually she looked like an elf—round face, wide-set, brown eyes that angled up on the outer edges, a decided pug nose, wide forehead, and pointed chin. She grinned openly and told everyone her name was Da-Da. Everything about her made us laugh. Dawn had on red knit shorts and a yellow- and red-striped top; Margey wore the parallel outfit in blue and yellow from K-Mart.

Margey was painfully shy; Dawn was equally outgoing. Margey held back and wouldn't take either of our hands. She kept looking around her, fearfully, her eyes squinting as if she might cry any minute. Dawn smiled broadly, hugged both of us and held our hands. She went up to everyone we passed and said, "Hi. I Da-Da. I like you," and tried to take their hands. The girls were also completely different in the way they fed the animals. Margey reluctantly followed me to the fence and held out grass pellets for the deer. When the deer came up to her, she got scared, pulled her hand away, and looked as if she would cry. Dawn put her hand right through the fence and let the deer nibble from her palm. She laughed out loud when their tongues tickled her skin, and she gnawed at the pellets herself.

On the way to the petting barn, we passed a popcorn-and-soda stand. Dawn started to cry. Mark asked what was wrong. She pointed at the food. Mark and I told the girls we'd go through the barn and then come back for treats. Dawn kept crying, so Mark put her on his shoulders and carried her through the barn. When we came out, we got pop and popcorn and ate at a picnic table. Both girls were happy then. They jumped up and down on the bench and squealed.

After Maureen had returned the girls to their foster family, she called and asked how everything had gone. I said just fine, they were both very sweet and cute. She asked when we'd like to see them again. I said as soon as possible, and we settled on the next weekend for a swim in Lake Harriet and supper afterwards.

Maureen told us that the foster mother thought it was unfair for people who already had three children of their own to be allowed to adopt two more. She believed families without children should be given preference over us. As we would never have dreamed of taking precedence over childless couples, Mark and I felt a bit indignant at her opinion.

The following weekend, Maureen dropped the girls off all dressed up in their bathing suits. They were tiny and adorable and vulnerable looking. When we got down to the beach, both were excited. Margey jumped up and down, crying "Eeh, eeh, eeh, eeh." There was probably more water than they had ever seen up close. They both stayed on the beach and watched the water from a safe distance. Dawn was a little unsteady on the shifting ground. She couldn't seem to get her footing and remained seated, cautious. Margey filled up a bucket with sand and poured it out, over and over. Kate, Sam, and Jack were delighted with everything the girls did. They couldn't seem to take their eyes off Margey and Dawn, as if they were fascinating new toys. The older three kept trying to get the girls to swim, and when they wouldn't, Kate, Sam, and Jack played in the sand. The three of them finally headed into the water, but one at a time they kept returning to check on Margey and Dawn, bringing them toys and telling them about the little fish that nibbled their toes out in the water. There was no way Margey and Dawn would consider a swim, though they did wade in to check out the fish. When a fish nipped Margey's toe, she began to scream and shake. She cried for several minutes. Poor Jack, who had urged her to come see the fish, felt terrible.

When it was time to go home, the girls whined until we mentioned supper. Kate, Sam, and Jack showed them the house, all their toys, and haunts in the yard. The girls paid little attention; they seemed to want to explore everything on their own. Margey went all over the house, upstairs and downstairs, in and out of every room. Then she got under the dining-room table and cried again, "Eeh, eeh, eeh, eeh." Dawn stayed in the kitchen the whole time, unable to take her eyes off the food. As soon as Margey and Dawn saw Maureen, they told her they wanted to stay with us. We all were touched and proud.

Kate, Sam, and Jack had a thousand questions: When were they coming back? What about their parents? Would their Mom and Dad ever come back to get them? What were their last names, anyhow? Mark and I didn't know their last names; we had assumed we weren't supposed to ask.

The next weekend, Margey and Dawn came to live with us for good, three weeks after we had first met. Maureen brought them in her car. They each had a dozen or so dresses on hangers: their foster father was a minister and no doubt they went to church a lot. Each girl had a paper bag filled with the rest of her clothes and a stuffed animal. Kate, Sam, and Jack put the girls' clothes away in less than two minutes. Kate was especially happy with the new little sisters, but she was also taken aback. "Where is the rest of their stuff? Margey and Dawn don't have much, do they, Mom?" They certainly didn't. Kate went off to pick out some of her toys for them.

Maureen had brought scrapbooks—records their foster mother had kept for Margey and Dawn. All five children paged through those scrapbooks again and again, looking at the pictures and cards. They showed us a valentine signed *Grandma*. "Are Margey and Dawn going to call their grandmother?" Jack wanted to know. "She's probably wondering where they are by now." Kate worried too, "Margey and Dawn can invite her to come over on Monday, show her their new toys. She'll like the trolley. Is their granddaddy dead, do you think? Will he come too?"

They flipped to the next page, filled with three more red and pink valentines. "Look, it says these are from their Sunday school friends." The next page had three pictures taken at someone's home. The top two were of Margey, her blonde hair tousled, her pajamas stretched across her bony body, the background dark. The last picture was of Margey, another little girl, and Dawn all sitting on an orange couch. Margey looked excited, bright, the middle child sleepy, and Dawn soft. Her dark complexion and hair stood out next to the two fair girls to her left. "Are we going to leave these pictures in this notebook," Kate asked, "or should we put them in our picture book?"

"No," I said, "we're going to save these scrapbooks just like they are for Margey and Dawn when they grow up."

The children turned to the last page and found a white envelope marked, "Margey's first haircut." Sam opened it. Inside was a clump of blonde hair. Kate unraveled it until it stretched out about six inches. "Look at this. Look at all this hair, how long it is." Kate was amazed. According to the date written in red crayon, Margey was three and a half years old. Kate, Sam, and Jack fingered the dull blonde strand. Kate checked the color to make sure it was Margey's. "Look, it's exactly the same."

Sam wanted to know if I'd saved hair from their first haircuts. I had to admit I hadn't. "We'll have to save some of Dawn's hair the next time she gets it cut," Sam said. "I know it's not her first hair cut, but she'll want to see hers, too, someday."

We put the hair back in the envelope, and I wondered about the person who had saved it. Then we put Margey's and Dawn's scrapbooks away in a safe place.

Over the next few hours, Kate, Sam, and Jack followed the girls around, asking one question after another, trying to get them to play. Margey loved for them to tickle her and roughhouse with her. She rolled around on the couch and the beds, laughing and laughing. She had a high-pitched giggle and once she got going couldn't stop, even when she was almost hysterical. Her pleasure seemed frantic, hectic; she pouted and cried when the others stopped tickling her.

The older kids couldn't get all the answers they wanted. "What was your house like?" "Do you remember your mother?" "Did you like the people you lived with before us?" "What was your father like?" Margey and Dawn weren't able to talk much, and they had difficulty processing so many questions in a row. They didn't seem to remember anything about their mother except that she smoked, but they both had plenty of dramatic information about their foster family, especially the family's little girl, Shelly, who was about their age. Dawn said Shelly always took her toys away from her, then bit her whenever Shelly got mad. And Shelly never got punished.

"Did you ever get punished, Dawn?" the kids asked her.

"Spanked, I spanked. No, no, no wading pool. Sit, sit, sit in grass. Shelly, she—Shelly play in pool. Grass, grass in pool. I spanked. I spanked a lot. I spanked. Shelly no spank, no, no, Shelly no spank."

Did they like the wading pool, was the spanking hard, did Dawn ever bite Shelly back, did Shelly ever bite Margey? On and on came the questions. Both Margey and Dawn thought their foster family had been very nice, but they didn't want to go back. They wanted to live at our house now. Our house was going to be their house. They liked their new house. Yes, they would like a wading pool; they had loved the wading pool at Shelly's house.

Finally it was time for dinner, the first dinner of our new family. It was then that we began to encounter problems. Dawn never chewed; she swallowed her food as fast as she could put it into her mouth. They each gulped down five or six glasses of milk. If anyone asked them a question, they answered as briefly as possible and kept eating. Every time someone offered, they wanted more. They kept checking everyone else's plates until all were empty.

When the rest of us got up from the picnic table, Dawn stayed in her seat and started to whimper. I asked her what was the matter; she kept whimpering. Her little stomach was tight and distended; I worried that we had let her eat too much. She and Margey had eaten twice as much as the other children, and they were serious eaters. I asked her did her stomach hurt; she said no. I told her supper was over, we'd have a snack later, it was time to go and play. She stayed at the table. She refused to go play—refused all invitations and teasing.

Margey had left the table, but she didn't want to play with the other children. Instead she went to the sandbox. She tunneled in the sand for a few minutes and then began taking buckets of sand out of the box and pouring them in heaps around the yard. I asked her to stop. She looked over into the yard next door as if she were seeing into another country. I picked up the sand and put it back in the sandbox and asked her to play with the sand inside the box. As soon as I moved back to the patio, Margey got another bucket of sand, took it behind the garage, and dumped it out. I went to her and showed her how to scoop up the sand and put it back in the sandbox. Again, she looked past me as I talked to her, cocking her head to one side. When I sat back down, she dumped out another bucket. I asked her to put the sand back in the box. She turned her head as if she were listening, but she didn't seem to hear anything. She didn't move to put the sand back. It was like dealing with a post. Margey wasn't there.

No matter how I went about it, I simply could not reach Margey.

Bedtime came and the three girls settled down in their room, Kate and Margey on the twin beds, Dawn on a cot across the room. Kate was excited to begin the first night of their perpetual slumber party. After sending the boys back to their bedroom half a dozen times, and after a stretch of giggling, and three or four times of being told to quiet down during loud wrestling, all the children simmered down. About an hour later, Kate came downstairs saying she couldn't sleep because Margey was making so much noise rolling from side to side in her bed. She rolled from one edge of the bed to the other, shaking the walls and the floor. We tried several arrangements and eventually settled Kate on the cot way back in the clothes closet, the only place in the room where it was quiet enough for her to fall asleep. Dawn slept soundly through it all.

Life did *not* settle down during the next three weeks. I read and reread with increasing understanding the terse lines in the foster mother's notes: "They never want to stop eating, they don't know when they're full." "Dawn is very friendly, she'll go to anyone." After every meal, Dawn cried when it was time to get up from the table. Regardless of what she'd just eaten, she hung around in the kitchen and stared at any food—bananas, potatoes, cereal, milk—that was sitting out on the counters until I either gave it to her or put it away. She cried if I asked her to leave; she cried harder if I carried her out. When I made Dawn go out in the backyard to play, she sat on the seat of the sandbox facing the kitchen window. She would not move or play with the sand.

One of the few ways we could divert Dawn's attention was to swing her back and forth across the yard on the trolley that hung on a wire between two oak trees. Dawn couldn't reach the trapeze bar herself so she had to be lifted up and then pulled back and forth. She was content up there—we never understood how she could cling on so long—well after everyone else wearied of pulling her back and forth, back and forth. It took Margey a long time to muster the courage to try the trolley, but eventually she, too, came to love the ride. She was also sweet about treating Dawn.

We discovered that Dawn was hypersensitive to noise. She became upset during thunderstorms, when the teakettle whistled, when the oven timer rang, when the vacuum cleaner or Mark's electric shaver was running. She typically put her hands over her ears and cried, sometimes leaving the room and attempting to hide. I tried to soothe her by explaining thunder or letting her use the vacuum cleaner or touch Mark's razor. My efforts, however, did not make her less frightened the next time she heard the noise.

As time passed, I began to notice that a lot of food was disappearing from the kitchen and no one ever knew what had happened to it. Eventually I had to hide goodies, neither a pleasant nor an easy task, but necessary in view of the amounts missing. Mark and I often wondered if the girls got up in the middle of the night and searched through the refrigerator, as some deprived children do, but we don't think they ever did.

Another behavior troubled us. Kate often came into our room in the middle of the night, crying and asking why Margey rocked so. Margey groaned and moaned and even frowned and flinched in her sleep. She herself never woke up; nor did she waken Dawn. Actually, Margey seemed to be soundest asleep when she rocked most vigorously; it was virtually impossible to wake her enough to soothe her. We all wondered what was disturbing her.

One afternoon during the second week after Margey and Dawn arrived, a friend came to pay a call on our new family, bringing a gift, a book called *The Giving Tree*. The girls were playing out in the yard and she stopped to speak to them. Dawn began to whimper and told Vittoria that she was so full she had pains in her tummy. Her daddy had made her eat a whole bowl of food that she didn't like. Vittoria didn't tell me that story until years later, which was a kindness. She said she hadn't known quite what to think at the time.

Vittoria asked the children if they would like for her to read *The Giving Tree* aloud, a book especially for them because it was about generosity, like in our family. Margey and Dawn sat still for the first two or three pages, then they wandered out of the room. I sat with the other children and listened to Vittoria reading, in her Italian accent, about the tree that kept giving to the little boy who kept coming back for more. By the time the boy was an old man, he had taken everything, and the tree had nothing to give except her stump, where she welcomed him to rest his old bones. For some reason, I felt more and more repulsed as the tree gave away part after part of herself—her branches, her trunk, finally her stump. I was disgusted with my reaction and immediately felt guilty. What a violent reaction! Where had it come from? Mark and I felt like accomplices to a crime when he confessed that he had had exactly the same response to the story.

At the end of that second week, Maureen O'Brien came for dinner to see how we were getting along. I told her something was wrong, I didn't know what—things did not seem right. Margey and Dawn wouldn't obey, wouldn't listen, wouldn't meet my eyes, couldn't seem to understand when anyone asked them to do something. They didn't like to be read to, they giggled and tussled when I tried to read to the other children until I had to give up or send them out of the room. Nothing I gave them or did for them seemed to satisfy them; in just a few minutes they wanted something more. I was beginning not to want to try. Mark said that he often felt violently angry, but he wasn't sure why or what to do about it. And it seemed to him that those occasions were becoming more frequent and turbulent. He was also getting depressed because he could not decide what was wrong, could not figure out how to talk about our problems. Not being able to articulate his feelings, he said, was terribly difficult for someone so analytic and verbal.

Maureen dismissed our concerns. "You have a beautiful family. You're making such a good home for these girls. God is going to reward you. He will give you strength."

I told her I was very worried. It didn't feel like I was loving Margey and Dawn. I wanted to love them; I kept waiting and hoping, but love was not coming. If anything, I was beginning to feel the opposite of love—not wanting to look at them, not wanting to touch them, not wanting to be around them. I told Maureen I didn't want to kiss Margey and Dawn good-night when I went into the other children's rooms and that made me feel guilty.

"Of course these things take time," Maureen said. "You have to think how many years you have been with your other children. Remember, you held them in your arms right after they were born and nursed them when they were babies. Don't worry," she said, "time will give you as much love for these new children as you have for your biological children."

"I'm not sure," I told her, "not so sure."

I told her about Dawn's and my trip to the doctor's office. Dawn had gone up to a woman sitting across the room eating cherry Life Savers, climbed into the empty chair beside the woman, and patted her on the arm. The woman had smiled and patted Dawn's arm. Dawn told the woman she was such a nice lady. The woman told Dawn she was such a nice little girl. Then Dawn asked the woman, "You be my mommy?" The woman told Dawn she was mighty sweet, but she had her own little girl, and a little boy. Dawn stayed by the woman until the nurse called us into the examining room.

After the third week I felt even more despairing. Mark and I were completely in sympathy with one another, and we tried to talk things through, but it was not possible to describe the problem well enough to make anyone else understand, at least not Maureen, and she was the only one with whom we talked about the adoption. Something always felt vaguely amiss; the ease and naturalness of parenting had disappeared. Mark and I weren't sleeping well; we worried and kept trying for solutions way into the night. We had troubled dreams, that we were on treadmills and would never be released or were perpetually hauling boulders up mountains. We were obviously anxious about how things would turn out in the end. There seemed to be so little communication: not much between Margey and Dawn, and less and less between them, the other children, and us. Of course, the girls' verbal skills were minimal, and the family context was more than usually verbal, but something essential seemed to be missing. Margey made no eye contact at all; Dawn spread a grazing, full-toothed smile, but nothing sustained.

Always having to worry about food was a perpetual strain: how to get the girls to know what full meant; how to deal with their taking treats meant for everyone. For me, this new relationship with food was particularly troublesome, because my family, both in my childhood and at present, had always gotten great pleasure from eating together. One of life's pure pleasures was becoming self-conscious and uncertain, reflecting exactly how I felt as a mother.

Finally Mark and I agreed that we needed to call Maureen and ask her to arrange a meeting with the social worker who had handled the family's case from the beginning. We needed to know more about Margey's and Dawn's background. All we had learned before the adoption were the few second-hand facts Maureen had recalled hearing from the social worker at the Department of Public Welfare. Maureen said she was sure we were going through the inevitable problems of moving from a family of five to a family of seven, to be patient, and let time settle everything. I said I had been waiting three weeks; something was wrong and I wanted to know more about the girls' history.

The social worker who had handled the case at the welfare office was on maternity leave, Maureen said, but she arranged a meeting with the woman who had taken her place. The meeting occurred two weeks later, in a cramped, partitioned-off section of a much larger, over-crowded room. The substitute social worker read through a manila folder of records she had never seen before and rattled off details she thought might be of interest:

Once when the Department of Public Welfare placed Margey with a relative, her mother kidnapped her. . . . Since their birth, Margey and Dawn had each been placed in foster care at least six months out of every year. . . . Protective Services had removed Dawn from the home the first time when she was three months old—and taken her to the hospital for malnutrition. . . . They'd removed Margey several times because she had bruises around her head. . . . They'd removed both children when their mother didn't have a suitable place to live; at one point the house they were living in burned to the ground. . . . Both parents were alcoholics. . . . The mother wasn't married when she had Margey, then she got pregnant with Dawn right away and didn't want another baby. For some reason she decided not to get an abortion as initially planned but to keep Dawn. Maybe she got married, maybe she didn't, the record wasn't clear. . . . The girls had the same father, probably. . . . [The substitute social worker was having difficulty deciphering the original case worker's handwriting.] *When she was charged with physical abuse and neglect, the mother appeared in court and fought to keep the children from being removed from her custody. . . . One of the doctors who'd examined the girls thought maybe Dawn's skull was enlarged, indicating water on the brain or retardation. He'd run a series of tests, but had found nothing. . . . In most cases of abuse, the father, or the mother's male friend (or friends) does the most harm; in Margey's and Dawn's case their mother was probably equally responsible.*

That's all we were told that day, and that was enough. Neither Mark nor I wanted to hear any more; we were overwhelmed. Shocked and appalled. During the next few weeks we found ourselves swept from one emotion to another: anger that no one had told us the truth initially, curiosity over what else had been left out, fear for the future, relief that there was some explanation for all we'd been going through. No wonder Dawn always wanted to eat. No wonder her hair fell out in clumps. Phrases like "three months old and in the hospital for malnutrition" played over and over again in our heads. Only six months in one place at a time their whole lives? No wonder they moved with such apparent ease.

We couldn't tell much about intelligence. Neither of the girls was able to pay attention to anything for more than a few seconds, with the important exceptions of food and television. Their verbal skills, however, were improving rapidly, and they had learned where every object in the house was in an astonishingly short period of time.

The evening after the meeting, I told my neighbor, who was a nurse, about the conversation with the social worker. She said, "You do know they must have been sexually abused, don't you?" I told her I knew no such thing. "That's the only reason they take children away from their parents in this state," she said.

Mark and I were furious: she couldn't possibly know what she was talking about, we agreed, and if she did, what kind of monster would say something like that so nonchalantly?

Dawn was too young to remember anything from her first day with us. Margey says she vividly remembers the day she came to our house, though she remembers nothing of her mother and very little about the foster family. She remembers the macaroni and cheese and the sandbox and the trolley. What she remembers most, though, was her overwhelming desire to crawl up under the dark green Rambler parked in the driveway so no one could find her, not ever again.

Expectations

Margey and Dawn came into the family in the middle of July. We celebrated Margey's fourth birthday on 21 July, a week after she arrived, and Dawn's third birthday on 10 September. Children's birthdays were always big productions—a day-long celebration, a party, lots of presents and treats. Margey and Dawn were absolutely delighted with the events. Margey was scarcely able to believe the piles of presents that appeared, from the family in the morning and from guests at her party in the afternoon. She kissed each item before she unwrapped it and afterwards clutched her toys and clothes to her chest, refusing to let anyone touch "hers." As soon as she could get away, she took everything upstairs and tucked the piles under her bed.

Only one thing marred the day. While I was busy outside with party games, someone scaled the refrigerator and ate the frosting off Margey's birthday cake. Dawn was the leading suspect, but she vehemently denied that she'd been in the kitchen.

Dawn enjoyed her birthday equally, but was less particular about her gifts. Except for a favorite outfit and a stuffed raccoon, she willingly gave other things away to whoever wanted to play with them. By the end of the day, parts of new games and items of clothing were scattered all over the house.

Both sets of grandparents welcomed the new additions to the family that summer. Mark's parents came to visit as soon as the girls were settled in. Da-Da charmed Mark's father; she climbed up beside him and patted his hand. Margey was much more standoffish, of course. From the first, she and Mark's mom struck a discordant note. For some reason, Margey vanished when Mom Kimble appeared in the room. If there was any way out, she never obeyed the simplest requests from her grandmother. In fact, whenever she was asked to do something, Margey wandered off and disappeared for long periods. Although it was years before my mother-in-law described these details, no one ever sensed much warmth between the two. Perhaps Mom Kimble reminded Margey of someone who had been unkind to her; perhaps Margey found it difficult to adjust to yet another authority figure—she had had a number in her short life. The Kimbles, however, did their best to accept the girls as their grandchildren. Mark was an only child, so grandchildren were rare and precious.

Grandchildren in my family totaled a dozen and they inhabited their own kingdom, far removed from the adults. The children, biological and adopted, disappeared in a jumble of family combinations: two of my brothers had adopted their wives' children from earlier unions, and several bachelor brothers, only a few years older than the grandchildren, kept the children cooking on high until they fell exhausted into bed. My parents made every effort to speak with the girls and be kind to them, but mostly all additions joined "the gang" and weren't noticed one way or the other.

By the end of the summer we expected the enlarged family to settle into something of a routine. But it didn't.

From her first days in the house Margey knew where *everything* was; gradually, she tried to move as much as possible into her room. She borrowed freely from the other children but never returned anything, and she became fiercely resentful if anyone touched her clothes or toys. Soon no one was willing to lend her anything, but she continued to "borrow," increasingly without permission.

Especially problematic were occasions when someone else received something new and Margey didn't, such as birthdays. Margey seemed to grow sad, almost to shrink when others were opening presents: all eyes were on the birthday-child. Particularly disturbing were stories from a past that Margey didn't share: "Remember his first birthday when Sam put his face in the cake." "Remember that jello cake Kate asked for when we were in Italy?" These events probably kindled painful feelings for Margey, because we had no "remember whens" for her and Dawn. Margey was so self-conscious that we stopped indulging in reminiscences.

As time went on, we discovered that Margey had her own system of justice. If, for example, one of the other children offended her in any way, something they treasured would disappear a short while later. Again and again these missing objects turned up, weeks or months later, obviously having been secreted away by human hands. The problem was difficult to deal with because, of course, no one ever saw her hide anything and Margey always vehemently denied responsibility.

With increasing frequency, the other children retaliated and hid Margey's clothes and toys, or, if no adults were around, they used physical force to get her to confess. When she felt she had been wronged, Margey at first grew almost hysterical, then she utterly withdrew. It took her a very long time to forgive anyone who had offended her. On the occasions when Margey's things were simply misplaced, she was positive that someone had deliberately hidden them. When her clothes or toys turned up where she had left them, Margey could never be persuaded that they had been there all along.

Gradually everyone in the house became uneasy whenever they were missing something. The first response was rarely, "Darn, I've lost my book," or "Shoot, I left my coat at Michael's," but something more like, "Margey, where did you put my book?" or "Who took my coat?" As we were all somewhat forgetful and a little disorganized, we became involved in far too many nasty, blame-laying scenes.

Several years later, a young woman who was herself adopted explained how she felt to blame for everything that went awry in her family. She felt that she caused everything from tense pauses and strained conversations at the dinner table to full-fledged verbal fights. Comments like "Nice going," "Now look what you've done," "Cute," from her sisters and parents cut her to the quick. Every session of finger-pointing reinforced her sense of responsibility, and it must have been the same for Margey and Dawn.

The young woman said she had always assumed that life was perfect before she arrived and finally that life in the family would have been better without her. Probably Margey and Dawn felt the same way in our home. Since things were not going smoothly for Mark and me, and the older kids were easily annoyed, Margey and Dawn may well have felt as if the family's unhappiness rested on their small shoulders.

Such troubles encouraged Margey's already well-established instinct for isolation. Bony and nonverbal, she wandered about the house not meeting anyone's eye or addressing anyone directly. She was involved in her own world, sometimes even conversing with voices no one else heard. She crept around the floor or in the dirt and scampered like a little mouse from room to room, from object to object, from toy to toy, playing intensely for a few minutes, then moving on, never lingering, never questioning. Her movements were so erratic they seemed cut off in the middle of one motion, already halfway into the next.

Once in a while, Margey came up to me and said in her high-pitched voice something completely out of the blue like, "She really bad. *Really* bad. She in a whole lot of trouble. She not my friend any-more," or "I don't like her, she mean to me. How come she so so so mean? Tell her no mean me." But there wasn't anyone to warn; Mar-gey had been all alone or with some imaginary companion she never introduced.

Bodies fascinated her, especially injuries. She often came up, held out her arm and said, "Look at this scratch he got on me. It hurt. Me look your arm. Any owie on your arm? Me see." She wanted to look, but not to touch or be touched. She pointed out first one and then an-other tiny mark on her own body and complained about how much they had hurt when they were new. But she wouldn't let you pat or rub any of them.

The social worker had warned us that Margey seemed to be afraid of her foster father; she cried when she was left alone with him. Appar-ently some man had hurt her. We were, therefore, not surprised when she avoided Mark, and they spent little time with one another. Actually, she played alone most of the time. Sometimes she played with Jack or Dawn but never for more than a few minutes. Kate and Sam gave up approaching Margey or expecting her to play with them. And she didn't talk or play with any of the neighborhood children. On occasion Mark and I realized that we'd forgotten to worry about our vanishing child.

Dawn was as forward as Margey was reticent; dark and large-boned, she looked a little like Sophia Loren. She was friendly and bold and crawled up on any empty and willing lap and chattered until she was put down. She went from person to person, kissing, patting, cud-dling, asking what they were doing, where they were going, where they'd gotten their clothes, what they liked. This pattern made Mark and me a little uncomfortable. Of the two of us, she was more likely to approach Mark, but he's an active person, preferring hugs and kisses on the run, and he'd put her down fairly quickly. For some reason I can't entirely articulate—perhaps she seemed wiggly and intrusive—I was never comfortable cuddling with Dawn for more than a brief period, and she approached me less and less frequently. It must have been hard for Dawn that I didn't respond patiently and affectionately because I tend to be fairly demonstrative. Clearly Dawn needed approval, to bond with Mark and me, with someone, but she was too profuse and indiscriminate for either of us. Unknowingly, we may have reinforced negative experiences from the past.

Dawn continued to crave and sneak food. We tried two things with her, without much success: getting her to chew her food, and to acknowledge when she was full. We also kept all food out of sight. With time, we hoped Dawn would conclude that because food was always available on schedule, she didn't need to steal or stuff herself. Things would go smoothly for a while and then something unsettling would happen to remind us that Dawn still had no internal control over her food craving. For a while, Dawn had been more than agreeable about jumping over the back seat and riding in the undesirable "way-back" of the station wagon. One day we discovered her in the "way-back" munching Puppy Chow.

Her preoccupation with the kitchen continued. She insisted on being at my elbow whenever I was in there. If I asked her to play in the yard while I was cooking, she stood outside the window looking in, and then, instead of using the toilet just inside the back door, she would soil herself. That always made me feel trapped and manipulated.

Despite the problems, I enrolled Margey and Dawn in a new preschool that fall. The Happy Day preschool was organized by a member of the psychology department at the college where I taught. I hoped with their help to make more progress with the girls.

I mentioned to the staff that Dawn was not yet able to set her own limits with food; that at home we had to monitor her eating carefully, or we were afraid she would eat all the time. The teacher looked at me as if I was exaggerating. She was positive no child would exhibit such behaviors in a normal school setting. She had never heard of such a thing. I tried to tell the director that Dawn had been in the hospital with malnutrition when she was three months old and that apparently her early experiences had left her perpetually "hungry." She said, no problem, the children were always closely supervised.

Within weeks, however, the director of the preschool called for an emergency conference. She described how Dawn crawled under the table after meals in search of crumbs and chunks of food, continually went through the garbage can and swallowed—she never seemed to chew—whatever she found, especially the remains of cookies and brownies. If someone took what she'd found in the trash away from her, Dawn screamed and scratched. The woman was clearly distraught. She mentioned that two days earlier, when the class was on a field trip, Dawn had stationed herself right beside the teacher carrying a box of cupcakes and refused to take her eyes off the box. No matter what the teachers asked her to do that day, Dawn would not leave that box. All the teachers were in turmoil.

I asked the director why things had gotten to such a point. I reminded her of my warnings that Dawn needed extra attention around food. She said, frankly, she had thought I was upset with the child and exaggerating the situation. Such a beautiful little thing, so roly-poly and friendly. The long and short of it was, she said, Happy Day was not equipped to handle a child with such severe behavioral problems; most of their children were from middle-class backgrounds and none of them acted anything like Dawn. For just one child, they were not prepared to do everything that was necessary to accommodate her special needs.

Perhaps, she ventured, I should keep Dawn at home alone with me while the others were in school. She also recommended another morning program that attracted children from a variety of backgrounds, including some children who had been abused.

I was angry with the staff at Happy Day because they had not taken my warnings seriously. But they were new as teachers, just as I was a new mother of a traumatized child. I was also sorely disappointed not to have a few hours in the morning when the children were cared for. Dawn and I needed some time away from one another, I reasoned; I needed someone's help in dealing with her.

Mark and I acknowledged to one another that these events gave us some perverse satisfaction: it wasn't just us—or the combination of Dawn and us. We had always felt alone in our efforts with Dawn, increasingly frustrated by the lack of progress over the months. Now someone else was unsuccessful in their attempts to help Dawn change her behavior.

I realize now that I should have spent the mornings with Dawn; that was my best, perhaps my only, opportunity to bond with her. Alas, being thoroughly annoyed with her and not knowing anything about what was causing her compulsions, what they meant, or how they might be changed, I never considered our staying at home together.

Instead, I made an appointment with the psychologist in town who was described as having experience dealing with the victims of abuse and neglect. Mark and I hoped he would agree to counsel Dawn. Dr. Stein didn't respond as anticipated. He said a three-year-old child was too young for therapy; he would be happy to see Mark and me as much as we needed. The three of us talked; we detailed how things were going, especially with Dawn. We described how she soiled her pants, deliberately we thought, when she didn't want to do something we had asked her to do.

Mark told the most recent family joke: that Dawn would sell us all down river for an Oreo cookie. The trouble with that joke, an obvious exaggeration, was that at some level we both felt that it expressed Dawn's character. "Never getting enough" was the flip side of "going to anyone."

Dr. Stein was very sympathetic, but he told us that we should not assume that Dawn had motives behind her actions. Or, even if she did, not to assume we were capable of determining what those motives were.

Dr. Stein had identified the motive-attributing game Mark and I were playing with Dawn, but we were not persuaded that his analysis was more correct than ours. We felt strongly that Dawn could do better; that it was not necessary for her to sneak and steal. We both continued to feel that she was manipulating us and causing considerable stress within the family. We yearned for the psychiatric profession to deal with her directly—to wipe away her fixation.

Family members are all too likely to assume, perhaps not even consciously, that the "newcomers" or "outsiders" cause trouble on purpose. "They don't have to act like this." "They've learned how to punch our buttons." "They know exactly what they're doing to all the rest of us when they steal." We treated Margey and Dawn as adults, as if they had mature reasoning abilities and were capable of plotting and scheming to get what they wanted. Margey and Dawn were as close to plotting and scheming at the ages of four and three as Mark and I were to understanding them at the ages of thirty-two and thirty-one.

Years later, I understand the far-reaching insight in Dr. Stein's advice and have since endorsed it as the best available for parents who attribute too many motives to their children's behaviors. But I also wish that Dr. Stein could have helped us more. Perhaps he missed our desperation or felt we weren't yet ready to listen. But he must have known how common Dawn's behaviors were among neglected children. Hypothetical scenarios of what can happen to the developing personality of a deprived child might have helped us considerably.

Dr. Hanley, the pediatrician, and I discussed whether Dawn's cravings might be caused by a nutritional deficit. She suggested, as a long shot, that Dawn might have a zinc deficiency—a common characteristic of children who have suffered from malnutrition. For years Dawn took zinc pills, with no apparent effect. Dr. Hanley eventually concluded that her cravings had no physical origin.

Around this time, a friend who had worked at the Orthogenic School in Chicago told me that Bruno Bettelheim permitted children with cravings for food to eat all they wanted when they first came to the hospital. Eventually, in Bettelheim's experience, they got enough, or he knew when to stop them. Mark and I discussed that idea, but decided to stick with the steady and controlled approach we had been using. We didn't think we could stand watching Dawn eat and eat, and besides, we were not at all sure she would find her own limit. Mark and I have often wondered since if we should have tried Bettelheim's approach. Maybe we would have been more able to experiment at the outset and that method might well have worked, but by the time we heard of the idea, we were already entrenched in our limit-setting approach.

All this attention to Dawn's food problem was hard on the conscience of the whole family. It was no longer a simple matter to bake a cake, for example, and set it in the middle of the table so everyone could anticipate enjoying it, or to leave the leftovers out for snacks. Over time, I baked less and less and eventually gave it up, except for special occasions. Feeling deprived of something we were accustomed to, the original family all began to hoard and indulge in twos and threes or in private. We all felt mean and selfish when we didn't want to share with one another, or with the youngest of all. Dawn must have known and been hurt by what was going on. Nothing was less likely to change her actions. Resentment of Dawn's "greediness" also spread to many other aspects of her behavior, and Mark and I often realized in retrospect that we had overresponded to fairly innocuous misbehaviors.

Jack was always the most generous with both Dawn and Margey, perhaps because they were nearest in age. He often felt sorry for Dawn and took her side when she was in the doghouse. Sam did not have much sympathy for her at all; he alternated between generosity and annoyance with both her cravings and the family upset. There never seemed to be any effective way to use his typical approach, humor, to help us all out of the situation. Kate occasionally found Dawn sweet and endearing, but then she would become angry with her misbehavior. Since they shared a bedroom, Kate was most often the victim of Dawn's thefts. As time went on and Dawn continued to act out, all three biological children became less sympathetic and more resentful of what they perceived as greed and lack of consideration on Dawn's part and anger and ineffectiveness on Mark's and mine.

Throughout this time, the family received a monthly counseling visit from Maureen O'Brien. Mark and I told Maureen of our frustrations and fears. She was continually reassuring, perpetually confident that all would turn out well. How could it not, with such good parents?

She urged patience and understanding. She reminded me of the girls' cruel and damaging past. She promised that all those scars and memories would fade away, with time, in a loving home.

"Yes, I keep telling myself all those things every day," I said, "but none of the past horrors make it any easier to live with Margey's and Dawn's behaviors in the present. I never know why things go wrong, or if anything I am doing is right."

In December, six months after Margey and Dawn came, it was time to go to court and formalize the adoption. The whole family dressed up and appeared in the courtroom. The judge asked Mark and me if we would swear to become the legal parents of Margey and Dawn, to care for all their needs, to love them as our own children. We each swore to do so, but it was impossible not to have serious doubts about our abilities to fulfill such an ambitious oath.

Mark and I asked each other a thousand "what if" and "if only" questions. What if we'd had another baby and never thought about adoption? What if we'd gotten an African American or Asian child? What if we'd taken in foster children instead of adopting? Mark was so discouraged; one decision and six months, he felt, had taken away so much of our joy as parents. Would we ever regain that pleasure, he kept asking. I kept thinking, if only we could break through and get the girls to listen, to obey. If only we could let go, not care so much. If only we could find help, for the whole family. We both wished we could discover how to keep from getting so angry; we were horrified by how terrible our tempers had become. Was there no way out, no way to return to "normal"? Knowing the answer made our complaints all the more bitter.

Though at such times we were full of self-pity, both Mark and I knew that our sufferings did not compare with those of many other people—not even with those of our parents, on both sides. Mark and his parents had lost a fourteen-year-old son; as pre–Vatican II Catholics, my parents had continued to have children they didn't want and couldn't care for adequately.

Margey's and Dawn's surnames were obliterated from their original birth certificates. They received my family name and Mark's family name. The secretary of the court handed over the birth certificates of Margey Brown Kimble and Dawn Brown Kimble.

Mark and I had not known that their original names would be

obliterated from all public records—hadn't thought about it. But the erasure troubled us. It seemed arrogant to eradicate their mother's name—a deliberate denial of the influence of the past upon the present; a rigid insistence that biology and four years of experience— three in Dawn's case—were immaterial in the face of a new environment. It felt as if Mark and I were being given possession of two children who had come from no-telling-where and been through no-telling-what, but everyone agreed nevertheless never to raise the subject again.

We celebrated the legal event and planned the next celebration, the baptism of the girls. All our friends attended the baptism, as did Maureen O'Brien, the social worker. The guests were awash with what a wonderful thing we were doing. We received letters from around the country congratulating us. I kept wondering what those offering congratulations would think if they walked into our house on one of the frequently difficult days or if they heard our real misgivings.

After the adoption was finalized, Maureen no longer came to visit. I was relieved; sometimes trying to communicate with her seemed as difficult as with Margey and Dawn, only the opposite extreme. Maureen made me feel guilty—fully conscious of not living up to the ideal—and when she brushed aside my anguished and angry confessions, I felt all alone.

Failing to achieve something I had set my mind to was new for me. Not that I hadn't witnessed a fair share of tragedies in my own family, but as the eldest of eight, spread out over twenty years, I had plenty of opportunities to be and feel helpful. In Greenville, Mississippi, I grew up as a good student and went on to Maryville College in Saint Louis to graduate with honors and receive a scholarship to the University of Chicago. Mark was even less accustomed to personal failure than I was, though he and his family had suffered terribly when his older brother died at fourteen. Mark grew up an only child from the age of seven. A star student at Nazareth Hall Seminary, Saint Paul, during high school, he worked his way through Saint Thomas College, also in Saint Paul, and attended the University of Chicago on a Woodrow Wilson Fellowship.

Although Mark and I were always able to talk about how helpless we felt as parents of Margey and Dawn, I, as the mother, was mainly the one who dealt day in and day out with the children. Mark was working hard and receiving affirmation as a teacher and author. I was teaching part-time—never more than two or three courses, and many days that seemed to be too many. Mark was growing confident in his profession; I was feeling voiceless and helpless, as if I could not do anything well.

"Love these children," I urged, prayed, commanded myself. "All they need is for you to love them. Love them just like you love your other children." I was never able to take my own advice.

Christmas brought a period of respite. Margey and Dawn were delighted with everything that happened, small and large. For the first time, they showed generosity; they really seemed to think about what gifts they might get for others in the family. They also delighted in every decoration, picked up ornaments from the tree or the mantle and carried them around the house, took them to their bedrooms and slept with their favorites. They sat still and watched the lights. That year I made each of the three girls a long, blue-checked dress complete with ruffles and a white apron. They were delighted, I think, to be all the same and so pretty. Dawn's apron was the joke of the day; it kept slipping beneath her belly.

Margey and Dawn were fascinated with the building of the traditional gingerbread house. They got to choose the design of the house that year. They didn't want their mother's house or their foster parents' house; they wanted the house to look exactly like ours—two stories, lots of windows and shutters. They checked every side of the house for accurate placement of windows and doors. And they wanted to decorate gingerbread figures to look like themselves and locate them inside the house.

Something magical happened with the gingerbread house and Dawn. She seemed so awestruck by the whole production that she didn't fixate on the house as food. She didn't stare at it or pull more than her share of goodies away from the roof and walls. She led all visitors straight to the gingerbread house and told them, "No, No, you can't eat anything, no, no, not until after Christmas." Mark and I wondered what those magic ingredients were and if there was any way to spread them over the rest of Dawn's life. One answer may have been that during those special times, visits with family, birthdays and Christmas, Margey and Dawn felt as if they were getting enough, but the rest of the time they were much less comfortable. Maybe during those times of great hustle and bustle, they felt like everyone else, not special in either a good or a bad way.

One of my friends says that Christmas cannot possibly come up to what the average American child imagines. The opposite was true of Margey and Dawn, who were always absolutely delighted on Christmas

Day, as if their wildest dreams had been realized. Their joy always made me remember those two brown paper bags that contained all their possessions the day they moved in.

A year to the day after the adoption, Maureen O'Brien called and asked Mark and me to speak before a group of prospective adoptive parents. Far from anxious to accept that invitation, I told Maureen that much of what we had to say would not be positive. She said this group of parents needed to hear everything. It was only fair that they understand what they were getting into.

The one-year marker then became more of an occasion for summing up than it might otherwise have been. Mark and I thought about all that had happened to the family in just one year. The whole lay of the land felt completely different. Nothing had turned out as we'd expected. We had come into the adoption with more than our share of warm and fuzzy expectations. We had anticipated a brief "honeymoon" where the girls would be extremely well-behaved and polite, then some acting out, followed by a return to the normal that would last forever. It never occurred to Mark or to me that it would take more than a few months, much more than a year, to jump-start even the most traumatized kid back to normal.

On the panel of speakers was another couple who had also adopted two children—two older girls. No mention was made of the girls' history. Their parents, who were otherwise childless, described the perfect adoption; they fairly glowed with success—with new love and fulfillment. At first I didn't know whether or not to believe my ears. They told one endearing story after another. The audience was near tears, exultant at the couple's success, identifying with them all along the way. I did, however, feel uneasy when the father mentioned that on occasion he had to "belt" the girls, and "belt em good."

Then it was my turn to speak. I told the story, beginning with our visit to the zoo, describing our first night together, telling of sleepless nights spent trying to understand why we weren't able to communicate with the girls. Every time Mark and I had ourselves convinced that we were all making progress, something seemed to slide all the way back to the beginning. Just a week earlier, for example, on the occasion of Margey's fifth birthday, Dawn had repeated her performance from the previous year: she had scaled a great height and eaten all the cupcakes hidden for Margey's party. I told of trying so hard and unsuccessfully to love as I wanted to—the heart of our problems, I thought.

I finished with the hope that the physical and social progress Margey and Dawn were making was as significant in the long run as it was dramatic in the present. When they came, both Margey and Dawn were "failing to thrive"; they were tiny and underdeveloped physically. In the first year, Margey had grown five inches, Dawn four inches. When they arrived, Margey and Dawn were both way behind in their speech development; a year later they were talking fine. Such marked physical improvements, everyone hoped, would have psychological parallels.

When it was Mark's turn, he spoke regretfully about how all our lives had been changed by the adoption, and the disparity between what we had hoped for and what we were living. He ended by saying that he did not feel that we had been warned, or supported in any meaningful way, and he wanted others to have a better experience, if that was at all possible.

There was a prolonged silence in the room after Mark sat down. Maureen O'Brien looked out the window. In the milling about after the talks, not one person met my eye or came up to speak. I could feel their revulsion. As a proficient-people pleaser, I yearned to be received more favorably. Mark and I ardently wished we had refused Maureen's invitation to speak to that audience.

Of course, I envied the other couple's happiness. I often wondered, still wonder, if Margey and Dawn would have been better off, as their foster mother had suggested, with a couple who had no other children. For days afterwards, I tried to make out the profile of the perfect adoptive mother so I could advise people more positively: she should be plump, generous, and religious; she should be completely accepting, well-organized, patient, and absolutely consistent. It didn't seem as if I had any of the qualities on that list.

Mark and I were never asked to speak to a preadoptive group again, but to our surprise a year or so later Maureen sent a couple to discuss adoption with us. Later Maureen confessed that she hadn't thought they would be suitable parents; she had expected us to discourage them.

About a month after our talk to adoptive parents, I heard in a lecture by the director of Child Protective Services that four children out of seven placed for adoption in our community that year had been returned to the Department of Public Welfare. I was stunned. One previously abused little girl was reputed to be so taken with masturbation that her first knuckle was noticeably worn down by continual friction. After she had been in her adoptive home for almost a year, she was returned to the Welfare Department because of the persistent and public nature of her habit. What a horror story. For a brief time, I felt grateful that Margey and Dawn didn't have such embarrassing and compulsive habits.

But before long I began to wonder about that figure: four out of seven placements terminated. How did Margey's and Dawn's background compare with the backgrounds of those four children? What about the other three stories? Why had no one told Mark and me about such cases? One good reason was that we never asked. Even after we heard that statistic, we didn't ask anyone for further details. If we had heard more stories, we might have been unable to congratulate ourselves that at least we were doing better than those four families. But to be truthful, although I pitied those families their anguish, I also envied their release.

Adoption manuals and counselors advise parents to be realistic in their expectations of adopted children and of themselves. Here we have a tall order, perhaps itself the first in a long line of unrealistic expectations.

How can parents whose only experiences are with normally developing children have realistic perspectives on children who have been threatened and tortured? How can those who are lied to, or told little to nothing about a child's troubled early life, anticipate the effects of the past?

Adoptive parents of course need to have realistic expectations of their children, but adoption agencies also need to have realistic expectations about the typical responses and limits of adoptive parents. A way to best help adoptive parents might well be to discourage them from regarding an adopted child as a blank slate with infinite potential; such expectations encourage high achievers to dream and dream big. Providing parents with as much information as possible about the child's life prior to the adoption might be the best way to help high-achieving parents develop realistic expectations of their adoptive children. Although many of us yearn to defy the laws of nature, we also understand that without a strong wind an apple does not fall far from the tree.

Many social workers fear that giving parents negative information will cause adoptive children's lives to become self-fulfilling prophecies.

After adoptive parents are informed, for example, that their children's fathers were alcoholics, according to this reasoning, parents' anxiety and expectation turn their children toward alcoholism. Social workers are also terrified that parents who hear the truth will grow faint-hearted and run away from adoption.

As an adoptive parent, I can think of several plausible scenarios that might work out better for everyone. Knowing that a child, adopted or biological, has a predisposition toward alcoholism is information parents can use to increase a child's receptivity to alcohol counseling. The hard truths about a child's past, I believe, are more likely to make parents sympathetic and understanding, rather than negative and fearful. After all, usually we are not shielded from the bad news in our biological families.

For years I have struggled with how hopeful but naive the professionals were about the risks my family undertook in adopting Margey and Dawn. I understand that we were all coming out of a behaviorist framework, that we believed a new environment would bring about radical changes. Everyone wanted to believe that children could begin anew; no one wanted us to worry, question, or anticipate trouble. Now I believe that such blind hope was not in the best interest of our family. If large portions of society treat adoption of at-risk children as unproblematic, the family is left to shoulder all of the blame and guilt.

Years later, both Sam and Jack, in writing their college entrance essays, chose to write about living in a family with adopted children, describing an experience that had influenced their lives. Both essays were diplomatic masterpieces: they walked a delicate balance between criticizing their family and honestly analyzing the difficulties of adoption. I thought at the time that their writing paralleled the way the biological children treated Mark and me on the subject of the adoption: with a combination of respect for our efforts and regard for our feelings, annoyance at our behaviors, and a longing for the utopian family that might have been had it not been for the adoption. In his essay, Jack suggested that Margey and Dawn might well have been better off in a family that expected less of them, in a family where competition was less stiff, in a family more tolerant than ours proved to be. Sam wrote about how difficult the adjustment to the adoption had been, how much his family had needed help, why he might someday choose to work in the field of adoption counseling.

Childhood

More obviously than any of the other children, Kate wanted the family to be happy. She tried her darndest to make up to her parents, especially to me, for the disappointment we clearly felt with the new family. She tried every bit as hard as I did to mother Margey and Dawn and integrate them into the family. Above all, she tried to be perfect herself so that Mark and I would be satisfied. Seeing a seven-year-old in this role troubled me; she had to grow up too soon, take on too much responsibility too young. Hers was a role similar to the one I had taken in my own family, and that made me extremely uneasy. Of course, as the mother, I had hoped above all else to create a world for all the children, as my mother had yearned to before me, where their childhood years would be uninterrupted by family conflict.

Sam was also affected, but less obviously. Once in a while he came up to Mark or me and asked a pointed question like, "Are you glad you adopted children?" or "How many children do you think I will have? I know the answer—three." One birthday, Sam asked to take a group of little boys to the skating rink rather than have the usual family-neighborhood party. He wanted an escape. In about the fourth grade, Sam became a serious worrier, especially during the time he was trying to fall asleep at night. Night after night he cried about "the dark hole" he kept seeing in his dreams. Often he had to get out of bed and finish up homework he had forgotten, because he didn't dare go to school without it. Kate had had the same demanding teacher two years earlier, and we hoped the problem was just Sam's carelessness and the resulting worry and guilt when he hadn't done his work. But the dark hole seemed more of a deep-seated fear than a phase with an individual teacher. And of course we wondered to what extent it was affected by Margey's and Dawn's coming.

Of the three children, Jack fared best after the adoption, perhaps because he was less ambivalent toward the two girls. He liked to play with both of them and spent more time with Margey than anyone else; they were only four months apart in age. He felt less guilt over wishing the girls out of the family, as Sam did on occasion. He also tended to be absorbed in his own agenda and not as concerned about Mark's and my discomfort, as Kate was.

Among the five children themselves, things were far from smooth. The main conflict was usually between Margey and the older three. The biological children had always organized complicated games among the neighborhood children, and numerous players were always necessary. But Margey wasn't sociable; she didn't want to be enlisted. Her communication skills were also limited, and so she usually ended up wandering off by herself, after being subjected to considerable abuse. Because Dawn wasn't able to keep up with the rest, she usually followed Margey, who was sometimes glad to have her but at other times harsh and rejecting.

Margey must have felt little in common with the other children. Maybe they seemed too carefree, too secure for her. Previously the eldest child, Margey had grown accustomed to being her own boss. She had probably had to watch out for the trusting, defenseless Dawn as well as for herself. Her life had never been predictable. Moving around all the time, never in one home for more than six months, must have given her a basis of distrust, especially of adults. They were guaranteed to abandon her, and in a short time. She must always have been on the lookout for cloudbursts of change, danger, harm. Accustomed as she was to serious drama, the usual neighborhood games must have seemed to her predictable, dull. She had good cause not to invest in conversations or games or friendships or family, all of which had been repeatedly taken from her.

At times, Margey seemed to view Dawn as a companion, her fellow "outsider," at other times as an anchor to the past she would like to forget. During the periods when Margey needed someone to stand by her unquestioningly, she could always count on Dawn. Dawn accepted a wide range of treatment from Margey as if she knew no better: Margey could be warm, rough, indifferent. Dawn gave Margey what all children yearn for: unconditional love, unquestioning approval. Yet when Margey wanted to stand on her own or move closer to the family, she ignored and denied Dawn, knowing Dawn would never abandon her. Margey's treatment of Dawn may well have damaged her in the eyes of the other children, whereas Dawn's loyalty to Margey commanded respect from the group.

Kate, Sam, and Jack all distinctly remember beating up on Margey and Dawn when there were no adults around to intervene. Those events are especially complicated in the biological children's memories: even they don't know whether they beat up on Margey and Dawn more than is typical with biological siblings; they don't know whether Margey and Dawn were unusually provocative. All in all, there seemed to have been more than the usual amount of resentment among the five children. Margey and Dawn must have been resentful toward the older children for being more intimate with Mark and me, for the time we had been together, the memories of the past, and the comfort of the present. Kate, Sam, and Jack resented the two younger girls for seeming to cause such havoc with the family. They remembered the time before Margey and Dawn as a kind of golden age, when the five of us were happy and well-rested. They also seemed to be afraid of their own feelings: they had wanted to adopt and love their sisters, but finding a common ground was much harder than they'd expected.

Whatever the reasons or context, all three of the older children have painful, guilty memories of pushing, shoving, hitting, and verbally abusing their little sisters. As the household was committed in principle to nonviolence, such outbreaks of abuse were troubling to us all. What's more, Mark and I worried that we had somehow set an example to the children through our own behavior that such cruelty was acceptable.

The year Dawn was six and ready to begin kindergarten, Mark decided to take a visiting appointment at the University of Virginia. I was less than thrilled with the idea of moving five children for a year and leaving behind what was just becoming a full-time job. But as long as we were going to be in Virginia, I decided to check out the possibilities of working toward a Ph.D., a degree I needed to teach full-time at the college level. And, indeed, the University of Virginia program seemed manageable.

As long as the family was going to be on the road in the fall, we decided to make a year of it and spend the summer in Mexico before moving to Virginia. That way the family could have an adventure, and I could learn Spanish. Never short on nerve, we decided not to take a car but to travel by train, our belongings on our backs, five children between the ages of six and ten, all the way down to Oaxaca, Mexico.

Of course, the physical components of the trip were hard work, but the strange land was good for the family. There were none of the old occasions of worry; we lived way out in the country with only one English-speaking family nearby. The children played fairly well with one another on the patio, around the large gardens of the farm, and in the river that ran behind the house. Mostly they disappeared for long hours. Our diet was simple: tortillas delivered fresh every morning and many, many beans, eggs, and vegetables from the garden. Perhaps because the meals were so repetitious, food was not an issue with Dawn that summer. There were no stores nearby and the children didn't have much of anything except what they'd brought in their backpacks and what they found on the grounds: a pet chicken, acres of orange trees and vegetables, a backyard river, and sunshine. The summer in Oaxaca still feels like a reprieve in Eden.

We set out for Virginia in the fall, after having great difficulty finding housing: no one wanted to rent to any family with five children; no telling what kind of folks they must be. Mark had a light teaching load and few extra responsibilities as a visitor, so he did much of the child care while I embarked on the doctoral program. The children loved the large house and yard, the hills of Charlottesville, and trips with their dad into the Blue Ridge Mountains. I had to work long hours reading and writing, but I did well and by the second semester some of the pressure was off. The four older kids did fine in Venable school. Kate even won a speech contest with a detailed explanation about what the devaluation of the peso meant to the Mexican people. Kindergarten didn't go well for Dawn, though; she was restless and not at all attracted to any of the tasks the teachers suggested. They encouraged Mark and me to start Dawn again in kindergarten when we returned to Saint Paul.

Venable kindergarten was the first whiff of the misadventures-to-be with the public school system once Margey and Dawn were enrolled in school back home. Mark and I are both dedicated teachers, and we hoped that our children would be well served by the educational system. Mark was only the second child in his extended family to attend college, and both became college professors. According to my mother, her family was full of Baptist preachers and schoolteachers. My original career aspiration had been to teach English in an inner-city high school, and to inspire students like Margey and Dawn to love to read and to write letters like those in *To Sir, With Love*, a popular book in the 1960s about an educator who worked in the slums of London.

Again, all our high hopes were dashed; in no time at all Mark and I realized how inadequate public school education was for children who did not like to read, who were nonverbal, and who did not take work sheets seriously. Of course, our sympathies were not entirely with Margey and Dawn; we ourselves knew how difficult they were to teach.

Things were, as usual, much different for Kate, Sam, and Jack. Kate, always a worrier, pushed herself too hard; Sam and Jack found school easy, even though there was often a good-sized discrepancy between their achievement and their abilities. At least Margey and Dawn were more consistent; they both tested and performed poorly.

Margey and Dawn were well aware of how they measured against Kate, Sam, and Jack. They left their report cards for us to find when they were not at home, or lost them, or kept them until we asked for them. The envelopes always looked worn and well-handled. The report cards themselves were folded and refolded, oddly wrinkled and creased, evidence of worried hands.

Mark and I tried to minimize the importance of grades—both to keep Kate from killing herself and to keep Margey and Dawn from feeling their differences. But children love to win and gloat. "They have to compete over every grain of rice," my mother used to say. The main competition was between Kate and the boys. Since the boys were more verbal, Kate had to have better grades. Margey and Dawn pretty much dropped out of the race as soon as they began school. They didn't seem to care about anything that resembled a book. Mark and I worried that the family was putting too much pressure on them, but we also wondered what would happen to them if they couldn't manage school at all, not at all.

Margey and Dawn were also left out of the lively discussions and bantering among the children, their friends, and us. Kate, Sam, and Jack were loud and energetic and oh, yes, verbal. Margey and Dawn, by contrast, had very concrete patterns of thinking, were not at all comfortable with abstractions, and often wandered off in the middle of conversations. Their vocabularies were also limited. No doubt they felt lonely during those discussions, uncomfortable at some level that the rest of us did not grasp how much they could not understand.

Within weeks of the beginning of school I would be invited by Margey's and Dawn's teachers to chat about their problems. All five teachers from Margey's "team" once called me in, sat me up on a high stool in their midst, and began cataloging Margey's performance and attitude problems—after a thrice-repeated introduction, "So you're Margey's mother, so you're. . . ." Dawn's crimes were variations on the refrain: "I've never seen such behavior; whatever is going to become of this child?" Dawn scaled windowsills and slithered across floors. She disturbed everyone. Had the family doctor been consulted about drugs to combat hyperactivity? (Yes, none were prescribed.) Would I give permission for paddling? (Under no circumstances.)

Sometimes my sympathies were with the teachers and I said so; at other times I heard myself sounding like Maureen O'Brien—these two little girls had a rough early start, they were doing the best they could; we all had to be patient and hope for the best.

How about special education, I asked every year; how about some-place where they could learn something—it didn't matter what—and feel good about themselves? Well, no, special education did not seem called for, not quite. Did I understand what kind of children they would be mixing with in special education? But they were failing mis-erably where they were; wasn't there something else we could try? The teachers weren't at all sure that Margey and Dawn were all that slow in-tellectually; they were convinced that if the girls worked on several as-pects of their behavior everything would be fine: their lack of impulse control, their inability to concentrate, their failure to follow directions, and so on.

What was the cause of these behaviors, did they have any idea? Possibly their early history, but no one could be sure. It seemed clear to Mark and me that if there were ever children with "special needs," Margey and Dawn were among them. Still, we could find nothing in the educational system that came close to meeting their needs. What happened to all the other children like Margey and Dawn? I asked. Well, there weren't that many like them, one teacher said, or she'd have quit long ago. Of course I knew what she meant, but what kind of an answer was that? In truth, there was no telling how many children were like Dawn and Margey and needed to be taught entirely different ma-terial using entirely different methods. Margey and Dawn needed to put their hands all over things; they could learn if they were able to manipulate objects. They seemed to be senseless before any abstrac-tion—numbers or words or even pictures in a book. Mark and I used to say that if they'd had a mud-pie education available, both of them would have been awarded master's degrees.

Years later, I learned that many psychologists and educators agree that a history of rejection and neglect slows down a child's cognitive de-velopment—the ability to concentrate and sustain interest, verbal facil-ity, curiosity, the ability to conceptualize. When they don't do well in school, children like Margey and Dawn feel terrible about themselves. Then in a vicious circle, that lack of self-confidence makes them do even worse, at school and everywhere else, too.

When Dawn was given an IQ test at age fifteen at the local mental health center, her therapist reported her score as eighty-one, her reading level at third grade, and her mathematical competence as nonexistent. No, Dawn was not technically retarded, but her ability to learn was so minimal, surely she had needed some kind of "special" education from kindergarten on up.

School was not the only matter of concern during Margey's and Dawn's early years. There was still food with Dawn and social relationships with both of the girls. When Dawn was in third grade, her teacher called me in for a conference. She said the class had had a project selling apples to raise money for a trip. Dawn had brought in money to buy apples like the other children, but she had kept all her apples in her desk. During the week of their project, Dawn had had an apple in her mouth every minute of the day. The teacher's real concern, though, was that several of the children had complained that Dawn was taking treats out of their lunch boxes and eating them in the bathroom. Many of the children, she said, had confronted Dawn directly, but, if anything, their disapproval had increased her pilfering.

In the fourth grade, Dawn began to call home three or four times a week saying she had a stomachache and someone needed to pick her up. Mark and I were both working full-time and the inconvenience was considerable. After several episodes I took Dawn to Dr. Hanley, but she found no physical problem. Still Dawn continued to complain and to call. Then Mark and I agreed to ask her teacher to send Dawn to the nurse and let her wait in the infirmary until she felt better. Eventually, the nurse called and said that she'd discovered a pattern: since Dawn frequently came in complaining shortly after lunch, the nurse had gone to the cafeteria to check things out and found that Dawn was eating all her lunch and then everything that remained on the other children's trays. The nurse thought there was a good chance that Dawn was uncomfortable after lunch because she had overeaten. Mark confronted Dawn, and I asked the lunchroom attendant to send her out to play as soon as she finished her own meal. Dawn stopped calling, but there was no kidding ourselves that we were doing anything more than handling each symptom as it arose.

As time went by and there seemed to be so little progress, Mark and I became more and more discouraged about the intractability of Dawn's eating behaviors. Then one of Dawn's teachers suggested that she might be addicted to sweets and that taking her off sugar might help; she felt that when Dawn ate sweets, she lost control completely. This same pattern was well established at home. Dawn often disgusted everyone because she had no limits. She would eat all thirty pieces of gum at a sitting, the whole bag of cookies, the entire bottle of honey—and then repeat bold-faced denials with maddening stubbornness.

I spoke with Dr. Hanley, who said that in some people eating sugar caused the brain to crave more sugar. She agreed that it might be a good idea to try taking Dawn off sweets.

The other children were resentful that they often weren't allowed to have rich treats because of Dawn. They were furious when she stole their things and then lied about it. Dawn seemed to grow more defiant in the face of her difficulties. Everyone felt she could make a better show than she did: at least she could admit the truth after she'd enjoyed the goodies. None of us interpreted Dawn's lying as a sign of her ardent wish not to have offended anyone. Instead, we all assumed that she could control her actions and her words, if she'd listen and try harder.

The most destructive aspect of the sugar regime was the constant vigilance, the virtual guarding of Dawn and the contents of the house to keep her away from sugar. The trunk of my car was always filled with pancake syrup, brown sugar, honey—all of the things Dawn would finish off if they were left in the cupboards. As for the long-term relationship between Dawn and me, I began to despair of ever being able to persuade her to do anything she didn't want to do.

Dawn's seemingly endless emotional needs frightened Mark and me as much as her apparently endless craving for food did. Guilty over our inability to satisfy Dawn's inner cravings, we became more and more frustrated by her lack of progress and increasingly rigid in our attempts to control her behavior.

Mark and I began to doubt that the environment was having the impact it was supposed to. In our worst moments we questioned whether our parenting was any better than Dawn's birth parents'. I became more discouraged than Mark. For some reason, Dawn's personality was more difficult for me to enjoy; Mark was much better at appreciating her virtues. He liked her jokes, liked to gossip with her about the go-ings on at school and in the house. They had good moments to balance the tensions.

Margey's and Dawn's inability to listen to directions or correc-tions began to have larger ramifications as they grew older. Either they didn't want to accept that toasters had limitations or they didn't believe us when we said that putting buttered toast in a toaster would ruin the appliance and possibly cause a fire. Toaster after toaster burned out. With imaginative versatility, the girls abused and broke everything mechani-cal. Any attempts at retributive justice, such as making them scrub out the toaster or buy a new one, provoked vehement objection and retali-ation. Apparently, they could not admit that they had ruined the waffle iron by using it to make grilled-cheese sandwiches, or that they popped a bicycle tube a week, no one ever knew how. It was never possible, ei-ther, to decide whether they were just stubborn or whether they did not have good cause-to-effect reasoning skills.

Margey and Dawn were very different from most relatively secure and self-confident biological children in terms of their ability to accept responsibility for what they had done. An apology would have been so cleansing. Without that simple act, transgressions kept building, and with each addition the anger seemed to start way up high rather than back at the beginning. Why couldn't the girls apologize? Perhaps be-cause in their early years they had been punished at random or way out of proportion to what they had done. They had probably lived in terror of provoking rage and violence, of being obliterated if they displeased anyone, so much so that they could not admit to doing anything that anyone could possibly criticize.

They also may not have accepted other members of the family as deserving of an apology. Their lack of consistent and loving authority figures in the past seemed to have taught them not to respect and trust anyone in authority. In the past they had never known how long those in charge would be around, or when they'd be abusive or drunk. Why should they listen to any of us?

The whole family played a lot of soccer during those energy-filled years. Everyone played but Mark, and he—in spite of a trick knee—became a dedicated coach. Mark constructed a goal in the yard at the side of the house; the children wiped out all the grass, kicking their soccer balls around. They were all nearly the same size, so they gave one another fair competition. Margey ran like a gazelle; she was fearless in attack, aggressive in defense. When she was eleven and twelve she became a star on the girls' team at school. I went to watch one of her games in a nearby town, and I don't know which of us was more thrilled to see her take out the formidable opposing team's leading scorer and make the winning goal for her team in the final seconds of the game.

Margey's attraction to soccer was her first attempt to mimic the older children and to get approval from Mark and me. She saw that soccer included her in an activity the family prized, in discussions about technique and strategy.

Dawn did not take to soccer like the rest of us; the game was too complicated and moved too quickly for her. She developed asthma, and the exercise often left her exhausted. Many articles on adoption refer indirectly to the large proportion of adopted children with histories of breathing difficulties, perhaps a result of prenatal or postnatal factors, perhaps triggered by anxiety. Dawn suffered from sinus infections from the first. But when she was twelve, her breathing problems became much more severe and quickly turned into asthma. The allergist brought her symptoms under control and began Dawn on shots to build up her immunities.

Although Mark and I kept signing the girls up in the soccer league hoping they would make friends among their teammates, we did so with mixed feelings. The other girls on their teams always seemed to form cliques, leaving Margey and Dawn to wander around on the outside. Their teammates were usually polite enough, but they never invited Margey and Dawn to informal after-game activities, which were often planned in their presence. It was clear who "fit" and who didn't. We had to admire the girls for continuing with their soccer teams as many years as they did.

Dawn still seemed like a very young child as she approached adolescence. Unable to manage the new requirements of hygiene, she left her soiled items all over the house. She would put on any combination of colors and styles. When she was twelve, I brought her a pair of red Chinese pajamas from San Francisco. The next day, before anyone else was awake, Dawn walked to school in her new pajamas. Alas, my response was not to acknowledge how much Dawn must have loved the pajamas, a long-awaited sign of my approval, but dismay at her impetuous behavior. In another episode, that spring she cut a daffodil and planted the stem beside the back door, telling me it would grow. I tried to explain that a daffodil grew from a bulb, and that all plants had roots of some kind. She said her flower was going to grow and be pretty; her teacher had told her to plant it exactly the way she'd done it. Again my response was not to applaud Dawn for her attempt to make the yard pretty, but amazement at her lack of maturity.

A week later, I went into Dawn's room and found a bag of Tender Vittles on her bed. I thought, "Oh, no, now Dawn's eating cat food." It was almost a relief when I opened the door of her closet and discovered a kitten meowing inside—without food or water or litter. Mark and I never were able to anticipate what Dawn understood and what she didn't: what she knew or learned from experience seemed entirely random. Mostly she seemed determined to command the world to do her will, regardless of the world's response—the way a young child presumes that its desires and reality are synonymous.

As Margey entered adolescence, her personal fastidiousness evolved directly into typical teen narcissism. She spent hours and hours in front of the mirror, snipping the strands of hair that didn't quite please her. She loved clothes and dressed herself carefully, always with a flair—a turned-up collar, a headscarf, dramatic earrings. Every year she designed extraordinary Halloween costumes—she worked at it for weeks—using fabrics and gloves and jewelry long-forgotten in drawers and cupboards. One year she dressed as a "horror," a lady of the evening.

Almost on the day she turned twelve, Margey began to wear heavy eye makeup of every shade, which was typical of her age, and a mask of cake makeup, not so typical. Her mask never matched her skin tone, and to Mark and me she looked deathly. She seemed to want to recreate herself, complete with new wardrobe and painted face.

Looking back, I realize that Margey's attraction to the feminine arts was connected with her first out-and-out theft. During the winter in Virginia, she took a tube of lipstick from her grandmother Kimble's pocketbook. Although there was a good-sized family upset at the time, no one thought there were larger implications in the deed. Years later, a friend commented after reading this passage in a draft manuscript, "You know that was the only way she had of getting what she wanted." Those words tumbled around in my brain. Indeed, stealing was the only way for Margey to get lipstick, since neither Margey nor Dawn ever figured out how to ask for what they wanted. They always seemed to be afraid we would disapprove of their requests, with some validity. I rarely wore lipstick and would have missed my one tube had she taken that, and her grandmother didn't use the lipstick she carried in her purse.

The larger issue, I realized much too late, was that Margey had landed in a house where the values differed greatly from those in her previous experience. She had no doubt spent her first years in highly role-polarized settings. Mark and I are feminists—we believe that males and females are equal—and we tried not to emphasize the differences between the two at home. We didn't believe in sex-typed toys, neither dolls nor soldiers. We specialized in building equipment— Legos, blocks, crystals, cards, sand—and athletic equipment—a swing set, the trolley, soccer balls. There was nothing in the house that Margey and Dawn would have loved, like a drawerful of shiny necklaces, a box of high-heeled shoes, a closet filled with long, silky dresses. How difficult it must have been for Margey and Dawn to make so many shifts in values and lifestyles! how they must have longed for the comfort of some of their old ways! Not being able to talk about their secret desires must have made their losses all the more painful.

Adolescence

The one warning Mark and I had gotten from the social workers during the adoption interviews was a cryptic "Watch out for adolescence."

When Margey entered seventh grade, she changed virtually overnight. Her soccer skills evaporated. She was chosen for the city select team but suddenly became afraid of the ball. If a high kick came her way, she lifted her arms over her head and ducked. Her run, so swift and free a year earlier, became checked and uneven, full of spurts and fallings off. Mostly, she stood around on the field and swished her hair back and forth between her fingers. Before long, she began to complain of how unfriendly her teammates were; they didn't like her anymore. She went with her team to a state tournament in Duluth, Minnesota and came home angry, because, she said, she hadn't gotten to play. Later that evening her coach called to say that Margey had infuriated the whole team: she had laughed and taunted the players after they'd lost the championship game. In the weeks following that trip, she began cutting practice and the next season was not invited to join the team.

The only thing in her life that seemed to matter to Margey was her appearance, and that mattered tremendously. A natural blonde— small and pretty—she had imagination in advertising her strengths. Her whole ego seemed tied up in her body. Every day, she wanted something new to wear. She would go into her room, throw all her clothes on the floor, and ask how anyone could expect her to wear that old junk. Apparently because she thought her clothes didn't suit her and she didn't feel she had enough makeup, she began to borrow from her friends, but never returned their things. When her friends and their mothers objected, she seemed incapable of admitting the truth or of apologizing.

I was never sure that Margey really understood that my things did not belong to her. Her favorite targets were anything new, underwear, and jewelry. I toyed with the idea of getting a lock for my door, but decided against it. I often wondered if I should take her shopping everyday, thinking back over the earlier advice to let Dawn eat all she wanted. But somehow I couldn't bring myself to do that, either. Her behavior was so troublesome in every area that I was always too angry to want to reward her in any way. But I also felt guilty for not buying her all she wanted—for not making my way into her heart in that relatively simple way.

On the other hand, how fair would such an approach have been to the other children, who of course measured out what each other received in milligrams? Also, would it ever have been possible to buy Margey enough to satisfy her?

One evening, I received a call from the mother of one of Margey's friends, asking me to go to her house so the adults could straighten up the matter of borrowed clothes among our daughters. I went over with Margey, hoping along the way to retrieve a new blouse that had just disappeared. In the living room I found the family's three daughters, each with a list of items she had lent Margey. Margey, in turn, demanded various things from each of the other girls. Then she and I went home to search for the missing items. Margey claimed the girls were lying; she had not borrowed anything from them, wouldn't be the slightest bit interested in any such trash. But everything on their lists turned up in Margey's piles of clothes waiting to be laundered. When we returned the collection, the mother met me at the door to say that if Margey ever again set foot on her property, she was going to call the police immediately. In the bag of Margey's things returned by the other family, I found my new blouse, which Margey insisted she had never seen.

The step from borrowing at this level to stealing was not a big one. Soon, makeup and clothes stolen from the shopping center across the street began to appear in Margey's room. She never got caught shoplifting, and none of the store managers seemed much concerned when she and I dragged in to return what she had stolen. They said little beside, "Yes, these items are from our store. No, these others aren't. Thank you for returning these stolen articles; not many people do."

One of the other children, Jack, did get caught stealing—taking candy from Target. The store security called the police, who called me. I had to go pick up the offender. The following week, Jack and I were required to visit the juvenile officer. Jack was thoroughly humiliated. I wanted the same thing to happen to Margey, but it never did. She could not have cared less when time and again I found what she had stolen and made her return things to the stores. I considered turning her in to the police but couldn't bring myself to do what felt like a betrayal.

A major stress point in the house was the bedroom the three girls shared. Kate insisted that she had to move out of the room—a physical and emotional disaster area. She had nothing to herself, no privacy, not even clothes she could call her own. Margey took whatever she wanted whenever she wanted and Kate stayed furious, both with Margey and with Mark and me for not being able to control Margey. The boys' bedroom was right across the hall, and one or the other of them often got embroiled in the quarrels going on in the girls' room.

Mark and I looked over the house and decided we had to add bedrooms somewhere. A soccer friend of Mark's drew up plans for an expansion that would have added two bedrooms, a family room, and a downstairs bath, but the proposed addition would have cost as much as the original house. We considered raising the roof and making a couple of bedrooms in the attic. One of my brothers suggested that we put electric heat in the basement, which turned out to be the easiest and quickest solution. We painted and carpeted the tiny canning room, and Kate finally had her own "cave." The former TV room became Sam's bedroom. With the older two downstairs and the younger three upstairs, everyone had more room to breathe. Margey and Dawn still shared a bedroom, but that seemed to be a good thing. Dawn rarely was bold enough to take anything from Margey, and she forgave Margey right away for taking, and even losing, anything of hers.

That was the end of easily achievable expansions of the house. Even though the children had privacy in their bedrooms, we all shared a single bathtub-shower, and one telephone, located in the middle of the central hall. The one telephone was a deliberate choice—the better to keep an ear on teenage goings on. We all suffered from living with one bath that received so much use that either floor or wall tiles were always coming off. The children arranged a schedule in the mornings, each of them with four to seven minutes in the shower, and surprisingly that worked well.

What pushed us to the edge was Mark's mother's coming to live with us the year she was recovering from uterine cancer—the year the children were between eleven and fifteen. Mom Kimble was too ill to live alone after the operation and during chemotherapy, so she moved into the basement alcove off Sam's room. We put in a wall and door so they both had privacy, but Mom Kimble had to go through Sam's room to get to her space. The house was full to capacity physically, and emotionally we were all overextended. Though Mark's mother remained relatively cheerful, given all she had to go through, she was terribly ill and needed a great deal of tending and patience. When she recovered and returned home after the year, everyone was relieved.

In junior high, school went from being a serious irritation to a hideous problem for both girls; no teacher and no bribes or threats could persuade them that the goings-on at school were worth their while.

The first marking period in the seventh grade, Margey changed her two Fs to Bs. The counterfeit was so skillful no one noticed. In retrospect, I'm astonished at how dumb Mark and I were, but Margey had never failed outright; we weren't expecting that. She had also destroyed or forged my signature on failure notices, intercepted the mail, and torn up teachers' notes home. Although they had tried, they said, none of the teachers managed to get through on the phone.

By the time the second report was due after Christmas, the teachers had called, and Mark and I warned Margey that we were on the lookout for forgery. She failed three classes and very carefully changed the grades a second time. Her actions seemed inexplicable to us. Why did she have to compound the crime? Didn't she know she was sure to get caught?

After the first release of fury, Margey and I had a good talk and she wrote a most convincing letter of apology. Fortunately, she and I had discovered that Margey could get down on paper exactly the words and sentiments she was "supposed" to have—though she still couldn't say "I'm sorry" face-to-face.

Mom,

I know when I changed my report card I made you mad and mostly disapointed after I lied and had done it before. But at the moment I didn't care about anyone but *me*. And when I did it was about my punishment. But I've thought things over and know I did wrong about changing it and lieing, and I know I deserve worse than what I got. I have to say I'm ashamed of what I got on the 1st semester but didn't care enough because I went and changed it only thinking of the trouble I would get in if I didn't. I am sorry I did this but am also sorry I got caught, but then I'm glad I did because you guys would have been so mad at me if I would of gotten caught later and would have probably flunked. So I'm thankful you caught me more than I am sorry for myself. I just hope you guys can learn to trust me soon again, and that I won't blow it.

Love you, Margey

Margey and I agreed that it would be helpful if she went in with me on school nights and did her homework in my office. During that next marking period, we cheerfully marched off in the evening and crunched M&Ms while we both went through our assignments. We enjoyed being with one another those evenings, and Margey assured me she was doing much, much better in school and that her grades would be all Bs.

They weren't. They were Ds and Fs. And she changed the Fs to Bs again. This third episode was beyond maddening. I kept thinking back to that little girl who wouldn't return the sand to the sandbox. There seemed to be no way to communicate with her once she had established a pattern.

Margey was furious that anyone expected her to pass. Her grades were not anyone's business but her own. Nor was her lying. Nor was her stealing.

Margey's grade-changing may well have been some fantasy of pleasing her parents—and, at least on some level, a clear admission of guilt, but Mark and I interpreted her actions chiefly as a denial of responsibility. I also felt betrayed and taken advantage of, and unwilling to try to help her when she did so little in return. The final marking period of the year, she changed her grades again. This time the counterfeit was sloppy and obvious, as if her hand wasn't steady enough for the delicate work.

Margey and I were at such loggerheads over school and her lying and stealing that I sought counseling. Linda Bradshaw at the Mental Health Center spoke with both Margey and me, spent several sessions alone with Margey, recommended a full battery of personality and intelligence tests, and then spoke with both of us about the results and how we might live with each other.

Somehow Linda managed to soothe both of us with a single speech. She told Margey that her test scores indicated that she was normally intelligent and should be making Bs and Cs. She said that school was probably hard for her, though, especially math, and that she was undoubtedly too active to like sitting still for long. Maybe I could find her a good math tutor. Linda talked with Margey about how upset people were bound to become when she did the same thing over and over, like changing her grades and stealing. Linda told me that school would never be Margey's favorite place, but that she had good life-skills and would probably do fine once she had school behind her. She recommended that Margey take vocational classes.

Margey and I left the last session with Linda more at peace than we had been in several months. A counselor at the high school said that if her attendance and grades were good, when she was a junior Margey would be eligible for their cosmetology program or for training in food services; there were no vocational courses available between eighth and eleventh grades. That amount of time stretched out before us like an unfamiliar road with far too many risky turnoffs.

I asked Linda if she thought a summer camp would be a good idea for Margey. Mark and I had heard about a Quaker camp in Maine that put a lot of emphasis on the kids' building their own camp facilities and planning their own schedules. Farm and Wilderness specialized in developing self-confidence through helping adolescents accomplish physical feats of all sorts. Their program seemed tailor-made for Margey. They had experience working with struggling teenagers.

Linda liked the plan; so did Margey. It wasn't entirely easy to decide to spend $2,000 for a month of camp after the year's performance, but something radical seemed called for. The whole family needed respite.

Margey and I shopped and packed. Mark planned her bus trip East. All the other children were envious. Margey was excited, and frightened; she knew the decision to send her away to camp was extreme, if not desperate, but she looked forward to the adventure. The morning she left we all breathed easier.

Within hours, however, I found several hundred dollars' worth of clothes from Target in her closet. I was furious. I had tried to please her in buying outfits for camp—a new swimsuit, everything on a long list. But she hadn't asked me for what she really wanted—a bikini— well aware that I wouldn't have thought that appropriate. In the stash from Target were three bikinis. With time away from Margey I began to feel guilty. Perhaps Margey was forced to steal when we couldn't communicate about our differences in values. What I took as an opportunity for Margey, a sacrifice for the family, she could have taken as desertion. Feeling both abandoned and terrified by the "opportunity," she wanted to build her confidence in the only way she knew how, with new clothes. It was also the case that Margey seemed to do things that would most displease me when I was most engaged in helping her, and satisfied that we were making progress.

I called to make an appointment with Linda, for when Margey returned, only to find that she had moved to Hawaii. I've always wondered if Margey and I might have fared better through the next few years if Linda had been around to help us.

The summer at Farm and Wilderness left Margey glowing with stories about her adventures, which she described with such skill that the other children were envious. She'd been on a two-day mountain climb, on a three-day canoe trip, built her own cabin, and learned to cook over a fire. She wanted to try out her recipes and everyone praised her prowess. Her counselors had been as much fun as the children her own age. And the boys, the cutest—she'd been in love, truly, three, no five times. Jeff . . . they were going to write . . . but could he ever kiss!

Things continued to go well for Margey through that summer and the next school year. Her teacher that year had decided that something must be done for the children who were failing to learn in the traditional system. Mr. Melrose developed a cooperative, individualized curriculum and was able to set a limit of fifteen students on his class. For Margey the eighth grade was a period of peace and acceptance. She did well and felt good about herself; apparently none of the students in the class hated themselves or felt like failures or acted out as they had in the past. At the end of the year, all of the parents wrote letters praising the experimental class and begging that it be continued. Mr. Melrose's class was cut the following year.

With Dawn, too, the first sign of her entering adolescence was an excessive concern with her appearance, sudden and surprising given her past inattention. She became almost as fixated on clothes as Margey. Regardless of how many outfits they had to choose from, both girls wore their single favorite day in and day out. But no matter how often I repeated instructions, Dawn ruined even her favorites in the washing machine, or left them somewhere. After innumerable mishaps, the bottle of bleach had to be stored in the trunk of my car.

Dawn's actions were never as dramatic as Margey's, but they were as desperate in their own way. Whereas Margey stormed through one relationship after another, Dawn maintained a symbiotic relationship with one girlfriend from seventh grade on. Dawn and her friend Angie slammed down the phones and parted forever virtually every night, then continued on as Best Friends. Angie's mother fought the relationship: Dawn was a Roman Catholic whereas Angie's family were devout Jehovah Witness; the mother insisted that Angie choose her friends from the church youth group.

In eighth grade, Dawn decided she had to be as thin as Angie. Diabetic and skinny as a rail, at five feet Angie couldn't have weighed a hundred pounds. By thirteen, Dawn had shot up to five feet ten. At about 140 pounds, she was shapely, though with a large frame and a full face she never looked thin. Dawn wasn't eager to diet, so she began purging, which involved a performance before as large an audience as possible at school and leaving her journal open on the kitchen table several nights a week. If she'd been more secretive, Mark and I probably would have worried more. She sometimes addressed the journal as Di:

Dear Di,

Hi How are ya? Well Angie & I are still Best friends but guess what her fuckin Mom read her diary and read about Kevin, my diet, everything I was sooooo pissed off! I cant believe she did that! I am sooooo pissed Well Today I havent eaten a thing! I will eat dinner and decide wheather to throw it up! I don't want to die anytime soon!

Diary

Hi its fat me again I just trew-up! And to top it off Doug Like Jenny! I cant believe it! I am so sad, and tierd I had bad dreams and I didn't get that much sleep at all! I wish he would Love me not her! I want to just go somewhere where I cant be hurt!

Dear Diary,

Today was a Shity day I just got in an argument with my Mom and brother and my throat hurts sooooo bad! Well at dinner I threw up all of my food which is good but then I tried to throw up & now my throt hurts!

Smile, Love Always, Porky & Fatty

I've got to Lose weight I'm a 15 year old True Blue Blimp!
I wish I could Lose tons of pounds.
           FATTY

Hi I'm back! My throt really hurts! And I feel really losey!
I ate today I just throw up & I have to eat Dinner & I'm
going to *have* to throw that up to! I wish I would be thin! I hate
to be sooooo fat! I weigh just a sec! about 124 or 125 that really
suck My goal is 115 to *110* 110 is just great I would look great!
I hate throwing up but if I stick to this scudle then it should
work
     1. Breakfast—None
     2. Lunch—None
     3. Afternoon snack—1 carret
     4. Dinner—throw it up!
I should lose weight fast I can't believe I weighed 145
                         125

        20 pounds I lost I am glad I'm not weighing that now.
I still feel like a 15 year old blimp! I just broke the bed I'm so
fat! OH yea I have an appoontment at 7:00 at Madison Center
on Thrusday that sucks! I'm reading *Tons* of Diet books to lose
weight! P.S.S. Angie hates it when I throw up and talk about
my diet & I cant help it I want to be thin so much!!!

Mark and I kept an eye on Dawn after meals that she ate as usual.
We thought that the performance in the journal was mostly attention-
getting. Then the counselor from school called. Dawn was going to the
bathroom when she arrived at school to vomit her breakfast. After a
large lunch, she did the same thing. Every afternoon there were several
trips to the toilet. Dawn's friend Angie had become alarmed and told
the school counselor she thought Dawn was bulimic. The counselor,
the teacher, the whole group around Dawn and Angie became involved; they all tried to get Dawn to stop. To no effect.
        I took Dawn to the doctor. By then she had lost almost twenty
pounds. Dr. Hanley spoke graphically to her about the possible physical damage from induced vomiting and convinced her that her weight
was normal for her size.
        Dawn's brief period of bulimic activity never seriously troubled
Mark and me; both the counselor and the doctor assured us that many
adolescent girls go through a similar stage, and we knew that Kate had.

Besides, Mark and I were convinced that Dawn was too involved with food to continue such self-punishment; for Dawn to have become seriously bulimic would have been too ironic. Mostly I was annoyed that she was making such a specimen of herself, as my grandmother used to say. She clearly needed more attention, but her manipulation made me angry. And of course I also felt terribly guilty that she had lost so much weight.

It was difficult to concentrate on Dawn's comparatively pallid acting out while Margey was becoming so uncontrollable. In her freshman year, Margey began to drink, she continued to steal, and problems with her peers mounted. She was angry all the time. The counselor at school called and said Margey had beaten up another girl, badly. Then, when she was asked to apologize, Margey not only refused, she insisted that she would do exactly the same thing the minute she got another chance. The counselor said girls often fought, but that she was seriously concerned about how remorseless Margey had become—how hard.

When she had to repeat math and history in summer school after her freshman year, Margey was furious. Perhaps she figured that after failing seventh grade and not being held back, nothing much would happen this time, either. Probably more to the point, Margey never seemed to grasp that her actions had consequences.

I was hoping that after summer school in the mornings, Margey could work and earn money to buy some of the things she wanted so desperately. Early in June, she got a job catering with the food service at Saint Catherine's College, where I taught. The first day she rode her bike into work. She called, an hour later than we'd agreed on, to say she'd had to stay late and clean up. When I picked Margey up at two o'clock, she tried to stuff her bicycle into the back seat instead of putting it on the rack behind the car. She seemed groggy, and fell asleep in midsentence as we drove home. The next day, the director of food service called to let me know that Margey and another faculty kid had stolen a bottle of bourbon from a party they were catering and gotten drunk on the lawn after they finished cleaning up at 11:00 P.M. Margey wasn't called to work again.

Everyone was thrilled, on the other hand, when Dawn landed a summer job as a junior counselor at the YMCA camp she had attended for two years. She handled the interview and was chosen, along with twenty-four others. Each cabin had two junior counselors and one senior. Mark and I were ecstatic—the directors of the camp knew Dawn's strengths and weaknesses from the previous summers; she would be in such a healthy situation all summer, and we would have some rare relief.

One week after she left for camp, the director called and said that they'd had to take Dawn to the hospital. She'd gotten so drunk the night before she had gone into shock. No, they weren't going to send her home; they'd give her one more chance. Tamed by the scare, Dawn made it through the rest of the summer without major incident.

Dawn's assignment was to supervise the craft room. She had large, awkward hands and fingers and not much confidence, and was not terribly skilled with crafts herself, but she was an adequate supervisor and clean-up person. She was asked to develop two additional skills, archery and swimming, but she wasn't able to complete either at a satisfactory level by the end of the summer. We all held our breath in the hopes that she would be allowed to return as a junior counselor the following summer. Mark and I resolved to leave all our money to the YMCA in gratitude. It was such a relief to see Dawn doing well. Margey passed both her summer school classes with Ds.

One afternoon in the middle of Margey's first semester, sophomore year, I was walking out to the parking lot at school with two mothers of large families, one with several adopted children. The mother of seven biological children said she had realized when her son was Margey's age that the family might not survive if he continued to live at home; he went away to boarding school for the rest of high school. The other mother said that one of her adopted daughters was in an institution because she was having troubles similar to Margey's, and the family had decided they could no longer cope. Something clicked in my head. It had never seemed possible to send one of my children away—boarding schools were too expensive, and adolescence was not a good time for a child to be away from home. And yet I remembered that one of my brothers had gone to the Christian Brothers in Arkansas, which had turned out to be a good experience for him. Why couldn't Margey go away? Certainly nothing good was happening at home. Just the thought made me feel as if rocks were falling off my shoulders.

I began to search out a boarding school for Margey. She wasn't happy with the idea, but she didn't refuse, either. She was miserable at home, but also, as always, terrified of trying anything new. Margey and I traveled to Saint Mary's Academy, in Nauvoo, Illinois, looked over the facilities, and the admissions staff evaluated Margey. They agreed to accept her at midsemester. Margey was most attracted to the weight room and the rooftop where the girls were allowed to "lay out."

Margey and I both enjoyed the trip to Nauvoo, the time alone together. It was exciting to think that there might actually be a way out for her. She seemed pleased that I was concerned about her. We kept talking about a new beginning, about forgetting the mess from the past. Margey liked the idea of a new group of friends, a whole new setting. Her favorite part of the preparation was choosing the various parts of her new uniforms. Almost enthusiastic, she promised to do her best.

And she did, for her first three months at Saint Mary's. The first marking period she was passing everything, even doing well in sewing and business math. The track coach saw her run and invited her to attend a practice. She tried out for the team and was the fastest runner in the school, but after a while she didn't return to practice: she had "too much schoolwork."

Late in the spring, calls began to come from the dean of students at Saint Mary's. Were we sure we weren't giving Margey more than the suggested allowance? She seemed to be accumulating much more than five dollars a week would buy. The other girls were wondering if she was taking their things. Did we know she was getting sick and missing classes? Would we make an appointment with the doctor for a checkup on her next visit home?

That summer when Margey returned home from Saint Mary's—without a single item of her own clothing—we embarked on the worst period in our lives together. From what Linda Bradshaw had said about Margey's having good life-skills, I was hopeful that she could find a job, make some money, and build her self-esteem. Nothing doing. Margey was as determined not to work as I was determined that she would. With me shoving her every inch of the way, she got three jobs and lost each of them within the first week. She refused to look further; there didn't seem much point. We were straitjacketed in one garment: she would not earn her own money; I wouldn't buy her much beyond necessities. Her desires were undiminished and she stole whenever she could. I was furious with her, but felt responsible somehow for driving her to steal.

All day long, Margey lay around in her room listening to the radio, alternating between rages and depression. She acted listless and far away, as if she was taking drugs, but none of us had any idea if she was or where she could be getting them. At dinnertime she appeared when she was called to the table, slammed her food around, clattered the dishes if it was her turn to wash them, and then returned to her room. Time and time again she came up to supper with a red, swollen face. No one had any idea from what.

After Margey returned to school and we were cleaning her room, one of the children saw a piece of cloth hanging from the ceiling tiles above her bed. We pulled out the tile and found Margey's stash—piles of stolen clothes and makeup, empty cigarette packages, and quantities of cigarette butts. Things she had stolen from me—underwear, clothes, and jewelry—came tumbling down. The empty box from the birthday present my mother had sent me in July fell into my lap. Mother had asked and asked if I'd received that package. Margey had denied having seen it, repeatedly and convincingly. Margey's destroying the present from my mother hurt me deeply. It also made me realize how sad it was that Margey and I would never have a relationship like my mother's and mine. Perhaps Margey had the same regrets.

In September, the previous months' canceled checks arrived in the mail and I found two checks for forty dollars that Margey had forged. For drugs? For clothes and makeup? No one knew.

Dawn returned from her second summer as a junior counselor at Camp Minnehaha with her trunk, as well as some milk crates, filled with other people's things: half a dozen sweat shirts, two sweat suits, twenty-nine T-shirts, innumerable bottles of shampoo and cream rinse, towels, and hairbrushes—all items she said she'd claimed from Lost and Found, many of which no doubt she had. She was furious with me for sending everything that wasn't hers to Goodwill and for the letter I wrote to her explaining why I thought she was much closer to stealing than she would admit.

It was overwhelming to start all over again down a path so worn by Margey. Dawn kept insisting that she was not Margey, that I was over-responding to her actions because of what Margey had done in the past. Of course, Dawn wasn't Margey; the two were very different, but it felt like an old wound being scraped when Dawn continued to steal, even if less aggressively than Margey. Dawn couldn't understand why her actions seemed so serious to me. I tried to explain that indeed I was oversensitive; after so many bouts with Margey, I was bound to be. Couldn't she think about that in advance and not steal, rather than blame me afterwards for overresponding?

Dawn said none of her friends cared if she borrowed things; she didn't care if they borrowed hers—and none of them had weird mothers like me. All of them could buy whatever they wanted and borrow whatever they wanted. Why did I have to be different? I reminded her of all the phone calls from Angie's mother trying to locate various items Dawn had borrowed and not returned.

I worried all the time that I was being too strict. If she had been someone's else's daughter, I probably would have agreed with Dawn's analysis. Instead of being responsive and sympathetic, I became hard and unyielding. The only soft spots were angry bruises. I know now that I was too attentive to my own feelings and not enough to Dawn's.

As she got on the bus headed for boarding school in September of her junior year, Margey bragged that she wouldn't be stuck in our prison much longer. None of us expected that she would last long at Saint Mary's, either.

I'll always be grateful to the Benedictine sisters in Nauvoo for giving the family a year's respite before they decided it was necessary to tell Mark and me that Margey could not return to their school. She started sneaking out at night and meeting migrant workers at a local bar, returning drunk in the wee hours. The dean of students said she thought Margey was into drugs, and the staff was afraid to take responsibility for what might happen next.

One of the main reasons Mark and I decided to send Margey away to school was so she wouldn't be a negative influence on Dawn. But losing Margey had been hard for Dawn. The two of them had spent a lot of their time quarreling violently, but the link between them was as strong as their feelings of being outsiders in the family. With Margey gone, Dawn had spent most of her time at home alone; she didn't have much to say and was rarely enthusiastic about anything. She held me responsible for sending her sister away.

The night before Margey was due to arrive home, Dawn and I were alone, eating supper. Dawn sensed how much I was dreading her sister's return, and we had a grim discussion.

"Mom, do you wish Margey was dead?"

"No. I wish she did a lot of things differently though."

"Would you miss her if she was dead?"

"Miss her? I have to think about that one. What do you think I should miss?"

"What would you miss about her if she was dead?"

"That's what I just asked you. For sure I would not miss being so angry with her. What do you think I should miss?"

"Well, she's nice."

"When? To me?"

"She's nice to me."

"What does she do?"

"She lets me borrow her clothes."

"She steals mine. Gives them to her friends."

"Mom, do you wish you hadn't adopted kids?"

"I don't know. A lot of the time I feel like my adopted kids need a different kind of mother."

"Why did you adopt kids?"

"Why did we adopt kids? We wanted more children and didn't think we should have any more. We wanted another girl, a sister for Kate. We liked kids."

"Are you glad you did it?"

"Glad we did it? What do you think?"

"Why do you wish Margey was dead?"

"I do not wish anyone were dead. I may wish that things were different, but you just can't wish people dead. That's the worst thing possible."

"Do you hate Margey?"

"Of course I don't hate Margey, but there's no question that I hate some of the stuff she does. How do you feel about her getting kicked out of that school, getting almost all Fs, meeting the bus back to school dead drunk? Do you know how many terrible things she has done since I saw her last?"

"Why do you wish that Margey was dead?"

"Dawn, would you think about what you are saying about me?"

"I'm not saying anything about you."

"You don't think these questions are a little bit insulting?"

"Why do you wish that Margey was dead?"

"Dawn, are you listening? I already told you—I do not wish Margey was dead. Why do you keep on attacking me like this?"

"I'm not attacking you."

"Are you mad because Margey is coming home tomorrow and nobody is doing anything to get ready for her?"

"No. I don't know. Do you wish she wasn't coming home?"

"Dawn, I'm very angry with the way Margey has behaved. I can't tell you honestly that I'm happy to see her right now. Why are you asking all this tonight? Can't you see how these questions are making me feel?"

"Not really. It's just a question."

"You don't think that people ask questions for reasons?"

"Not really."

"Dawn, you expect me to forgive everything Margey does, just like you do. I wish I could, but I can't. You don't understand why I am angry with her, do you?"

"Yeah, I guess I do."

"Do you really?"

"Yeah. But I don't see why you wish she was dead."

"Dawn, you are making me furious. You are being so mean. And I don't think very honest."

"I'm being just fine. Why are you getting so upset?"

"I think you are saying all this because I'm the only one home and you are mad that no one beside you much wants to see Margey."

"No. I'm not."

"Damn it, Dawn, I can't believe you are not listening to yourself at all. Get out of this room. Just go to your room. I don't want to deal with you right now."

I didn't do well by Dawn in that conversation. She was right: I didn't want Margey to come home and I should have granted her point instead of taking her worries personally. Dawn was no doubt feeling that she and Margey were a pair and that I didn't want her around either—that I wanted both of them dead. She was also on target asking me if I wished I had not adopted children. That question had always been at the heart of the matter, but I didn't know the answer, not really, not once and for all. Of course I didn't wish Margey and Dawn dead, but I was guilty enough, now and again, of wishing our paths had never crossed. What's the difference to a child? Rather than answer Dawn honestly, I pushed questions back at her. As so often happened, our timing was terrible—I was too angry about Margey's behavior and upset by her imminent return to listen to Dawn's concerns, and express some support for her.

During this period, Margey, Dawn and I struggled with our vastly different relationships to the material world. It wasn't that I was less materialistic: I preferred a few expensive items, and they wanted quantities of cheap ones. They were solid citizens of a consumer society; I was a snob. I kept wishing for them an environment like my mother-in-law's house, filled to the brim with knickknacks and mementos. They wanted me to show my love by buying them things. For me, buying things didn't signify love, though *not* buying them signified more than I was prepared to admit. I wanted them to show their love and respect by doing their work and communicating with me. All three of us yearned to be a better match for one another.

Our five children reached adolescence just as I approached the most difficult part of my career—the struggle for tenure. Mark was comfortable and successful as a full professor, but my progress from a part-time position to full-time and tenure had been much harder. English departments are notoriously complicated and divided, and mine sank to the depths in both areas. Work was extremely stressful much of the time; home, equally so. But the affirmation I received as a teacher helped give me the confidence to survive life with five teenagers. When I won the college's teaching award, I thanked my family publicly for sharing my time with students. Finally, when the children were between fifteen and nineteen, I did receive tenure, after being, as Mark said, a "cliff-hanger to the end." The fear of being turned out of the job then disappeared, even though the work of reading all those books and responding to all those papers remained. At least I was usually still up reading when the teenagers' curfews rolled around, and we often had long chats at the hours when adolescents are most loquacious.

Life at home grew more chaotic. The kitchen became a wet mess: once in a while, water leaked from the bathroom above the kitchen and trailed from the refrigerator to the center of the floor. Our yard was in such bad shape that neighbors considered offering to pay the children to mow the lawn and clean up the leaves. Paint was peeling off the outside of the house in wide strips and it took Sam and Jack the entire summer to repaint the place. Every room inside needed cleaning and scrubbing and painting. A summer visitor from Mexico lingered a whole month painting the living room. I resisted to the end getting help with cleaning because I'd grown up with a housekeeper in Mississippi and didn't think that having "help" was good for children. In desperation, I called a cleaning service. A crew of five did one stint in the house, then left a note that this particular place was too much for them.

Kate and her boyfriend from college created one particularly memorable event. The tub had gotten plugged—no wonder, considering the amount of hair it swallowed—and was about one-quarter full of water and the bottle of muriatic acid that had been ineffectual in unclogging the drain. I'd left a printed note on the door saying NO ONE was to use the tub unless they were prepared to risk burning precious parts. Kate and her boyfriend laughed, thinking it was a joke, and proceeded to take their showers, filling the tub even higher with the poison that eventually had to be bailed out.

The five members of the original family attempted to defend themselves from the stress of so much chaos by fleeing the house, which by default became Margey's and Dawn's domain. They, too, would no doubt have preferred flight, but they had fewer options. Mark immersed himself in work and coaching soccer teams that played all over the state and in regional and national tournaments. I worked long hours and lingered with my friends. Kate, Sam, and Jack became involved in school activities and sports or closed the doors of their rooms and turned up the volume on their stereos. Margey and Dawn stayed at home and grew angrier. They had nowhere to go. They had few friends or invitations.

The abandonment of the house, in particular the kitchen, meant that the cupboards and freezers were no longer filled with food. There was always enough to eat if you worked at it—things that took time to prepare, noodles, or macaroni and cheese, sandwich fixings, and fresh fruits and vegetables from the farmers' market—but rarely cookies or ice cream, or chips, the sources of immediate satisfaction that kids love. I would stop by the grocery on the way home from work, buy fixings, claim the kitchen for the night, then return it to Margey and Dawn the next morning. This desertion of what my Spanish cookbook calls "the soul of the home" contributed to the empty feeling of the house and to some of the empty feelings of those who lived there.

Flight

When Margey came home from Saint Mary's Academy the Christmas of her junior year, Mark and I were desperate. She'd been dismissed from the boarding school, and we had already decided that there was no point in her returning to school in Saint Paul. We briefly toyed with the idea of declaring her incorrigible and ending our parental responsibilities, as another adoptive family had done with their daughter. I was more in favor of the idea than Mark and checked into the legalities. But neither of us had the nerve, and we were also not convinced it was the right decision.

I admitted, I insisted, that I could not live with Margey, that we must find a placement for her. But no other school I contacted would agree to admit her. Mark talked with another adoptive family about the placements they had tried. They recommended Clayton Home, a Methodist group home for adolescents, not far from the Twin Cities. Margey, Mark, and I visited Clayton Home shortly after Christmas. Margey was furious with the idea of our sending her away again: who could know what her fears were about the consequences of her dismissal from Saint Mary's? She was rude and aggressive with the staff at Clayton Home, informed everyone that she wasn't going to stay long, she would run away the first chance she got, and that at sixteen she was perfectly capable of taking care of herself. The staff seemed unflappable. They said they'd seen lots of the same and agreed to accept her.

Karen Harty, the social worker in charge of discipline at Clayton Home, was tall and stringy—tough enough for her job; indeed, for any job. "Margey simply has to take responsibility for her actions," she told me. "We try and teach them that every action has consequences. We let them make their own choices and then force them to take the consequences."

How well I knew that litany. It felt as if Margey had done little but take consequences since the seventh grade. She was always "under the jail," I told Karen. Before she got out from under one consequence, she'd have piled up six more. She made me want to punish her until I broke through her endurance—grounding, chores, silence . . . the previous year we scarcely spoke for six months. I wasn't sure she would ever break.

I wondered aloud whether punishment had escalated her defiance, her lying, and stealing. Karen doubted it; Margey was probably going to do what she was going to do. Because Margey observed me so closely, she had a genius for hooking into my weaknesses. At this point in our lives, the hook was her acting out and my retaliation and inability to quit before the finish. If she pulled one way, I followed; neither of us ever missed a cue. We were as mean as we could be with one another. A friend once told me, "If you keep on, you'll eventually have to cut off her hand for stealing. Why don't you take comfort in thinking about all the societies where Margey's and Dawn's skill as thieves would have been not only socially acceptable, but necessary for survival?"

Karen insisted that a kid had to hit bottom before she could face her problems and do anything about them. But, but . . . I kept thinking, what if she has no bottom? . . . I don't think she does . . . except maybe dead.

In the meantime, I received a call from Dawn's counselor at school asking me if I knew about the burns on her legs; they were extremely serious, she thought. I told her I didn't know what she was talking about. It turned out that Margey had given Dawn her sunlamp when she left for school—through which we finally gleaned the cause of Margey's swollen and blistered face the previous summer. Now Dawn had burned her thighs under the lamp and was in so much pain that she had shown her burns to the school nurse.

I was stunned when I saw the huge blisters on Dawn's legs. And angry with her for following Margey's lead in everything, even when she was no longer at home. It also hurt that Dawn hadn't shown me the burns and asked me to take her to the doctor instead of going to the school nurse. Then guilt kicked in: if I'd looked after her better, she would not have burned herself; if Dawn had felt comfortable with me, she wouldn't have had to confide in someone else. I felt punished, like a naughty mother. Dawn and I went to Dr. Hanley, who gave Dawn a salve for her legs and another of her talks.

During the winter—under Clayton Home's sink-to-the-bottom policy—Margey broke into the boys' dorm every weekend, cut more than half of her classes at school, did drugs and had sex in the parking lot, wrecked the kitchen in the dorm so severely—not once but twice—that the police had to come and lock her up for twenty-four hours. Karen kept saying each time she called with another story that Margey hadn't yet hit bottom, she didn't think.

"Isn't there any other way?" The question came up when Mark and I were having a meeting with Karen and the school psychologist. "She doesn't give a damn about your consequences as long as she can do whatever she wants. It sounds like she's getting worse and worse."

"We work on the level system here," one of them said. "Margey has yet to get off level zero, so she never has any privileges. It's pretty hard to talk to her. She's walked out of therapy and slammed the door three weeks running. She shouts over your voice if you tell her something. If you ask her a question, she refuses to answer you."

"Can't you make her stay for therapy?" Mark asked them. "Why do you let her walk out when she's here for therapy?"

"We don't force them here. We don't have restraints. Even if someone is tied down, they won't talk if they don't want to. Much less listen."

"And you can't persuade her?" Mark couldn't believe his ears.

"Not so far. She is nothing but her anger right now. Nobody is going to take that away from her. Do you know how she eats?"

"Awfully fast," I said.

"It almost makes you sick to sit beside her."

"Yeah, I know," I said.

"She stuffs food down her throat, talks with her mouth full, sprays food all over the table and everyone within range. When she's mad, which is practically all the time, she's twice as bad."

"Have you tried to get her to eat more slowly?" Mark kept pushing.

"When you tell her to do something, she knows she's getting you and she really puts on a show."

"Margey eats that way," I said, "because she knows how revolting that is for all of us."

"It's what she does to the appetites of those around her that bothers me. No one on the staff will sit by her or look at her during meals. Dr. Pembroke wants her to eat at least one meal somewhere else, to spare her audience."

That's exactly the response Margey's looking for, I thought, but Karen wasn't any angrier or more disgusted than Mark and I had been. We were in another city, far enough away to be a little calmer in the face of Margey's machinations. Besides, the angry part of me almost enjoyed it when other people seemed to provoke Margey as I had; they became my sympathy group. Still, it always seemed as if they thought it was my fault. Couldn't I at least have taught her table manners?

"I'm not overly impressed, are you?" Mark said when we got to the car. We tried to think of another alternative, wondered if Margey hadn't been doing somewhat better at home. The staff at Clayton Home tolerated far more than we did, we kept thinking. But we knew Margey had gotten much worse, much more aggressive, much, much angrier. Neither Mark nor I could even approach the thought of bringing her home.

Two weeks later, Mark and I attended a family counseling session at Clayton Home. Margey sat stone silent for the first thirty minutes and then left, slamming the door behind her. When she agreed to go out to eat with us the next family visitation day—because she couldn't stand having us hang around any of her friends—she crammed food in her mouth and splattered lettuce on me when she screamed how much she hated us, how much she wished we would go away and leave her alone. None of the other kids' parents kept bugging them. Karen Harty was just like me. She had the wrong name. Her name shoulda' been Ann Kimble.

Margey was right, except that watching Karen's approach made me more uncomfortable than ever with my own way of dealing with her. We were all ensnared in some perverse Skinner-inspired conditioning process—all very rational, commonsensical, and well organized; when the program didn't work with a child who broke rules to confirm her self-hatred, none of us knew what else to do.

Of course, Mark and I were trying to stand by Margey. That made her all the more furious, especially since it was on our terms. Who were we kidding, she yelled, coming and visiting, acting like we cared about her. Putting on a big show, like we were Olympic-class, concerned parents or something. What a joke! She'd be a hundred times better off if she never saw us again, if she had never seen us in the first place.

She accused me of being as happy as I could possibly be with how everything was going. The bottom line to her was that she had been shipped out yet again. "Easy for you to visit," Margey screamed as we drove away, "I have to stay in this prison."

Karen kept calling with unsettling stories. She had little doubt that Margey would soon be successful in her threats to run away. The weather was getting warmer; kids managed to get away from them every spring. Josh, the young man Margey had taken up with, was a member of one of the gangs in White Bear Lake; he had street smarts and contacts. The police had been alerted.

Karen was right.

"This is Karen from Clayton Home. I have to tell you Margey has run away."

"She did! Oh no! You said she was going to. When?"

"About an hour ago. The kids were going on an outing to the bowling alley. As soon as we opened up the back door of the van she ran off into the dark."

"Was she alone?"

"No, she was with a boy and another girl."

"Who are they? How old are they?"

"Well, Josh is sixteen—he's local—so he knows his way around. Penny, the other girl—she's fourteen—has run away a lot, she knows what to do."

"Do you have any idea where they're going?"

"One of the other kids told us that they'd been talking in school with some of the Rangers."

"They're the gang?"

"One of the gangs."

"What happens now?"

"We've reported them as runaways to the police."

"Do you think the police will find them?"

"They always do."

"How long does that take?"

"I've never known it to take more than a couple of weeks."

"A couple of weeks! Think what all could happen to her in a couple of weeks?"

Perhaps because she was so angry with me for sending Margey to Clayton Home, perhaps because she wanted something more from me herself, Dawn began taking my things. First there were the usual items most kids take from their mothers, like underwear when hers was in the wash. Then she moved to more valuable and disturbing objects—clothes, jewelry, and more and more underwear. I finally asked Dawn if she *could* stop herself from going in my room when I wasn't home, rummaging through my drawers and taking whatever pleased her.

She didn't answer.

I asked her again.

She didn't say anything.

I decided that she simply could not help herself. That meant I did not have to become furious every time I came home to find something missing. To protect both of us, I put a padlock on the bedroom door. That didn't help as much as I'd hoped, because both Mark and I were lousy gatekeepers, and Dawn was intent on getting into the room and removing something every time she found the lock unfastened. It became a foul game between us. The only way she would return anything she had taken, thereby admitting the theft, was if I threatened to deprive her of something she really wanted.

After she took and lost my leather coat, a treasured gift, Dawn and I discussed the matter with her therapist at the mental health center. More accurately, I raged at the therapist after she said it was my responsibility to keep the things I cared about under lock and key. What was going to happen to Dawn, I asked the therapist, if all controls remained external? I had no intention of serving as her jailer throughout her life.

It made me furious that Dawn's stealing was somehow my fault, but somewhere inside I also felt as if I were responsible. In a grim logic that was probably never conscious, it made perfect sense for Dawn to take something that had been given to me; after all, I was not giving her nearly enough. In addition, I had been given so much more than she had, from the start. From the opposite perspective, I imagined that if I'd been able to give her what she needed, be what she wanted, Dawn wouldn't have had to steal from me. She must have been trying to get back at me, to demand more of what I should have been willing to give—just as her sister had.

Nevertheless, as usual, I rummaged through possibilities for a punishment, no doubt more out of my own frustration than with any real hope of stopping Dawn's stealing. We were already at saturation point with chores, which brought their own nightmare of supervision; and I didn't want to ground her as I might have Kate, Sam, or Jack—she had precious few invitations and it seemed important that she be able to accept those. I decided to make Dawn replace the leather coat, a very expensive piece of clothing given her means. She was furious with that punishment; she had written an apology and wanted the matter to end there. I felt like an unjust judge knowing full well the money I removed from her savings account had no connection with her taking the coat:

Dawn didn't understand anything about the value of a leather coat or of money in her hand, much less money in the bank.

"This is Karen from Clayton Home. We had a call from the police today. They said that Margey and Josh showed up at the school cafeteria during lunch hour. In all new clothes. They told the other kids they were set up in an apartment and having a great time. Drugs, alcohol—they were fixed and ready for company."

"Did anyone try and stop them?"

"The school called the police right away. They caught Josh, but Margey got away."

"Got away?"

"She ran and hid in one classroom after another. Some of the girls may have helped her hide in the dressing room. Anyhow, they couldn't catch her."

"How could she manage that?"

"I don't know. She does have the nerve, let me tell you."

"Yeah . . . so she's alone now?"

"I doubt it. Josh won't say a word. He won't tell us where they were, who was with them, anything."

"So they have a place to stay? Is it safe?"

"Apparently they're some place."

"Does Josh seem okay?"

"I guess so, it's hard to tell."

"Do you think he'll tell you anything later?"

"I doubt it. He ran away last year, stayed away six months, and has never said one word about what happened."

"Six months? . . ."

"Yeah, he has a lot of contacts."

"Great. Where are his parents?"

"His mother moved to Ohio and never sent her address. His dad's in jail, still, I think."

"Do you think he might talk to me?"

"I asked him, he said not to try it, I'd be sorry."

"Well, maybe the police have a better chance of finding her now."

"Maybe so. The police think she's with the gang somewhere downtown. They think they pretty much know where. They're worried because of that killing last month; there's been a lot of gang fighting lately. It's always that way in the spring."

"I see. Should I call the police?"

"You can if you'd like. They know you're waiting to hear."

That night I dreamed of being called by the police to identify a body. I was standing in front of a drawer at the morgue. The policeman pulled the sheet off the naked body. It was Margey. Her whole body looked like it was covered with a thick layer of pancake makeup. I touched her toe—it felt like lard on a popsicle stick. A policeman asked me if that was my daughter. Yes and no—no, no, no.

Every time the phone rang during those nineteen days she was gone, everyone in the house jumped. Whenever the fear hit us, we couldn't think of anything else. Someone always had to be home to answer the phone.

The phone rang a lot those days, too. Dawn and her friend Angie had sent out fliers all over school advertising a "grand opening" sale of sex devices—pills guaranteed to produce "seismic organisms" (*sic*), giant phalluses, telephone titillation—and given our phone number to call for further information. At first the cracking voices on the phone provided comic relief. But eventually the phone's ringing every five minutes all night long became irritating. I threatened to turn the girls in to Angie's mother and to show her the catalog, illustrated in Angie's hand, if they didn't straighten up immediately. Dawn was a mighty good girl for one week: she even cleaned her room.

I worried that Dawn's acting out upset me less than Margey's because I wasn't as closely connected with her as with Margey. But perhaps Dawn's behavior hooked me less because it seemed more self-absorbed, coming more from her own agenda, which was bizarre enough but not always in direct opposition to me, as Margey's so often seemed.

"Mom, the police just left." Dawn was waiting for me when I walked in the door.

"What were they doing here? Was it Margey? Have they found her?"

"It's about our house."

"What about our house?"

"It's been robbed."

"No—. Margey?"

"The policemen think maybe."

"Damn, I forgot to lock the door. What did she take?"

"A lot of stuff. All my pants. Sam's box and all his tapes. The television. And we can't find Venus."

"Venus? What on earth would Margey want with a dog? She doesn't even *like* Venus."

"She isn't here."

"She isn't? Have you looked everywhere? Did you leave her out this morning?"

"Jack says he's positive she was in the house."

"He's been positive before. Did you go around the neighborhood and call for her?"

"Yeah. She isn't anywhere."

"Go out and call her again. Try across the street at Target; you know she goes that far if she gets a chance. What on earth does she want with Venus? The clothes, the tapes—those make sense. But Venus? She's the nicest person in the house."

"I don't know. Dad said maybe Margey left the door open and Venus ran away and got run over. He called the pound but nobody saw her."

"What did she take of yours?"

"All my pants. And my red sweater and the Coca-Cola sweatshirt."

"All Sam's tapes? What'd he say?"

"A lot."

"Where are the boys?"

"Out lifting."

"Go out and look for Venus, please."

"I just did five minutes ago."

"Go again, and try around back of the McDonald's. Check their dog pen."

Several months earlier, Mark had called a locksmith to put dead bolts on the back and front doors, hoping to prevent exactly what had happened. But having the locks on the doors hadn't helped; none of us could remember to use them.

In her raid, Margey also took Kate's jewelry—a gold bracelet that was a gift from her best friend, a ring Mark and I had given her for Christmas, and another ring, also a gift from a friend. I was thankful that I'd taken my jewelry case to school. Margey always stole the things that hurt most to lose, the pieces that represented all she must have wished she had. On a less psychoanalytic level, she stole what she could hock.

The household was beyond anger with Margey. Kate went out and bought a padlock for the door of her room. All of us mourned the dog. We were stunned by what Margey had done, terrified by what might happen to her at any moment. We all found ourselves thinking about that little girl who had rocked herself back and forth in her bed to stay asleep. Now she was fully awake.

"This is Officer Jacobs with the White Bear Lake City Police. Do you have a daughter named Margey who has been reported as a runaway?"

"Yes, have you found her?"

"She's down here at the station."

"Thank heavens. How is she?"

"Foulest mouth I've ever seen on a kid. Or else she shuts down like the morgue."

"Yes. . . . I'm so glad you have her. How did you find her? Where was she?"

"For about a week now we've been watching the house where she's been staying. We picked her up about thirty minutes ago. Along with a thirteen-year-old girl named Penny."

"Thank goodness. Is she okay?"

"She's hungry and furious."

"I'll bet. What a relief, officer."

"We need you to come to the station and identify the items missing from your house."

"Did you find a dog with Margey? Our dog has been missing since the day the things were taken from our house."

"As a matter of fact, we found two dogs locked up in the bathroom. We took them to the humane society to be checked out. The dogs have to remain at the shelter for twenty-four hours. Describe your dog for me?"

"She's a mix, but she looks mostly German shepherd."

"Yeah, sounds like one of them. And a little black-and-white terrier. Do you know anything about the other dog?"

"No. What in the world did they want with those dogs?"

"You asking *me*?"

When I went to the police station, Officer Jacobs was very kind and obviously curious about what kind of family had produced Margey. He said if she hadn't been a minor, one of the policemen would probably have been provoked into roughing her up, her mouth was so foul.

Officer Jacobs said he needed me to be present while he took a statement from Margey. He'd go get her and see if she would talk. I stared at a poster above his desk, LEAVE HOME NOW WHILE YOU STILL KNOW EVERYTHING. Cynical. And true.

I went through the pile the police had dropped on a big table in the hall—clothes, empty pop cans, McDonald's containers, cereal boxes and cartons of tapes, telephones, parts of stereos, bedding, makeup, hair dryers. Everything was covered with crumbs and ketchup and looked shabby and filthy, including socks and underwear. There was a lot I didn't recognize.

In a few minutes, Officer Jacobs came back with Margey. She looked rough—makeup smeared beneath her eyes, her bleached hair scraggly. She was wearing a boy's black-cotton sweater, loose and hanging, torn jeans, dirty tennis shoes without laces or socks. She'd been asleep.

Margey didn't look at me, "What's she doing in here? I told you I didn't want to see her."

"You're a minor. You have to have a parent or guardian or lawyer with you to protect your rights when I take your statement."

"You already know everything. What the fuck difference does it make? She doesn't give a fuck about me."

I asked Margey how she was doing. "Since when do you fucking care?"

"Want a cigarette?" the officer asked her.

"Yeah."

She snatched the cigarette, waited for him to light it, puffed hungrily. "I'm not going to tell you anything. It's a fucking waste of time."

Officer Jacobs told her he wasn't going to ask her anything; he was just going to read her the facts and she could sign the statement or not sign the statement—that was her business. But Margey had it right: the police already knew everything in their report was true.

If he knew everything, what the fuck was he asking her for? She wasn't going to tell him who she was with. She sat there. He told her she did not have to sign anything she didn't want to. She said what the fucking difference did it make anyhow and signed. I signed the statement and Officer Jacobs took Margey back to her cell.

I waited beside his desk for Officer Jacobs to return. In a cubicle across the room another officer was taking a report from a social worker.

The Child Protective Services worker had picked up a three-year-old client named Claire from her grandmother's house. As they pulled away from the curb, the little girl had started sobbing—choking and shaking. The social worker had asked what was wrong. Claire said they had put her up on the kitchen table—her grandmother and her boyfriend with the sticky-outie teeth—and looked at her and looked at her. She was up there for a long, long time. They tickled her. They had rough hands, they scratched her stomach. They laughed real loud all the time they were looking at her.

The social worker took Claire to the emergency room, but she'd been there before, and when the doctor tried to examine her, she got hysterical. So there was no evidence.

The officer was asking the social worker if there was any way she could get more information—maybe go out to the grandmother's house and ask some questions? The social worker didn't seem to think anyone could do anything, except report the facts. Probably they couldn't even terminate the grandmother's visiting rights. The child was too young for anyone to believe she knew what she was talking about.

Officer Jacobs came back a few minutes later and said Margey had given him considerable trouble. Did I mind if he asked why she was so angry? It was a long, long story, I told him. She was taken away from her birth mother for abuse and neglect, no telling what all she'd been through. I asked him was she really so much worse than the other kids he saw? He said she was worse than most, her mouth for sure. He said there was just no help for it, some kids were born without a conscience.

Driving home, I wondered whether Margey really didn't have a conscience. At first it felt good to think she might have been born that way, like Officer Jacobs said. That let Mark and me off the hook. But there seemed to be a lot more to the conscience thing than that. It had never seemed that Margey had any real desire to please anyone else— she was all alone on the planet. Or that she was ever sorry for anything she did, except for herself when she was punished. And she could never anticipate or accept consequences. All of these behaviors pointed to a nonexistent or weak conscience, but something terrible must have happened to stop what is so natural in children—to try to please their parents.

Then I really got into it with myself. But had Margey ever been able to please me, the critical one? And how often did I get the ball rolling?

Margey loved-hated everything about me because I had replaced her birth mother. She probably couldn't have done much else. But it didn't console me to hate Claire's grandmother for this mess, or Margey's and Dawn's mother, which I might have, if I'd had them to hate as Margey had me. Margey's mother was too far away to hate. I, Margey's mother, had also made plenty of mistakes.

A friend whose mother was mentally ill described the recurrent feeling that she was responsible, at some level, for her mother's actions, even though she knew her mother was clinically ill, and my friend was not. Indeed, my friend did provoke many of her mother's actions, simply by being who she was.

Similarly, by being who I was, I was an enormous provocation to Margey and Dawn. In some ways they knew me better than anyone in the world—especially Margey, who studied me so intently. The problem was that Margey used her close scrutiny to become everything I wasn't. She knew, for instance, that being a good mother was important to my sense of self-worth. "If I'm a bad daughter, you're a bad mother," she once told me.

Perhaps because biology and experience had left us little chance of actually being very much alike—Margey, and Dawn, too—went all the way in the opposite direction. If I crossed my legs, Margey spread her knees; if I was soft-spoken, she was loud; if I chewed with my mouth closed, she chewed with hers open; if I valued being a lady, she was going to be anything but. As for Dawn, if I wanted to be independent and autonomous, she was all the more likely to be dependent and passive.

It probably made matters worse that I was cast in clear opposition to their birth mother. At some level, they must have had fantasies of defending, or returning to, or becoming, the mother they had lost. Perhaps they yearned to get back at me for taking their mother away from them or for thinking I could ever take her place.

It was a strange feeling—being observed so carefully; being simultaneously admired and rejected. Like my friend with the disturbed mother, I felt responsible: being what I was set up our game of mirror images. Some of these responses I understood from my own experience. My mother and I were so different that I used to wonder where I'd come from, until one of her sisters came to visit and I realized the two of us were much more alike than my mother and I. But the ways Margey and Dawn worked out their differences from me were self-destructive for them. Our differences were not based on love and respect; they were much more closely linked with judgment and control.

One time, Margey admitted that she enjoyed the attention when she was in trouble. She got to be best at something—she was nothing if not competitive. It probably had not done her any good to be unseated as the oldest child in her biological family. She had inherited all the competitiveness of an eldest; but as fourth in our family, she had three tough acts to follow in terms of positive accomplishments. What she was best at she trumpeted: she was smaller and better coordinated than Kate, and she tormented her sister, who as a teen was vulnerable to the comparison. Margey's nickname for Kate, Big Kat, stuck, and it was only years later that it ceased to irritate Kate. Margey also signaled herself as the sexiest one, which embarrassed and puzzled all four other children, and their friends, who were much more self-conscious about their bodies.

Who knows, perhaps the original family of five grew more in opposition to Margey and Dawn than they to us; doubtless we all grew toward extremes. If the girls were materialistic, others of us became increasingly intolerant of consumerism. If they wanted to hang out, we had to work. When they were focused on sex, we made prudish judgments.

Yet if those with different backgrounds help us learn to question our assumptions, nothing could have been better for the original family than living with Margey and Dawn. The girls were always making us question: did they, for example, have a certain wisdom in not over-committing to the work ethic? Certainly it was not pleasant living with parents who sold themselves, at intervals, to their jobs.

The girls also provided exemplars for the other children of what happened to those who were disorganized and negative, who could not manage themselves or their environments, who never seemed to accept responsibility or learn from their mistakes. But witnessing frustration and defeat in the lives of those so close caused a great deal of turbulence in the family unconscious. Watching Margey and Dawn slip and fall instilled a dark terror in each of us: Why did we always feel more fortunate than they? Were we in truth more fortunate? Was there then a difference between *we* and *they*? Was it blood? Luck? Love? Intelligence? What was the cause and the meaning of all our differences?

Locked In

As the children moved through adolescence, Mark and I had become more and more housebound. The girls required so much supervision that one of us always had to be on duty: their attendance at school had to be carefully monitored; they both had to be delivered everywhere; because they were so rarely invited out, there were few nights off duty. A few times Margey had asked to be driven, alone, to a school function, then ended up getting into trouble with alcohol, or drugs, or sex, or all three. Someone had to be home as much as possible to keep the house from becoming a pleasure den when Dawn and her boyfriend became sexually active.

On the other hand, Kate, Sam, and Jack were always running in and out of the house, in transit to and from academic and social events. High school was tough enough on Margey and Dawn; having more active and accepted siblings made matters much worse. Margey and Dawn had grown angry, sullen, and worse.

These feelings of being imprisoned were compounded when Margey entered the legal system at age sixteen and other people began to make decisions about what was to happen to her. Mark and I were not given any choice: we had to follow along and pay the bill. It was infuriating. We felt powerless, not knowing what else to do.

This same eventful spring, Sam treated us all to his personal worst. He and a group of friends rented a newly remodeled hotel room for their senior prom after-party. As luck would have it, some pipes from the original building were still in the ceiling, just high enough to provide monkey bars. The partygoers did several-hundred-dollars-worth of damage, swinging from the ceiling pipes, crash-landing on brand-new mattresses, and spraying champagne all over the freshly painted walls. Widely recognized as one of the ringleaders, Sam was given the responsibility for collecting money from his fellows and helping re-paint the room. He did his painting chore almost cheerfully, hoping to cover up the whole event in all our minds. Though Mark and I were both horrified and furious with Sam for his inconsiderate behavior, we couldn't help feeling how simple the cleanup seemed in comparison with the way things often continued, unresolved and ominous, after an episode with Margey or Dawn.

After her arrest as a runaway, Margey was moved from the city jail in South Saint Paul to the juvenile detention center in nearby White Bear Lake. Visiting hours were from 4:00 P.M. to 6:00 P.M. on weekends; I was welcome to arrive anytime in those hours and stay for thirty minutes.

The matron at the detention center unlocked three doors and left me waiting in a cubicle with a table in the center and four chairs. The walls and the door were painted bright orange. The table was brown and the chairs a moss green. I heard the locks turn one at a time and saw the matron in the door of the cubicle, this time with Margey behind her. Margey turned around and faced back down the hall, "I don't want to see her. Take me back."

"Fine, if you're sure that's what you want," the matron said, "or if you'd like to stay a few minutes, you can press that button on the wall when you're ready to leave and I'll come and get you immediately." She turned to me, "Mrs. Kimble, you can also press that button at any point. Otherwise I'll be back in thirty minutes."

I asked Margey if she might want to talk a few minutes as long as I was there. She didn't say anything, but she didn't move to leave, either. The matron waited a minute and then backed out the door; the sound of her keys in the locks followed her.

Margey moved to the farthest green chair and slouched low. She was clean, dressed in a black sweatshirt and gray sweatpants, no makeup, straight hair. She looked at the floor, at her fingernails, at the wall behind me. "You don't think I'm going to talk to the world's biggest bitch . . . really . . . now do you?"

I didn't say anything.

"I gotta get the fuck outta this room. They think they can make me do any fucking thing they want."

"All you have to do is get up and press that button," I said. "But I can tell you, Margey, I'm *not* going to go near that button. I want to see you."

She looked up at the button to the right of the door. Then she tilted her chair up against the wall and worked hard on her gum. "I look like this because they won't give me my goddamn makeup. They won't give me nothing—no clothes, nothing—look how I look. Cigarettes—forget it. But don't think they don't smoke any time they want. Right in front of me. Look at my fingernails—this one's broken, this one's splitting, this one's plain disgusting. They don't even have a nail file here. You got one on you?"

"No, I'm sorry. There's some makeup in the things I picked up from Clayton Home. You want me to bring that to you, and a nail file?"

"Do I want you to. . . . You know what I want you to do? Go back to your house. Go back to the other children you love so much. Quit this fucking faking."

"Everyone said to tell you hello. They wanted me to ask if you'd like to see any of them. Dawn maybe, if they'll let her visit?"

"FUCK NO. Why the fuck can't every one of you assholes leave me alone? That's what I want. That's what you want, too, but you're too fucking pure to admit it."

"Okay. Fine."

"You know what? I'd a whole lot rather be here than in your house. This place is pretty cool. The best part about jail, you want to know what it is? I don't have to be around you. And that includes right this minute."

"Like the matron told you, all you have to do is press the button. I'm not going to, I told you, regardless of what you say. I want to see you."

"I'll punch that button when I get fucking ready, you hear?"

Her snarl split her face in two, but she seemed a tad softer—though only a mother could tell.

"I came to see how you're doing. Ask you if you want me to bring you anything."

"I want my makeup and curling iron. Look at me. You think I look like a witch on purpose?"

"You look pretty good to me."

"You don't know shit."

"How long will you be here?"

"How the fuck do you think I'd know?"

"The juvenile counselor, Mrs. Larson, she said she'd talked with you. How'd that go?"

"That bitch. You know who she's like? She's exactly like you. I told her not to try and talk to me again. And I wasn't going to talk with anyone the least bit like her. That happens to include . . . guess who—you."

"Mrs. Larson said she wanted you to go to a hospital in Rochester where they help teenagers."

"There's not one fucking thing wrong with me. Except my totally fucked up family. I did just great for three weeks all by myself. Now didn't I? Got high ALL the time. I mean ALL THE TIME, day and night. You can't stand thinking 'bout me having so much fun, can you?"

Margey had a point, I guess; she did always make me feel worn out and repressed.

"That was the best time in my whole life. And I'm going back. Don't think there's one thing you can do to stop me, you hear that . . . bitch?"

I skipped from topic to topic trying to find something we could talk about. "Is Josh in here with you?"

"What makes you think that's any of your business?"

"Karen from Clayton Home said he was in here with you."

"If you fucking know everything, how come you're asking me?"

"How's he doing?"

"You think I'd tell you one fucking thing? You gotta be kidding."

Another dead end. Another subject. "So, what do you do all day?"

"Shitty-ass school, workbooks for babies in math, group three times a day—you fucking satisfied? You know I really like it here. You know that?"

"That's good."

"We play games most of the time—ping-pong, pool. There's a workout room, the food's great, all you want. I'm going to be the leader in my group after this one guy leaves. He thinks he's God or something because he's been here over six months. When somebody new comes into group, he pushes them up against the wall, asks them why the fuck they're messing up their lives. I told him, he fucked with me, he'd wish he was dead."

Margey was meeting my eye more and had moved her chair so that she was no longer at exactly the farthest point possible from me.

"Nobody understands about me. They ask me how come I'm in here when I have parents who teach college. I tell them they don't know what they're talking about. They're so fucking lucky not to have parents bugging them all the fucking time. And I mean all the fucking *time*. Having parents don't mean nothing. Not fucking nothing. Except you end up with more problems than everybody else."

"Where are Josh's parents?"

"That lucky fucker don't got any. His mother moved out of state. She didn't leave her address. His dad—he can't remember the last time he saw him."

"Karen said they were sending him back to the Family and Children's Center in South Saint Paul."

"Fuck, yes. They get rid of him any way they can."

"He's sixteen?"

"Almost seventeen, same as me. We were born the same month."

Josh was Margey's first boyfriend. Mark and I wished we could meet him. "You going to miss him?"

"None a' your fucking business."

"Mrs. Larson asked if the two of us might talk with her sometime next week. You want to do that?"

"I told you already, I am not talking to that bitch. She looks like some bird carried her in outta' its nest. Scraggley-ass hair, orange lipstick. I refuse. I have rights."

Margey had Mrs. Larson dead to rights. "She's interested in you, Margey. She wants to see if there's any way to help all of us."

"The fuck she does. She's just nosy. Fucking nosy. She told me this was my last chance to straighten up, I better take advantage of it—that is, if it turns out she can do something for me. Oh my God, I got to be fucking grateful to this bitch. I hate her, I really hate her. You better keep her away from me."

Another bull's-eye for Margey.

"Otherwise, I'm going to end up in girls' school, [the Minnesota School for Girls], she says. Fine, I told her, fine—any place will be fucking great as long as I can be positive—and I mean positive—I won't have to see your ugly face."

"Would you rather go to girls' school than to the hospital?"

"Yeah, bitch, that's great. That's fucking terrific. How'd you like to have that choice?"

Right again. "Look, Margey, we're headed for trouble again. How about I stop by next weekend and bring you some makeup and clothes, good idea?"

"Do what you fucking want. That's all you ever do anyhow."

Our thirty minutes were up. The sound of turning locks approached.

Actually I was pleased with this meeting, though I felt as if I should have made a more direct statement of support, instead of switching channels. It was very important, it seemed, that Margey didn't press the button and that she got the message that I wasn't going to either. We'd managed to talk with one another, even if the conversation wasn't what you'd call intimate, for a full thirty minutes.

Possibly I was finally less angry and more able to see Margey's point of view. The longer Margey lived away from home, the easier it was to feel sympathy for her. Her insight was also growing keener as her situation worsened. Her arguments were irrefutable—who would have wanted her choices—that question described her whole life.

Margey did seem happier at the juvenile home than she had been in years. She worked up to level four (out of five) before the end of her three-month stay, and was indeed a leader in group therapy sessions. But somehow she got it into her head that after the detention home she would be set free. Her record of breaking and entering and theft had disappeared from her mind. During our next visits, she chattered on and on about how well she was doing in group, how she was taking over the place. But when Mrs. Larson brought up the question of what next, she flew into a rage.

The rest of us struggled with that question day in and day out. Since Margey was doing so well at the White Bear Lake Juvenile Center, I wondered if she should go on to the Minnesota School for Girls, where they followed the same highly-structured program. Perhaps the court could sentence her there until she was eighteen.

Mrs. Larson wasn't sure the court would sentence Margey to girls' school. Because I had protected her for so long, Margey did not have a police record that matched her past. Mrs. Larson asked me if I understood why I should have turned Margey over to the police for those previous episodes of stealing and forgery. On the other hand, girls' school had its drawbacks. A huge percentage of girls who spent time there moved on to adult facilities. At girls' school it was possible to make contacts that later led many young women into serious crimes.

Again Mark and I considered declaring Margey incorrigible and making her a ward of the state so that the State of Minnesota would assume financial responsibility for her care. Mrs. Larson did not support that alternative. She did not want us to give up custody, and she was adamant about pushing for a psychological diagnosis, which for some time Mark and I had wanted. If Margey's problems were psychological rather than criminal, Mrs. Larson argued, she needed to get help before she began a long career of incarceration. Of course, Mark and I agreed. But Margey had already received a good portion of the family's resources, and there were four other children to consider.

Mrs. Larson spoke glowingly of The Corners, an adolescent diagnostic hospital in Rochester, and the work of a Dr. Holmes. He had saved many of the problem adolescents she had sent him—most recently a young man who had threatened his mother with an ax. That young man, she said, had returned from The Corners a perfectly calm, solid citizen.

Mark and I were skeptical. The expenses involved were astronomical, but perhaps the insurance company would pay the hospital bills and we could cover school and other costs. However, we were not easily hopeful.

At home the tension was so thick there was scarcely air to breath. Dawn grew sullen and withdrawn. There's wasn't much attention left for her or the other children while Mark and I were expending so much energy dealing with Margey. Dawn soon found a way to break into our concentration: she swallowed half a dozen aspirins, then came downstairs and announced that she had tried to commit suicide. The whole family panicked. Mark and I thought of taking her to the emergency room to have her stomach pumped. That didn't seem necessary, but it might have served the purpose of scaring Dawn, which had its attraction. Instead, I called Dr. Hanley. She said we'd all be best sleeping it off and she would be happy to talk with Dawn the next day. Dr. Hanley was eloquent with Dawn about why teens do such things, and although her diary entry was more equivocal, Dawn promised Dr. Hanley not to pull such a stunt again.

Mrs. Diary,

Hi it's me when everyone was mad at me yesterday after I took those asprns I brooke down and cried and I felt that I really should of killed myself—nobody really knows how it feels or belives me which upsets me or makes me angry! I *really* can't believe I was going to do it! I feel ashmed but then I sorta wanta do it again but really go through with it! But I wont!

Dawn was right. No one really believed she'd been serious; we went through the motions because she needed us to get involved with her. Nor, I'm afraid, did anyone believe she was in real anguish. She was already in therapy, though she didn't seem to be making progress.

I tried to get her into a weekly adolescent group counseling session, without success. It was time to change therapists—yet another hassle.

I thought often of Maureen O'Brien's calling and asking, "Will you take two girls?"

The family had responded, "Why not?"

At this point I could easily think of other answers to that question. Going from one crisis with Margey to another with Dawn kept the whole family constantly in turmoil. The other children were up to a fair share of dangerous and illegal behaviors. By and large, however, they tried to keep us from finding out anything that would add hot water to a full kettle. Mark and I worried that they had to be so protective of us, so secretive. We were concerned that out of consideration for us, they might not come to us for help when they needed to. We did hear enough stories about Sam and alcohol to be extremely concerned, and at one point Sam went for alcohol counseling. His drinking to excess, however, continued way past the counseling.

As a Southerner transplanted to the Midwest, I was acutely aware of how the North avoided its own racial problems by focusing on those in the South—of how effectively scapegoating serves the guilty conscience. In my own family, too, I knew Margey and Dawn served as scapegoats. What would have happened with Sam, I often wonder, if Mark and I had focused on his drinking and tried to exert more control over him? What would have happened if his problems had not been overshadowed by Margey's? Sam, who is incredibly sensitive to other people, must have wondered, too. He told me of a dream he once had. Someone was driving a car, careening around corners at breakneck speed. He and Margey were in the back seat with someone else—someone he didn't recognize. Margey was offering him sausages somehow made from herself, dripping with grease. He was devouring them, feeling terrible that he found them so delicious and kept on eating more and more.

Sam and I decided, uncharacteristically, not to analyze that dream: it was clear enough.

Mental
Hospitals

From the very first, Margey didn't like to be touched. As a little girl she would pull her hand away, even if it was bleeding and needed to be cleaned and bandaged. If the aim was to soothe her, it was better to let her wash herself, climb up, and get the Band-Aid "by self." She was angular and brittle and wiggly when you did catch her and wouldn't stay put more than a few seconds.

During her rebellious phase, from thirteen to seventeen, there wasn't much chance of my approaching her physically. It had been years since I'd touched her. I couldn't even remember the last time. Then after our fourth therapy session at the hospital in Rochester—The Corners, where Margey had been struggling for nearly two months—Margey stopped talking and said to Linda, the therapist, "I want to do it now."

Linda said, "I think you should. Right now."

Margey came up to my chair, asked me to stand up, and said, "Hey, Mom, give me a hug."

We hugged and returned to our chairs. Margey was delighted with herself. She told me she'd been wanting to do that for a long time. She was glad she had. And now wasn't it time for lunch?

I told Margey I, too, was glad she had.

From then on, as soon as she saw me and when I left the hospital, Margey unfailingly said, "Hey, Mom, give me a hug." She'd halfway grab, halfway push or pull me up against her. Maybe hugs were clichés for the staff and the rest of the patients—they were always saying, "Hey, I need a hug," as part of the whole reassuring business they were about. But Margey and I weren't talking clichés; we were talking the first time in years, maybe the first time she had ever approached me for physical comfort.

What had changed? Perhaps Margey was getting along better with her own body; perhaps she was coming to trust me enough to tolerate physical closeness. Maybe she was so isolated in the locked unit that deprivation left her grateful to anyone who broke into the hospital routine. Perhaps her sexual relations were helping her connect bodies and love. No doubt all the hours of therapy were having some effect. I wasn't asking questions. Although our touches were somewhat staged, even jerky and self-conscious, I was glad that Margey was hugging someone, and that it was me.

Not that we had reached the end of our anger. Nothing of the kind. But Margey and I had made it all the way to the bottom and now we could gradually float upward. We were both cautious about maintaining our new equilibrium. Whichever one of us tipped the balance and lost her temper was sure to apologize.

Margey and I came upon this peace behind three locked doors in the White Bear Lake jail and in a Rochester hospital on the edge of the Zumbro River run by faultless, never-a-second-thought Dr. Joseph Holmes.

Dr. Holmes was busy, busy. Most of Mark's and my conversations with him involved money—how to coerce Blue Cross and Blue Shield at Saint Thomas and Saint Catherine's into paying for Margey's treatment at The Corners, his diagnostic hospital; how to convince the Saint Paul School Corporation to pay for Margey's schooling while she was at The Corners. Saint Thomas's Blue Cross and Blue Shield adjusters needed no arm-twisting; they were actually eager to find help for Margey after they heard her story.

Margey was no longer involved with the community mental health center or a nuns' school for young girls or an adolescent group home or detention center; she was now in a $475-a-day mental hospital, and that figure covered only her bed. Dr. Holmes called me Doctor Kimble throughout our acquaintance, although I asked him several times to call me Ann. He introduced Mark and me to his staff as the Doctors Kimble, which made me uncomfortable: I was coming to Dr. Holmes as a mother, not as a professional. In our meetings, he always addressed Mark, but since in the beginning so much of the conversation had to do with finances, that seemed natural. Later, when he had a message to convey or a question to ask, Dr. Holmes called Mark's office. I was more difficult to reach, it is true, and at first I thought it was good for Mark to get those calls: it was his turn and I thought maybe he'd get more involved.

But there wasn't any question of getting involved in a conversation with Dr. Holmes—it was business, business all the way. Telephone reports of Margey's progress sounded like interoffice memos.

This is Dr. Holmes at The Corners.

Margey had a psychotic episode today. I want permission to administer the maximum dose of Haldol, for her weight, until further notice.

Hello, The Corners Hospital here, Dr. Joseph Holmes.

Margey has refused to accept oral medication at this date. In fact she collected three doses of her medication and distributed the capsules to other patients, behavior we cannot tolerate. Henceforth Margey will receive her medication by injection.

Dr. Holmes here.

I have been repeatedly challenging Margey about her behaviors and her refusal to accept responsibility. This afternoon her defenses collapsed. She became catatonic and began rocking back and forth in her chair, curled up in a tight ball.

Dr. Holmes on the line.

I have requested copies of Margey's preadoptive records from the Department of Public Welfare in Minneapolis. I should receive these documents within the week. They may well contain information relevant to the case.

Dr. Holmes calling.

I received Margey's records from the Department of Public Welfare yesterday in the three P.M. mail. I plan to read Margey a section from her history, a line or two at a time if necessary. To date, Margey seems to have no memory of any of the events described. She does, however, have great interest in hearing about her early life.

Dr. Holmes.

Yesterday I read to Margey the report of her being treated for a fractured skull and bruises around her face and head.

Dr. Holmes.

Today I read to Margey that she had been diagnosed as having three broken ribs very near the date of her second birthday.

Dr. Holmes.

I am all but positive that there was considerable sexual abuse in Margey's preadoptive history. Early sexual abuse would explain her coquettish actions toward me, her craving for male attention in general, her lack of ego strength, her unfocused rage. To the best of my knowledge, given her symptoms, it is entirely likely that she was abused as a child by her father or some other male in her mother's household.

How astonishing, Mark and I thought, that this stranger could request and be handed Margey's early records while we, her parents, had no access to that information. I called the welfare department and voiced this objection. The social worker said, yes, she had mailed Margey's records to Dr. Holmes, and, yes, she completely agreed with me. If I came to her office she would give me whatever I requested. No, she said, such an action certainly was not standard procedure; she had no intention of asking her superior to okay her decision; she was acting on her own beliefs.

I never went down to that kind woman's office. The odd bits of information Dr. Holmes delivered and Margey relayed already took up too much room in my imagination.

Margey seemed bemused and distant, almost clinical when she recounted the details Dr. Holmes had read to her, probably imitating his manner: she was curious about what effect all the violence might have had on her; she didn't know what to think. She couldn't remember any of it, wasn't that strange? All that stuff about them hitting her was gone, completely gone. She didn't remember going to the doctor, running away with her mother, moving out of the house. Did I think it was better that way?

Clearly she liked the attention. Indeed, she had always liked to talk about herself. Now she talked about nothing else, and she never asked about anyone else. In her position she could be excused; she didn't need to hear anything about proms or state soccer championships.

Dr. Holmes seemed not to be interested in psychoanalysis; he simply read out the facts as recorded and asked Margey to tell him what she was thinking after she'd heard each line. He wanted to get all that past out in the open, so that Margey could go on.

After a month of treatment, I was able to visit Margey at The Corners. She'd been through hard times, but some of the anger was abating. About half of our phone calls progressed all the way to "Good-bye."

Dr. Holmes here.

Be prepared when you visit, Dr. Kimble, to notice some changes in your daughter's appearance and behavior resulting from the medication she is prescribed. There is often weight gain associated with psychotropic medications; undoubtedly you will notice some rocking-in-place.

Before lunch, Margey and I met with her therapist. Margey chattered about how angry she had been when she first came—all the outrageous things she'd done, like stripping off her orange entry uniform and running up and down the halls naked; cramming her food into her mouth like a lawn mower. She was proud of how much better she was doing and admitted how much she enjoyed earning privileges.

In the dining hall, Margey waited on me—brought my silverware, remembered water for both of us, insisted that I try the frozen yogurt so she could serve me. She ate three helpings of french fries, a small salad covered with half a cup of dressing, and a yogurt cone—her manners perfect. Although Margey had gained a lot of weight and looked puffy, the social worker assured me that the patients' diets were controlled and some of the weight gain was a side effect of the medication.

"Everyone is teasing me about rocking all the time," she said, "but I can't help it. Do I look funny?"

She did look a bit strange, sitting in a straight-backed chair steadily rocking, forward and backward, as if to her own drummer. She never quit, not in group, while eating, or in front of the TV. I told her it reminded me of how she used to rock in her sleep when she was little.

The visit went well. Both of us were relieved. I was so sad thinking on the drive home how little wholesome adolescent fun Margey had experienced in her life. When I got home that night, one of Jack's friends asked about Margey as the two boys headed out to pick up their dates for fireworks on Lake Harriet.

The next visit was two weeks later. As soon as I got through the locked door of the unit, Margey stepped out from where she'd been hiding and said, "Give me a hug, old lady." Earlier that week, she'd chattered on the phone about how excited she was to have earned a four-hour pass to Circus World. So many of the other guys had gone there with their families . . . they'd told her all the things we had to see . . . she couldn't wait.

At Circus World, Margey ate her popcorn and hot dog and caramel apple, looked at a few animals, talked about what would be going on at the hospital, asked the time every five minutes, and finally said she was ready to go back—a little over an hour after we'd left. "Them guys are about ready to go into group. Some gigantic stuff is going down with Neil and Tom. Neil's been messing up bad—Tom's his roommate—Tom turned Neil in—I gotta find out what for—I think for fucking Darla in the girls' Henry. Anyway, I'm not sure I took my meds this morning. I gotta go back and check on things. I'm missing them guys. Can you believe this shit?"

Back at the hospital, the nurse took Margey to her room and frisked her before she was free to come and tell me good-bye. "Hey, Mom, you ain't gonna leave without giving me a hug—don't even think about it."

During Margey's stay at The Corners, she and I learned to talk "normal" with one another—to talk trivia. No one wanted to rock the boat—not me, not Margey, not her therapist. We learned fast which topics guaranteed explosions: *her drugs* (no reasons for her to take them, no way she'd continue chemicals, other than those of her own choosing, once she got free); *her diagnosis* (nothing was wrong with her); *her next placement* (she was going to be out on her own); *her schoolwork* (forget it!). Margey's chatter was always, always self-absorbed and endlessly focused on her appearance, but infinitely preferable to insults and rage.

The rest of the family visited Margey in July, with pretty good success. We were all nervous, but by the time the visit was scheduled, two months into her stay at The Corners, Margey was a real smoothie: she put on her company manners and chronicled dozens of teen freak stories that were certain to entertain her siblings. Then there was her own behavior—rocking back and forth and manic; she never stopped talking, "There's Jeff, he's the one that used to go out with Angie's cousin, you remember him, Dawn? Can you see those bandages on his arm, he carved *Bruce* on his right arm, and *SSSS* on the other. You could read every letter in the scabs. See Andrea over there, she's the one I told you about, Mom, shaved off the hair all over her whole body, painted herself up with poster paint, and then strutted her stuff up and down the hall. And over there, that's. . . ." Sam cracked jokes sotto voce. Dawn seemed terrified, happy to see Margey, but mystified by her appearance, how much weight she'd gained, new perm, new hair color, constant rocking.

The hour of family therapy went quickly, mostly at the level of talk about the weather: nothing threatening. We went out for gyros at

Margey's and my favorite place and that pleased everyone. After supper was an hour of games in a playroom filled with possibilities. The whole family got into a rowdy game of bumper pool and we forgot our troubles. We'd worried needlessly; there wasn't much chance for conflict, nor for intimacy, but there was concern and civility.

After Margey had been at The Corners three months, Dr. Holmes was ready with his diagnosis. Margey needed long-term treatment: she was a severely damaged young woman. He was convinced she had a thought disorder: she was unable to process stimuli accurately or to think logically about her own actions. He recommended an extended placement at the adolescent treatment center of the Pembrook School in Houston, Texas.

Dr. Holmes said he had talked with the Blue Cross and Blue Shield claims adjuster; the company would pay only for a psychiatric hospital—all of which charged from $500 a day. Blue Cross and Blue Shield would not pay for a treatment center, costing about $170 a day. Doubtless, he said, $170 a day was out of the family's financial range.

Dr. Holmes insisted that the Pembrook School was far and away his first choice for Margey. He felt sure she would need years of treatment involving a gradual acclimation to the outer world. The Pembrook School offered a series of placements—from the locked unit Margey needed in the beginning, to an unlocked unit, to a supervised, independent work-living situation. Over the years, Pembrook School had developed contacts within the community so that their patients could find work and support themselves, one step at a time. No other hospital, he assured us, had such an extended program, and there was no disagreement among us that Margey needed a structured and gradual entry into independent living.

Still, Mark and I thought, there must be other options. It seemed impossible that there was not a good adolescent psychiatric hospital between the Twin Cities and Houston. Sending a child that far away seemed ridiculous. The cost was excessive, if not immoral. Five hundred dollars a day for an extended stay—nothing short of a year, and perhaps two or three. I dared not compute those figures. Dr. Holmes said those sums were nothing, nothing compared with what insurance companies had to shell out when a kid got in a motorcycle or automobile accident or overdosed on drugs and charred his brains. He'd convinced the adjuster to be happy that he'd saved Margey from that virtual inevitability.

In the meantime, Mark managed to extract from Holmes the name of a less-than-ideal group facility within our price range, and he visited Harwood, located on the outskirts of a small town near his mother's home in Saint Paul. Mark was quite satisfied with Harwood, but the director was afraid Harwood couldn't offer enough security for Margey; their staff had never accepted a patient from a locked unit. He felt unable to accept her.

Mark was clearly disappointed at our having to return to Holmes without an alternative to Pembrook School. We were paralyzed by our own ignorance, as well as angry to be presented with only one possibility, one so hugely expensive. We weren't at all sure the insurance companies should be asked to pay such sums, even if they were willing. I was also enormously frustrated that insurance-company policy made it all but impossible to consider a much less expensive, long-term treatment center rather than a hospital. The choice was to send Margey to Pembrook School or to send Margey to Pembrook School.

One week after her seventeenth birthday, Margey was scheduled to stand trial for breaking and entering and theft. She was blown all the way back to the beginning by the news. Rage. Storm. Destruction. Why did she try? Why had she bothered? It always ended up the same. Her therapist, Linda, and I wondered if we should have confronted her earlier instead of letting her forget there was a future, as was her wont. Unprepared, she was overwhelmed. We agreed it probably would have been fairer to introduce gradually the possibility of another mental hospital, but we were glad we hadn't. We had all needed a respite from rage and despair.

Dr. Holmes appeared in court with his staunchest supporter (and Margey's nemesis), the juvenile probation officer from White Bear Lake, Joanne Larson. With these two voices recommending Pembrook School, Pembrook School in chorus, the judge didn't have a chance to think of anything besides a mental hospital. Mark and I had nothing else to suggest, and the courtroom was no place to bring up our reservations. The judge sentenced Margey to Pembrook School Psychiatric Hospital until she reached the age of eighteen, at which time she would no longer be a minor and under the jurisdiction of his court.

As a minor, Margey had not been allowed in the courtroom during the proceedings. None of us—Mark, nor I, nor Dr. Holmes, nor Joanne Larson—dared tell her about her sentence. Watching how far Margey regressed when challenged made me wonder whether she would ever be able to control her emotions, even with the most expensive treatment in the world.

Margey, bless her, was able to express all the rebelliousness against the situation that her parents were forced to repress. The night before she and I were to fly to Texas, Margey—still, of course, at The Corners—completely lost control: she ripped the clothes off her back, tore out the stereo in her room, flung the pictures off the wall, and finally had to be restrained and sedated. Dr. Holmes was afraid she would act out on the airplane, and he arranged for an escort to go with Margey and me from Rochester to Texas. When I arrived at the hospital the next morning, I was upset with his arrangements, made without consultation or consideration of expense. Who could blame Margey for her rage? She was being deserted and carted off yet again. She had, however, never "gone off" in front of me, and I didn't expect trouble from her on the trip.

As soon as I came through the locked door of the unit to pick her up, Margey grabbed me and clung to me as if rescue had arrived in the nick of time. She told me what she'd done the night before, and laughed. When we arrived at the airport and found some confusion over the escort's ticket, I sent him back to The Corners, with my regards to Dr. Holmes. Margey and I traveled peacefully to Houston, where we found ourselves being escorted through low, comfortable bungalows that had once served as rest and recuperation quarters for military personnel. At dinner, all the patients, staff, and guests were served spicy chili and corn bread by three cooks who chatted with each of us as we passed through the line.

Over the years, Mark and I had focused on one child more than the other—he on Dawn, I on Margey. Dawn wasn't any less determined to go her own way than Margey, but at sixteen her fantasies went toward love and sex rather than toward alcohol and sex. Her taste in men was different from Margey's. Margey was attracted to strong, macho men; Dawn to soft, gentle men. Though not nearly as terrifying and disruptive as Margey's, Dawn's quest for sexual experience, detailed in the diary she often left in the living room, was unsettling in its combination of teenage gunk and compulsiveness.

Diary,

Hi, How are You? I'm in a wierd mood I am happy and

sad! Im sitting here in my thinking place which is small and it's just a place to sit and cry or be depressed and there are a few steps and there is a white fence! I'm cold but I dont care! David walked me all the way to my algeria shot place it was really nice of him! He's a great kid but Im worried. I *really really* am pretty sure I love him and I think he feels the same way! But we haven't kissed or anything! It's like we are just close friends! I wonder what will happen? I gave him his tape and candy for Valentine's day! And he gave me a really sweet necklace and a card. I love it! I am afriad I will lose him I love him so much Well I gotta go home!

Love ya

PS. You a great friend to talk to!

Diary,

Hi How are ya! Hey listen. Guess what Margey wrote me and I'm going to write her back in just a sec. Anyway Melissa Snyder and I are in a fight and so that is not good but anyway David and I are Doing really good I'm going over to his house on Friday!!! I'm so happy I hope we at least kiss! We haven't done anything at all But I love him so much! Chris has fucked 2 guys, Done Drugs, Drinks, lies and betrays people. I really dislike her a lot But I gotta call David I love him so much.

Love ya

Dear Diary,

Hey Babe. What's up Not Much here I'm here with Angie at David's staircase! But David isn't here which sucks! I Love him so much! Well Angie is going write & Say Hi! [The next dozen or so words are in Angie's handwriting.] Hi Diary—I'm Dawn's BEST FRIEND! Nice to meet you—Angie. Hi again I really want to See David & get a peice of his ass But that will never happen I am freezing! But oh yea Last night David was driving and he is a really good driver I told him I would never go crousing with him but I would love the chance to! But Shit I havent even kissed him it makes me sad. Melissa S and I are in another fight! fuck that woman well Gotta Go I Love you, I LOVE David.

Diary,

Hi Its me again & I talked to David & he was at his brothers house! I Love David so much & I dont want to smother
him I never would hurt him! When I have a kid I'm going to
let her date & Everything for names of kids I want
a girs—Angie!
a boy. David!

David lived only a couple of blocks from us; Dawn ran over to his
house every chance she got, according to his mother, or, again according to his mother, called for David to come visit her as soon as she was
alone in our house. One evening, David's mother called to ask if I knew
Dawn had come over to their apartment the night before—at three in
the morning—stood outside David's room, thrown stones at his window, and called out his name a dozen times at the top of her voice.
David had slept through it all, but she had been awakened and had
gotten up and told Dawn to run on home. Dawn was a nice girl, and
all, but she just didn't know about the ideas kids got into their heads
nowadays.

Not long afterwards, I drove up in time to see Dawn and David, as
if carved from one tree trunk, leaning into one another. I chased David
home, reminded Dawn that she was not to have guests when no one
else was home, and began to worry, seriously, how Mark and I could
keep track of those two and hold down jobs?

But David's mother and David himself saved us all. His mother
permitted David to drop out of school and work with his brother.
Dawn saw much less of him than when he'd been in school. Shortly afterwards, David broke the news to Dawn that he was a homosexual.
This admission didn't deter Dawn, but the relationship was over, anyway. Mark and I breathed a sigh of relief.

In the beginning of her stay at Pem-
brook School, Margey either sulked or raged; she "went off" repeatedly
and had to be restrained. She refused to participate in group except to
shout that there wasn't one fucking reason for her to try; look where
she'd ended up after all that work she'd done for six months at White
Bear Lake and The Corners.

Gradually, aided by her primary counselor in the unit, Hope, Margey became more compliant and curious about her surroundings. She

began to earn privileges and enjoyed the freedom of walking up and down the hill and from building to building. She even commented on how kind and helpful the staff had been during her rough transition. Maybe her turnaround time was getting shorter, I thought. Two weeks after she arrived, she wrote this touching letter.

Mom—

Hi, how's everything going? Me, ok I guess. I lost your letter I wrote you so here I am writing you another one. Guess what? I started school this week. It's pretty fun, at least it gives me something to do. I also got on campus activities which means that I get to go up to the gym and to swimming and play other sports which is super cool. In therapy I talk to Barbara about mainly how I'm feeling those couple of days she hasn't seen me and about the problems that I've had in the past. I know I haven't been that pleasant to talk to the last couple of times we've talked on the phone it's just it seemed like I wasn't accomplishing any thing here, I just felt like giving up and of course I do what I always do and that is take my frustrations out on you. I'm sorry I've done this I feel bad about it I know I hurt your feelings. I'm sorry. There's something I need to tell ya and it's easier to write than to say that's the way it's always been with me but it's that I've grown to love you so much since The Corners and that I can't wait to see you, it's just I miss you so much it makes me sad. I'm crying right now cuzz I miss you so much isn't that corny? I can't wait till you come up and make a visit so I can see ya and show you around the campus. Well I don't have much to say. Sorry so short.

Love you always, Margey

The following month, the adolescent unit of the Pembrook School was moved from its comfortable, wooded setting to a posh new facility in Pasadena, Texas, called Magnolia Ridge. Mark described the brand-new institution as an Art Deco mausoleum; I thought of it as B. F. Skinner, mission-style. Neither staff nor patients at Magnolia Ridge were allowed to replace the "art" work on their walls with anything of their own choosing.

This move was not what Margey needed. In the first weeks, the staff at Magnolia Ridge, about half of whom were newly hired, had difficulty establishing a routine. Margey sensed the instability, hated the new facility, and became increasingly angry and rebellious. She threatened to run, and spent all her time with patients who had run before. The staff assured me that the unit was locked; very few of the patients escaped.

Then Margey kicked open a fire door and escaped. On the loose again, halfway across the continent, with another female patient. The police were alerted. For days, for a week, there was no news. Ten days went by. No news. The girls must have gotten to the highway and out of town, we were told, otherwise the local police would have picked them up. There were alerts in a dozen states.

On the eleventh day, the phone rang at 6:00 P.M. It was Margey. "Mom, I just wanted to call you and tell you not to worry. You remember, you told me you worried so much last time I ran. Well, I'm just fine. I'll call you again tomorrow and tell you how everything's going."

"Margey, Margey, wait a minute. Where are you?"

"Hey, how dumb do you think I am? You think I'm going to tell you that so you can send the police after me? I'm having a great time, hitching with truckers. We're headed for Florida. You don't have to worry. That's all I want to tell ya."

"Thank you for calling, Margey. That was really sweet of you. But I'm more than worried, I'm terrified. How can I stop worrying with you running like this? Anything could happen. Anything. Listen to me. Margey . . . Margey—"

Two more days went by. On the evening of the thirteenth day, a highway patrolman in Kentucky called to say he had picked up two teenage girls at a truck stop. On his shortwave radio, he had heard a trucker trying to find two hot babes a ride to Florida. The staff at Magnolia Ridge had been notified, and someone was already en route to pick the girls up. They were both doing okay. Would I like to speak with my daughter? "Watch out," the officer said, "she's pretty upset."

"Margey, Margey, are you there?"

"Yeah."

"Are you all right?"

"Yeah."

"Are you mad?"

"Fuck, yeah."

"You wanted to keep running?"

"Fuck, yeah."

"I was scared to death, I kept dreaming a policeman would call to say he'd found your body in some wide Texas ditch."

"You were wasting your dreams. I had a great time. I was doing just fine. I told you that. Why the fuck don't you ever believe me? Because you think you know everything, that's why. Now comes the real fucking trouble. What's going to happen to me now? At Magnolia Ridge I go back to strict escort, I can't even go take a piss by myself. I'll lose all my privileges. I'm fucking nowhere. Nowhere and surrounded by a bunch of fucking assholes. You know what I'd do right now if I could? I'd fucking get the hell outta here forever—and I do mean forever."

"You sound so low. I'm so sorry."

"What the fuck do you know about it anyhow? How close have *you* ever been to a situation like this? You don't fucking know shit! Get your butt in here and change places with me. Then we can talk." Margey nailed down the truth every time. How would I be feeling if Kate were in Margey's position?

Hope called from Magnolia Ridge to say that the girls had arrived and were physically okay. They'd been checked out by the doctor, bathed, and were down for a long sleep. Margey had wanted to call, but she'd fallen asleep as soon as she got back to the unit.

On the phone the next day, Margey said it'd been fun. Real wild and real fun. Even better than the time she'd run in South Saint Paul with Josh. She and her friend Julie had met this nice guy on the highway right outside Magnolia Ridge. He gave them beer. The next driver gave them speed. This one really nice guy told them all about all the drugs he'd ever taken, what each pill did to you, how he'd made this big collection of every one he'd ever taken. He pulled out a kid's carrying case, made for matchbook cars but now filled with pills, and told her and Julie to pick out anything they wanted. He was really nice. When he had to turn west, he got them a ride with another guy he called on his radio.

She and her friend made all the money they wanted cleaning out rigs. That was even sorta' fun. Had I ever seen the inside of one of those rigs? Man, those drivers had everything they could possibly want; they were *equipped*. I had to see all they could fit into one a them trucks.

At first, the next guy was great, then. . . . He gave her and Julie a quart of whisky. She passed out. Then . . . then, she woke up. She woke up and . . . there he was . . . him, on top of her. She didn't have any clothes on. She couldn't breathe. He was smothering her. She didn't scream. She didn't know . . . didn't know where Julie was. Everything was dark. She was sick . . . she didn't know where to go. No one was around. She ran . . . didn't know where to go. Somehow she found Julie.

Julie was in the driver's seat the whole time. She couldn't find her clothes. She had to vomit. Now they had her back and at first it had been so much fun. She wasn't going to run again. It wasn't worth it. Her friend Julie was fine—No, he didn't get Julie . . . no, he got Julie first . . . while Julie was hiding in the rig. . . . She woke up . . . he got her, too. He was on top of her. Then she woke up. She didn't know where she was. She was all fucked up, couldn't find her clothes. She was sick. Back at the hospital they gave her a pill that made her throw up all day long. This was it. Now she had AIDS. She wasn't going to keep going any more. This was too much. She was going to get out any way she could. This was it.

Surely Margey had found her rocky bottom. Where could she fall further? What earthly good did it do to know she had set herself up for the whole thing. I listened, cried with her, promised to come see her as soon as possible. She said she loved me, wanted me to come as soon as I could. She promised not to run again. I begged her not to, told her how worried everyone had been, how sorry I was for her.

There was something I wanted to give her, I said, but she'd have to use her imagination to make it work over the phone.

She said, "What is it?"

I said, "The biggest hug we've ever had."

Margey said she wasn't going to run, not to worry about that, but she wasn't going to stick around either. "But anyhow—whatever happens—thanks for the hug. And for being my mother."

Margey is one of the pluckiest human beings I have ever known. She gets herself into horrible messes, but give her a day, a week, and she's eager to begin again. That's the good side of her waking up to a brand-new world every morning.

In her next letter she seemed already to have forgotten the events from her runaway. I envied her her slick memory.

> Mom—
>
> Hi, how are you doing? Me, I'm doing just great. I got my on campus activities back and I got off strict escort which means I got all of my privileges back from before I ran. In two weeks I'm gonna ask for my off campus, which means I'm going to be going to activities off the campus and I'm going to ask for my off escort which means I'll be able to walk around campus without staff. On Sat. I got to go on the Bonus Trip which means only people that are involved with their treatment get to

go. We went to the mall and went to an arcade and played video games it was so much fun.

Everybody has been giving me so much support cuzz I've been doing so well, it makes me feel so good. Guess what? Two girls ran away today, it was Dolly and Lois. I hope their ok cuzz I'm really worried about them. Now I see how worried you were about me. I'll never run away again things are going much to good for me. I still haven't gotten a letter from you so I'm gonna leave the address at the end of this letter. So, what's going on at home? Dawn seemed like she was doing well when I talked to her on the phone when you called. Well I don't have much to say so I'm gonna end this letter. But what I've had to say this whole letter and the most important part of it is that I miss you and love you. I guess now I'm gonna write a poem cuzz I feel like expressing my feelings.

It's gonna be called, Here's a hug for my old lady.

Love you Lots, Margey   Joshua Unit

The dynamic duo—Dawn and Angie—had made a new friend, a forty-five-year-old man who lived a block from Angie's house. Henry did everything the girls asked: delivered them wherever they wanted to go: Dawn back and forth to soccer practice so she no longer had to ride her bike, Angie back and forth to our house so she no longer had to walk or call her mother. The girls also spent hours at his house talking and messing around, playing with his kittens. If they wanted something to eat, he took them to McDonald's and paid for everything they ordered.

Henry was no longer working—he'd been in sales—because he had to take care of his invalid mother. Dawn and Angie said he was a nice, lonesome person who knew how to make other people happy. So . . . what in the world was wrong with that? Not every grown-up in the whole world had a sick mind.

I had no idea how to respond to this new development. Angie's mother didn't think there was much of a problem; Dawn's therapist and Mark thought there was a considerable problem. I went to his house, met Henry, and liked him. He seemed sweet and gentle. Maybe it was best to let it go.

Which we did for a while. Until I overheard Angie talking to Henry on the phone. "Didn't I tell you to get your butt over to Dawn's house at eight? What do you think you're doing? Get here. Now!" I called Angie's mother and said I didn't think it was good for the girls to be treating Henry as if he were their personal slave. Angie's mother said she had been worrying, too, about some conversations she'd overheard. She knew how nice Henry was and all; sometimes she had more questions about our daughters' manners.

I didn't want to, but I felt as if I had to talk with Henry. Henry was sweet and understanding. Of course, he knew the relationship was hard for others to understand. Yes, he understood our concern. Yes, he thought the girls were getting a little demanding, a bit rude even, and he couldn't quite figure out how to handle them. Of course, if that was what I wanted, he would not see them again. He'd only been trying to help out. When they'd talked about their problems, he'd tried to offer the best possible advice, just like a parent would, and they always seemed to have a lot of problems.

Henry was as good as his word; he told the girls his mother had taken a turn for the worse; he was too busy taking care of her needs to spend any more time with them.

Mark and I breathed easier—for a bit. We'd lucked out again. But with Dawn's bizarre choices we couldn't help wondering: how much longer?

During this dramatic period in Margey's life, Mark was less eager to talk about his children than he had been earlier, when he could describe their various adventures and conquests. He was deeply troubled by Margey's time in jail and the mental hospitals. He had memories of traumatic psychiatric events in his own biological family: one of his uncles had had to be forcibly committed to a state institution and had eventually been diagnosed as a paranoid schizophrenic. Uncle Thomas lived out his remaining thirty years at the mental hospital.

Jack and Margey were both seventeen years old. Jack was in the process of choosing a college. He had worked carefully on all the forms and essays. His choice was between Haverford and Swarthmore. Margey, by contrast, was sentenced to spend a year in a mental hospital. The differences, as always, seemed grossly unfair, far beyond one child or the other's responsibility or achievement. Again Mark and I wondered whether established families made the best placement for children with troubled backgrounds. If there had been no other children,

Margey and Dawn might have been able to move forward without being pushed back by jealousy and envy. Without the other children as points of reference, they might have developed more original and self-motivated goals. Both of the girls might have been much better off living under a single spotlight that softened their faults and swelled their successes.

Dawn had scored 81 on the IQ part of a diagnostic battery. We didn't know the reason, whether the cause was malnutrition, her mother's alcoholism, genetics, or maybe a bad test day. The choices available to Dawn, compared with Jack, seemed unfair.

Margey was told again and again to accept responsibility for her actions, but in fact she was not responsible for so much of her early life—the background for her present situation. She was actually being asked to assume responsibility for someone else's actions.

Diagnosis
and Dismissal

Kate was in Mexico studying and Margey was in Texas, so the rest of us decided to visit both girls for Christmas. Visiting Magnolia Ridge for Christmas was an ambitious undertaking. Too ambitious, as it turned out.

Perhaps most upsetting for the other children was seeing the new physical contact between Margey and me. Because of the stress of her whole family's descending upon her, Margey kept hold of my hand or had her arm around my shoulder virtually the whole time we were together. Sam and Jack were "grossed out"; Dawn was shocked and jealous—Margey had always been *her* special friend; Mark was astonished and uneasy. I felt divided into four or five pieces—annoyed at Margey's clinging, upset with the boys' intolerance, sad for Dawn's loss, glad only that Kate wasn't involved.

Expressing physical affection with so many different children had remained a problem over the years. Mark and I weren't publicly affectionate: we had actually had our first fight over whether holding hands had any significance. He took the negative and I the positive. With the babies, we were both very affectionate, but that gradually diminished. With Margey and Dawn, showing affection had never come easy for either Mark or me: Margey resisted being touched and Dawn was too gooey. Thus Kate and I were the only ones who were openly affectionate, which probably made the males somewhat uncomfortable and Margey and Dawn envious. I never quite knew how to handle the situation: I didn't want to suppress Kate's and my easy relationship—she always wanted to reassure me that one daughter loved me, and we both thought that Americans seemed repressed, unable to touch one another—but I also didn't want to make anyone else uncomfortable.

Margey's insistence on holding and patting me constantly during the visit seemed on one level to be the result of our never having resolved the issue, but—more importantly—an expression of her yearning for a relationship with me. The others took it, it must have been in part, as fear and rejection of them.

At the motel on Christmas Eve, Dawn told us about something none of us had seen: Margey had actually been vicious with Dawn when they were alone together on the river walk—once kicked her as hard as she could, once bit her arm and broke the skin, pretending to be playing. Dawn cried and cried; she didn't have any idea what she had done to make Margey so cruel. Probably she'd done nothing more than remain with the family.

Those two days in Texas seemed to last forever and to move the other children backwards in terms of understanding Margey—if that were possible. None of us managed to broach a serious subject; Margey dominated every conversation with endless chatter about doing her nails, perming her hair, this or that diet. Once Margey was going on about someone in the unit who had absolutely no self-control; finally, Sam said, "How can you be talking about someone who has no self-control when you have no control over anything?" We all fidgeted, but Sam was only saying what we all knew—the empress had no clothes. Without batting an eye, Margey pulled the headband off her head and asked me how I liked the flowers on it . . . she'd borrowed it from her roommate who was really crazy. Eventually the other children refused to say anything at all. Mark did great on the weather; I talked teen fashions, one of my least favorite subjects.

On the way to the airport after our last visit with Margey, the air in the car was thick and gray. Everyone was full of pent-up emotions. Jack was remote, Dawn hurt, Mark avoiding. Sam was angry, and said so; he blamed Mark and me for not having said anything real. Dawn worried about why Margey hadn't spent any time talking with her; Jack plugged himself into his Walkman. Mark and I talked about the arrangements for getting out of the country.

Fortunately, by the time we arrived in Mexico City, we had shaken off enough tension to take great pleasure in meeting Kate, who had been away from home since August. We finished off Christmas day with an ebullient dinner of margaritas and paella in the luxurious Zona Rosa. Mexicans, bless them, refuse to let anyone remain sad on a fiesta. Margey should have been adopted by a Mexican family, Sam commented.

Even when Margey and I were alone in therapy, there were still so many topics we dared not approach that a vast gap remained between our tender letters and our words face-to-face. Both of us wished for more honesty, as Margey indicated in the following letter.

> Mom—
> See, I told you I would write you. I really don't have much to say cuzz I just talked to you on the phone yesterday. Today I got upset but I talked it out with Shea, she always helps me out. Today Barbara told me that you wanted to become close to me well let me tell you a secret. That's what I've wanted nearly all my life is someone that I could tell all my problems to, someone I could tell all my secrets to. I've wanted to become close to you for so long now, and now I feel that for the 1st time in my life that we are finally getting close and that makes me very happy. I miss you alot, I cried for a long time when you left. I can't wait till you come up so I can tell you some of my secrets that I've been holding in for so long. Well I don't have much to say except that I'm gonna work real hard on being good so we can go out to dinner and that I miss you and love you a whole lot.
> Lots of love, Margey

Margey's letter had come shortly before my February visit, so I arrived at Magnolia Ridge expectant but nervous. Although I hoped we might talk about something other than the weather, I wasn't at all sure I wanted to know all of Margey's secrets. Her plea for intimacy frightened me.

I need not have worried. Margey didn't bring up anything she had suggested in that letter. She talked nonstop about her new boyfriend, all his problems, her new Orphan Annie perm, and the many ways she could arrange her curls. I was amazed, but also relieved. We had already reached an unspoken understanding that we would never be able to communicate about school, work, alcohol and drugs, sex, responsibility. Knowing our time together was limited, we settled for manners.

During that winter and spring, Margey seemed to be on hold at Magnolia Ridge. She attended GED classes but made no progress toward a certificate. For a while she worked a few hours a day at the school cafeteria, then she quit. She talked a lot about finding another job, but never did. Several times she reached the higher levels in the locked unit, then she broke a rule or two, got furious about being disciplined, "went off," lost her privileges, and began the cycle again.

When I asked her therapist if someone should confront Margey, Barbara said she already had, the previous week, and she was still bruised from the experience. Margey had screamed at her, asked her who she thought she was, did she think she was Ann Kimble or something. Where did she get the idea that she was able to help anybody? All she'd ever done was ask a bunch of stupid questions any idiot could answer. Margey had then swept over Barbara's vase of flowers and her daughter's picture, stomped out of the session, gone out into the unit, snatched up and ripped apart all the origami papers, marched into her room, torn both beds apart, piled all the mattresses on top of each other, then crawled under her comforter and fallen asleep. An hour later, Barbara said, Margey strolled out of her room and said she was hungry; had anyone saved her lunch? Not another word. Margey forgot immediately, Barbara said, but a therapist's memory—and fear of another encounter—was much more tenacious.

I asked Barbara if Margey wasn't manipulating us, leading us through some sort of aversion therapy. Barbara said no doubt she was. For both of us, confronting Margey felt like tormenting an animal until it became enraged and turned on us; everyone got hurt—to no lasting effect.

The psychiatrist at Magnolia Ridge had taken Margey off all drugs. They weren't helping her: Haldol caused double vision; lithium made her lethargic. I was both relieved and frightened at losing one more source of hope—for years I'd thought Margey might be bipolar because of the severity and frequency of her mood swings. Barbara explained that precisely because Margey's moods shifted so quickly—often in midsentence—she was not bipolar; the highs and lows of true bipolars or manic-depressives last much, much longer.

Anyway, it was clear that even if the drugs helped her, Margey would refuse to take them when she got out on her own: accepting the need for drug therapy meant accepting she had a problem. She was delighted to be victorious over Dr. Holmes and me.

On July 21, Margey turned eighteen. For some months she had been growing restive at Magnolia Ridge: after eleven months, she had been there twice as long as anyone else on her unit. She wanted to know why she should stay; she said she wasn't getting anywhere with her life, which was true. I wasn't any happier with her progress than she was, but I was more patient, and of course relieved knowing she was safe.

In late July, my brother Ray, a psychiatrist trained at the University of Mississippi, offered to go with me to visit Margey. He sensed that I needed his help. Ray made an appointment, granted as a professional courtesy, with the psychiatrist at Magnolia Ridge, a man I had spoken with only once, and then solely about financial details. Ray was curious about Margey's diagnosis and I was unable to answer his questions, except with vague phrases—*violently angry, no impulse control, no self-concept.* He kept saying, but that's not a diagnosis.

While Ray was talking with Margey, I had a session with her therapist during which Barbara dropped a bomb: the hospital staff had set Margey's date of release one month hence—one year after her entry. I was stunned. Why wasn't Margey able to follow the anticipated course at Magnolia Ridge—a gradual move from the locked unit to working and living outside the mental hospital? Margey was nowhere near ready to be released. What would happen to her? How could she possibly go, in one day—bang—from a locked unit—bang—into the real world?

Barbara agreed that Margey was not prepared for independent living. But the hospital had a new policy; they were no longer treating patients for more than one year. Barbara was kind and sympathetic, but policy was policy. I told her that the choice of Magnolia Ridge for Margey had been based on an entirely different set of expectations; I asked why the hospital was changing its policy at this point.

Barbara said Margey wasn't ready to leave the locked unit, but also no one could anticipate a time when she would be ready. I asked about another placement within their system. Barbara said that wasn't possible; none of their other facilities would admit Margey in her present condition; she was far too unstable and required too much supervision. Certainly Magnolia Ridge was nothing like the hospital described to Mark and me, where Margey could eventually work her way into the community. Magnolia Ridge was in the middle of a corporate development, right off Exit 8 of the superhighway. There was no community around for anyone to be integrated into. Magnolia Ridge was a for-profit hospital, first and foremost. None of that soft stuff about helping kids.

Immediately I suspected that Blue Cross and Blue Shield had finally decided they had done their share for Margey Kimble. Barbara's task was to ship her and the family out. Where? Irrelevant.

I said we all knew Margey should not come home.

Barbara agreed.

Where could she go then?

Barbara had no idea—that was up to the family.

When I met my brother after this session, Ray said he had arranged for both of us to talk with the psychiatrist: he and the psychiatrist would review Margey's diagnosis and help me understand it. I told him what had just happened. He said he needed to get Margey's diagnosis; then he might be able to deal better with the situation.

For a time, Ray and the psychiatrist talked technical terms. Ray kept pressing for a clearer response from Dr. Bradshaw. There was a great deal of hesitation about making a diagnosis for one so young— only eighteen. Many typically adolescent characteristics could be described as abnormal, but those often faded with maturity. It was difficult to pinpoint symptoms that might be less than stable; there was much resistance to making prophesies that might become self-fulfilling.

Ray understood the ins and outs of the drugs Margey had been prescribed and wanted to know why they had been discontinued. The diagnosis began to make sense to him. He asked about the long-term prognosis. Then he and the psychiatrist tried to help me understand.

Ray asked Dr. Bradshaw to hand me the third edition of *Diagnostic and Statistics Manual of Mental Disorders*, the standard text describing and classifying psychological disorders. As near as they could come, Dr. Bradshaw said, Margey's diagnosis was *severe borderline personality disorder*. As I read through the description, phrase after phrase rang true.

DIAGNOSTIC CRITERIA FOR BORDERLINE PERSONALITY DISORDER

The following are characteristic of the individual's current and long-term functioning, are not limited to episodes of illness, and cause either significant impairment in social or occupational functioning or subjective distress.

At least five of the following are required:

(1) impulsivity or unpredictability in at least two areas that are potentially self-damaging, e.g., spending, sex, gambling, substance use, shoplifting, overeating, physically self-damaging acts

(2) a pattern of unstable and intense interpersonal relationships, e.g., marked shifts of attitude, idealization, devaluation, manipulation (consistently using others for one's own ends)

(3) inappropriate, intense anger or lack of control of anger, e.g., frequent displays of temper, constant anger

(4) identity disturbance manifested by uncertainty about several issues relating to identity, such as self-image, gender identity, long-term goals or career choice, friendship patterns, values, and loyalties, e.g., "Who am I?", "I feel like I am my sister when I am good"

(5) affective instability: marked shifts from normal moods to depression, irritability, or anxiety, usually lasting a few hours and only rarely more than a few days, with a return to normal mood

(6) intolerance of being alone, e.g., frantic efforts to avoid being alone, depressed when alone

(7) physically self-damaging acts, e.g., suicidal gestures, self-mutilation, recurrent accidents or physical fights

(8) chronic feelings of emptiness or boredom

Dr. Bradshaw explained that Margey was not psychotic, not bipolar or manic-depressive, as I had feared (because such disorders are difficult to treat) but also had hoped (because such disorders are at least treatable). She had a personality disorder. Personality, he explained, is related to temperament, which is genetically determined and is established fairly early in life. It remains relatively stable through time. Drugs are usually ineffective with borderlines, he said, unless they are also psychotic. Although the borderline patient experiences intense mood swings, these are not the extended mood swings characteristic of bipolar patients or manic-depressives. Margey's mood swings were indeed extreme, but they occurred from moment to moment, from hour to hour. Medication, effective with bipolar patients, only blunted Margey's affective responses; her mood swings remained unchecked. On occasion, borderlines were clinically depressed and experienced relief from the use of antidepressants. That had not been the case with Margey.

The cause of borderline personality disorder, I asked?

In Margey's case, early maternal deprivation and, in all probability, sustained physical abuse, including sexual abuse. As the successor to her other mother, I was the main object of Margey's anger, and her dream of salvation. I was alternately devalued and idealized. When I

was not around, she shifted her anger and hope to other "mother" figures. She had done so with Barbara, her therapist.

Ray explained how the borderline person "splits" people into all-
good or all-evil, often switching the same person from one role to the
opposite in the middle of a sentence.

The prognosis?

A lifetime in and out of abusive relationships; probably a lifetime in
and out of penal and psychiatric institutions.

Could anything be done?

Probably not much.

Could anything have ever been done?

Probably not much.

Was it my fault?

Not likely—those early patterns were probably irreversible.

How could they release her in this condition?

Her condition had not changed appreciably in their facility. According to their new policy, patients were released after a maximum of
one year in treatment. Most patients made considerable progress over
such an extended period of time.

What would happen to Margey?

In all probability she would come home and sink lower and lower
until she broke under some crisis or other and had to be sent to the
state mental hospital. She was an adult now.

How could they recommend that I take her home with such a sce-
nario before us? Could she go directly to the state hospital?

Dr. Bradshaw didn't think the state hospital would admit her at this
point; she was relatively stable and not an immediate threat to herself
or anyone else. He couldn't in good conscience make that recommendation.

How could we all anticipate what was going to happen, then stand
by and watch? At such expense to all those involved?

That was something I would have to work out. They weren't releas-
ing her immediately; there would be time to make arrangements. Her
year was not up for one month.

One month!

I was desperate and furious. My brother talked to me about how he
treated his borderline patients; he warned me against my tendencies to
judge and overcommit. Ray suggested that I always be very clear about
my limits with Margey, and with myself. He had had more success, he
said, than Dr. Bradshaw had described, with a borderline patient who

was willing and able to undergo intense and sustained treatment—three or four times a week over a period of years. That's nice, I thought, but you are not describing behavior within Margey's range.

Ray said that he knew of few institutions equipped to treat borderlines; few therapists knew how to handle the conflicts borderlines created in a group, and within the therapists themselves. He could walk into a room filled with patients, he said, and spot the borderline—the patient at the center of the storm. A hospital staff needed a lot of training to handle such patients; as far as he could tell, Magnolia Ridge specialized in substance-abuse cases.

I've wondered many times what would have happened to both Margey and me and to my attitude about the psychiatric profession had it not been for my brother's intervention at this point in our family's case. I would not even have seen Dr. Bradshaw without Ray's arranging the appointment. I had never before realized how important it was to ask for a diagnosis. Although Barbara had a masters in social work and was an excellent family therapist, she and I had never discussed Margey's diagnosis. For example, she had never used the words *personality disorder* or *borderline*. Her observations were always at a much lower level of generalization: no impulse control, inability to form and sustain relationships with others, unfocused anger, self-destructive tendencies.

Only because Ray knew exactly how to help was I offered a clear outline of Margey's complex symptoms and, later, information on the origins and ramifications of the diagnosis, borderline, all of which I found enormously consoling.

After the diagnosis, I wondered why both Dr. Holmes and Dr. Bradshaw had agreed to such extensive hospitalization of a patient they suspected early on to be a borderline, since such a diagnosis ordinarily includes a patient's inability to make consistent progress in an institutional setting. During our conversation, I asked Dr. Bradshaw if Dr. Holmes concurred with his diagnosis. He said that, yes, Dr. Holmes's original thinking had been that Margey had a personality disorder; he'd thought borderline rather than narcissistic. Dr. Holmes had suspected depression and schizophrenia as further complications and he had had hopes that she might respond to medication.

In all fairness to Blue Cross and Blue Shield, I believe that the two doctors, Holmes and Bradshaw, should have released Margey much earlier, about halfway through the fifteen months she was institutionalized. After the first six months, we all realized she was making no real progress. The extra time behind bars cost more than $100,000 and only delayed the inevitable.

On the other hand, I had been completely complicitous. In fact, I begged Dr. Bradshaw at the end to continue to hospitalize my daughter, even after we all admitted that nothing was being accomplished. Desperate, I would have agreed to almost anything rather than worry about Margey's wandering the streets.

Still, it seemed that the two choices open to my family were woefully insufficient: to watch a family be destroyed or to spend close to quarter of a million dollars on hospitalization. Surely the psychiatric profession needs to offer—and insurance companies need to support—a variety of affordable options for treating troubled young adults within their communities. Adoptive parents need to know that such options are available, or have good insurance, before they take responsibility for a damaged child.

After experiencing the benefits of working with a therapist like my brother Ray, I came home determined to find a better counselor for Dawn. I had been on the verge of changing therapists for six months because I felt that Lettie and Dawn had been in cahoots from the beginning, both blaming everyone in the world for Dawn's problems—everyone except Dawn. The low point in this struggle came when I went to Lettie and described just one week's events: Dawn's math teacher had called. Dawn and Angie had switched their schedules and gotten themselves into the same class. Their behavior was atrocious. Dawn frequently dropped to the floor beside her desk in the front of the room and crawled back to Angie's desk in the back. If the teacher asked her what she was doing, Dawn had a ready excuse—she had to pick up some lint off the floor. The photography teacher had also called. Dawn and Angie were both failing; the two of them sat beside each other and gossiped; they refused to take even the pictures he assigned in class. Finally the volunteer in charge of Candy Stripers at Saint Joseph Hospital had called. Dawn was such a sweet little girl, came from such a nice family, her dad had even brought her in to volunteer and filled out all the papers, she had liked him so much, but she just had to ask us not to bring Dawn back to the hospital again. Dawn and another little girl just would not stop hopping aboard wheelchairs and racing one another through the halls.

Lettie's response to this litany was that the math teacher had clearly lost control of the class; her parents must have neglected to buy Dawn a camera for the photography class—and clearly the young and eager Candy Stripers were not receiving adequate supervision.

I went home and thought about Lettie's responses. Finally, I wrote her a letter explaining that she was doing a good job as Dawn's advocate, but I was afraid she was also reinforcing Dawn's tendency to blame everyone but herself. Teachers were not always at fault when children were naughty; in fact, this particular teacher had volunteered to give up her planning period so she could separate Dawn and Angie and help Dawn pass math. Parents often provided all the equipment their children needed, but those children sometimes chose to do other things than use that equipment. Yes, riding a wheelchair was great fun and we'd all yearned for the opportunity, but there was no excuse for someone's repeatedly disturbing the work of a hospital staff they were supposed to be helping.

I told Lettie that I had just read in a newsletter from Evergreen Attachment Center that therapists often assumed the parents of adoptive children were to blame for their children's difficulties—and typically held all parents responsible, especially if the parents were as angry and frustrated as I was. The newsletter suggested that therapists should always ask two questions before they made assumptions about adoptive parents: (1) What were the parents' relationships with the biological children like? (2) What was the adopted child's early history?

Both Dawn and I needed an inspired counselor to help us deal with one another. With Margey, I had grown more forgiving over time about who bore responsibility for her actions; with Dawn I still had a long way to go toward understanding and forgiveness.

Faced with Margey's imminent release from Magnolia Ridge, I made an appointment with Melanie Ross, the director of sustained care at our local mental health center. Melanie was horrified at Dr. Bradshaw's suggestion that Margey come home, sink to the bottom, and then be carted off to the state mental hospital. It was not possible, she felt sure, for the hospital to release Margey if Mark and I refused to take her. She would check into the Texas laws, but she was confident that the hospital staff was legally responsible for finding a suitable follow-up placement for their patients.

She said there were other things to be done—living situations dedicated to prevention; but she warned me, the diagnosis of borderline personality disorder was a serious one.

I asked Melanie about halfway houses in the area. She said that from my description Margey needed more security and supervision than any of those facilities were equipped to provide.

I told Melanie that I was desperate at the thought of Margey's returning home. She urged me to face one reality right then and there: Margey could never return home, except to visit. I could easily get trapped, she warned; borderlines were incredibly manipulative. Her staff, she said, was experienced and would help me learn to say no.

Margey was equally frantic when her therapist informed her that she was to be released in August; she insisted on knowing where she was going. Someone on the staff told her that she might be sent to the state mental hospital. She responded in characteristic fashion, by blaming me. This time she had all my sympathy.

Mom—

Hey, what's up? Me, just some shit that is going on our unit. Today this kid Jake threw up in my face that I'm going to State Hospital. That made me so mad, but I didn't say anything. Well what I mainly want to talk to you about is why I get so mad at you. It's mainly because that I get the impression that you don't care about what goes on with me anymore. It's like you used to get all excited and show that you were proud of me when I got a new privilege or when something happened to me that made me happy. When I told you when something was going wrong I could tell in your voice that you understood and you always supported me. Now it's just changed. You don't at all seem to really care about what's going on with me and that hurts my feelings and makes me feel insulted. I don't know and when I feel hurt I get mad, real mad, and that makes me mean and want to lash out at you. But then every time that happens I get depressed later on and feel like the biggest fuck up and I begin to hate myself for all the things that I've done. I don't think you understand how much I need to hear like I'm worth someone's while and feel cared for. Because I don't really get that around here that much and that's just something I need to hear to like make me feel good about myself and to go on. I know I've fucked it with us and I hate myself for it, but I just don't know how to come off to you. I mainly just want to say that I'm sorry for all the shit that I've done and that I love you, and I need you.

    Love ya, Margey

Margey was correct in sensing that I was deciding not to bring her home, that she was again being abandoned—this time for good. Yes, she was aggressive and manipulative, but she needed me—or someone or something—and I could not find help for her.

Though this period was another dark night for Margey and me, two things happened that were to bring release, in the beginning to me and, eventually, to both of us. The first, thanks to my brother, was my growing understanding of Margey's diagnosis and how hopeless it was to dream of her ever living a stable, independent life; the second was finding the strength, with the help of Melanie Ross, to admit that Margey and I should not live together.

Day in and day out we were not good for one another. There was no way I would or could tolerate her manipulation and abuse or a lifestyle involving multiple sexual partners, alcohol, and drugs, and no way she would agree to live under expectations that she go to school or work. She was eighteen; she dreamed of going her own wild way. It was torture to tell Margey that she no longer had a home, and the line had to be drawn again and again in the coming months; still, facing that truth made it possible, eventually, for both of us to speak honestly about many things beside the weather.

Although it might seem that Margey's diagnosis should have caused more despair than anything else, the opposite was the case. At last it was clear that her patterns of response were not going to change much; all my mistakes and best efforts had probably not affected her a whole lot one way or the other. And there was little, beside offering love—no small gift—I could do for Margey in the future.

At last I had to give up hope that things would go my way. I had to give up trying to solve Margey's problems and learn to relate to her in a whole new way.

Saying that I gave up my hopes for Margey sounds awful; it sounds inhumane. Giving up hope sounds like the end of the road, and it is. The end of the road spent trying to force a different possibility upon patterns that do not change; the end of sleepless nights spent trying to imagine yet another solution when there was none; the end of power and control; some lessening of responsibility and guilt.

Giving up my hopes meant drawing the line and saying, "Given who I am, I have done what I could." Giving up hope meant changing the words "will not" and "would not" into "could not" and "cannot." Giving up hope meant coming to understand that human beings are far from equally free.

Giving up hope did not mean giving up love.

Since walking into my first, brand-new 1980s mental hospital at Magnolia Ridge, I have been in several other new facilities for adolescents. They all looked exactly the same—all expensive new tile; they all charged the same—exactly as much as the insurance company covered. And they all dismissed their patients on the same schedule—when the insurance money was completely gone. Parents had gotten so desperate to find help for their children, who were usually suicidal, that they were easily victimized by facilities that had little to offer except time out and huge bills.

All too often, adolescents who were abused and neglected prior to adoption are likely to arrive, with their adoptive parents, at this point of desperation. These same parents had earlier suffered at the hands of the social service agencies who awarded them terribly troubled children and then disappeared from the scene.

Mark and I yearned for choices other than the three available:

our family in crisis

jail

mental hospitals

Halfway
to Where?

There was a great deal of difference between the sexual development of Margey and Dawn and that of the biological children. It wasn't easy with any of the five, but Margey and Dawn were much more focused on their sexuality as a potential solution to their problems rather than as a source of pleasure. They became sexually active at an earlier age and were more public about their sexual activity than the other children. Margey and Dawn were also uninterested in, even hostile toward, birth-control measures.

Kate, on the other hand, denied her first sexual relationship so vehemently that Mark and I almost doubted our intuitions. She didn't want us to worry or think negatively of her. In college, when the time came to choose some form of birth control, she considered every option and, for health reasons, finally chose a diaphragm to be used in conjunction with a condom. Sam's senior romance was a hot spot on the high school scene—he and Janet made a cute, sexy couple. They laughed happily when they had to be chased out of the basement after hours. He had no worries about birth control; good hedonist Janet was on the pill. Jack was a late bloomer, and his initiation was far from home, and private: Mark and I knew only by way of the grapevine. Both boys always had a stockpile of condoms.

At Magnolia Ridge, Margey resisted birth-control pills even though she was as sexually active as the circumstances of incarceration permitted. She simply did not want to take the pill.

"Why not?" Barbara and I asked her.

She just didn't. She didn't like it, didn't like to take any kind of pill. She'd heard it got you all bloated, shit like that.

Was the pill linked in her mind with psychotropic medications? Did Margey think taking a pill meant something was wrong with her? Barbara and I asked one another.

It seemed so.

Did she not want to take the pill because she could see that not getting pregnant meant so much to her family?

Entirely likely, Barbara and I thought.

A couple of months before she was released from Magnolia Ridge, Margey did agree to go on the birth-control pill. But her heart wasn't in it; she was only trying to meet the adults' standards and prove that she was ready to go free.

With Dawn, sex was at least as difficult. She was not as rebellious as Margey—not as motivated to do something only because her parents disapproved. But Dawn lived a romance novel. Dreaming of sex and love and babies provided the escape from reality that Margey found in drugs. From Dawn's point of view, there were positive side effects of sex, love, and babies: they had the power to release her from school, which she hated.

When Margey left Magnolia Ridge in September, Melanie Ross found a placement for her in a halfway house about thirty miles from Minneapolis, in Lakeville, Minnesota. Lakeville was close enough to visit and far enough away not to have Margey on the doorstep.

Lincoln Home was more depressing than a retirement home. The residents sat stolidly and stared at what was in front of them—food or television. Margey's room was small and crammed with clothes, stuffed animals, and cumbersome furniture—a space she shared with a woman exactly my age, who never spoke.

Each resident had certain chores, including cooking one night a week. Margey always planned my visit on the nights when she cooked. She went to great efforts to please me, asked about my best recipes, and always served my favorite—chocolate cake. Not once would she let me take her out; she was proud to be doing something for me.

Mom—

Hey, how's it going? Me, OK. I wrote to thank you for coming up to see me and for putting an extra effort to see me that made me feel happy. Everyone around here says your so nice and everything and saying they wish they had a mom like you and it made me stop and realize how lucky I am and to really appreciate you. I know that your very busy because of work & all & I'm really happy that you've made time for me. I'm going to work on not taking my shit out on you because you have alot of your own things to worry about and you've helped me out so much already. Larry liked getting to meet you, you know how hard it is to meet new people especially mothers (you know the ole hardness with peoples parents). He likes you alot. Thank you also for bringing that bread up for me and the house that's very nice, very welcoming. I love it when you come up here, I get so excited. And all I talk about when you leave is you I get kinda sad but then I know I'll see ya next week, so it's OK. Well I just wrote to say thank-you.

I love you, Margey

Dinners at Lincoln Home were unsettling. Margey and her friend Larry were the only ones who ever spoke a full sentence or introduced a topic of conversation other than the food. Margey's roommate was never there for a meal—she was painfully thin. The other residents—two large women about fifty and fifty-five and a changing group of four men of various ages—ate and ate and ate and gestured when they wanted more. Immediately after the meal, everyone disappeared from the table and reappeared five minutes later with cigarettes and plastic mugs of coffee from Dunkin' Donuts. Margey explained that the staff made coffee only in the morning. Everyone sat in silence, drank coffee, and smoked; the long, narrow dining room was saturated with cigarette smoke. Everyone except Margey and Larry was over forty-five. Larry had been released from prison, the rest from the state mental hospital. All were dull and heavy, probably from sedatives. Margey and Larry were the opposite—frantic and loud. It worried me to watch Margey talking all the time, speaking over Larry when he tried to get in a word.

From day one, Margey complained that she was bored and lonesome at Lincoln Home: nobody was young like her, except Larry, who was twenty-five and loony. When I asked if she had applied for a job, she shrugged, "Why should I?"

If she kept her curfew, Margey was able to go out at night. In no time she was keeping company with a young man who worked at a car wash, Ed Jenkins. He provided Margey with a way out. Who could blame her for taking it?

At Thanksgiving, Margey brought Ed to the family dinner. He was quiet and shy, small-boned, with long, brown hair. He looked a little like Margey. She talked all the time; he said little. Did I like her new clothes? How about these high heels, weren't they a smash? Didn't they go good with the green in her shirt? She'd gotten everything she had on at the community center down the street from Lincoln. Could you imagine that people gave away such good stuff?

Didn't the pie she'd brought look yummie? She'd gotten up at six and started cooking on it. Took her all morning. Didn't it look great? She'd made the crust from some of them sticks. They worked great. The cherry filling was a snap. Just pull it right outta' the can.

When Margey was busy in the living room, Ed came out to the kitchen. He said he wanted to get Margey out of the halfway house; that was no place for a beautiful, lively young girl like her. Why was she there, anyhow?

She'd told him there wasn't one thing wrong with her, except that she couldn't get along with her family. Half the folks he knew didn't get along with their families. He thought she was wonderful, and he'd been seeing a whole lot of her for two months. He had a chance to rent a trailer for a hundred dollars a month and get her away from there.

I told him she needed a lot of structure to keep going as well as she was. I begged him to think seriously about what he was trying to do. She had spent more than a year in mental hospitals, and her diagnosis was serious indeed.

He said she had no business living with all those whacked-out folks.

Beginning in December, Margey was never there, according to whoever answered the phone. Finally one of the staff volunteered, against the rules of confidentiality, that Margey had moved in with Ed. When she called before Christmas, I invited her and Ed to spend the day with the family. Margey said she'd think about it, but that she and Ed just didn't fit in. She knew it, I knew it, everyone knew it. She didn't know how to act around us; she never knew what to say, so she just shut up.

Shut up? Amazing! We had all been afraid neither she nor Ed was comfortable. Still, I told her we were her family, it was Christmas, everyone would do their best.

She thanked me for inviting them. She would really like to see me. She'd let me know later.

We didn't see Margey and Ed over the holidays.

About two weeks after Christmas, Margey called and started in: there was no way she was going to live with Ed; he was impossible. Drinking. Shouting at her. Getting blind drunk. Expecting her to be his nurse when he passed out, to drive him home when he was in a stupor, taking advantage of her sexually when she was drunk.

She was in a bind; what could she do? She didn't have any place to go?

I told her I'd help her move her stuff back to the halfway house the next day.

Ed called a few minutes later. He was doing all he could to take care of Margey. He had gotten her out of the house with all those fruit-cakes. He was working. Bringing home food to feed her. Taking her out to eat if she was hungry. He loved her. Loved her so much, he'd go without food himself rather than see her hungry.

Oh, yes, he was drinking, but what could he do when she threw him out of his own trailer. She never cleaned it up, never let up bitching. Now she'd locked him out in the middle of the cold night. Would I come and get her for the night? Give her time to cool off. She was throwing things around, breaking up all the dishes. He didn't want to get the police involved or nothing like that.

Oh, yes, she was telling everyone she was pregnant, quite a ways along, too, but none of his friends believed her. She was drinking way too much alcohol for any woman who was pregnant.

I took a deep breath. No, I said, it wouldn't help if she came back home for the night. What she needed was to assume some responsibility for herself. He wasn't helping by trying to do everything for her.

The next day I called the halfway house to see if they'd take her back. They said, no, she'd checked out against their advice. She'd have to petition to get back in and promise to get with the program.

The next morning I called the number at the trailer park and after ten minutes or so Margey came to the phone. She wanted me to help her get all her stuff out of Ed's trailer and take it to some friend's place—someone Ed didn't know. We had to move fast while he was at work. He was trying to keep her captive in his sorry-ass, nasty-ass trailer, so far out in the cornfields she never could see her friends. He didn't want her to have any fun, to meet anyone. He got all jealous if she talked to anyone else. They never had anything to eat; she hadn't eaten in days.

I told her that I wouldn't help her move in on strangers; it wasn't fair to impose on someone else because she and Ed were having a bad time.

She said to leave if I wouldn't help her.

I wished her well and hung up.

For once I wasn't particularly upset. Margey was practically out on the street, to hear her describe it. I believed Ed, though, and thought she would be too desperate to let him go. If she and Ed couldn't straighten things out, she would have to go back to the halfway house and commit to the program. Mostly I was furious with her for being pregnant and drinking.

No word came from either Margey or Ed for the next month. Then in late January at 4:00 A.M. a policeman knocked on the door of our house. He had a message for someone to call Saint Joseph's Hospital in Lakeville. A friend of Margey's answered. Margey had just had a miscarriage. Did we have any insurance on her?

I said, no, she was no longer covered under our policy. I'd come and see her in the morning.

I called a friend to help me calm down. Becky volunteered to go to Lakeville with me to visit Margey, and I was grateful.

Up against the white hospital sheets, Margey looked pale and tired. Ed was with her, his clothes, hands, and fingernails lined with heavy black grease. He wasn't at all comfortable having Becky and me around. Margey was full of her story. Ed wanted to talk, too, but she kept him out.

"God, Mom, you can't imagine how much blood came out. And talk about something that hurt. You wouldn't believe it. At first I thought it was a regular period. Then it got worse and I thought I musta' done something, pulled something loose inside or hurt my stomach from not eating right. I went to the bathroom, and all this blood come pouring out. All around the toilet and on the floor. I was cramping so bad I couldn't sit still on the toilet seat. I had to roll up in a ball on the bathroom floor with a towel between my legs.

"Ed, he didn't have any idea what was going on. He kept saying, 'You want to go to a doctor, Margey? You sick or something, Margey? You got to go to the hospital. Let me go get somebody to help you.'

"He came back a few minutes later because I was screaming so loud. Then he went to get Ida and George from next door. She's about nine and a half months pregnant by now. They're about to get evicted for not paying their electricity. Now you tell me how they're going to have a baby without heat in that trailer—it'll freeze to death.

"They got this trashed red pickup. I was in pain big time by then. Blood pouring out of me, like a faucet, I'm not kidding, Mom, just like you turned on the handle of a faucet. These big old clots coming out, I'm talking about nasty. I am not going to do this again. No way. I mean it, I'm never going through anything like that again. Never.

"Mom, do you know what they brought me in for dinner—meat loaf with tomato sauce! I'm not kidding you. After all the blood I've been looking at, they bring me something that looks exactly like one a them big old clots. Ed ate it, I couldn't look at it.

"They told me after the operation I was twelve weeks pregnant. Hey, Mom, do you have insurance on me? This is gonna cost big bucks. An operation and everything."

I told her she was no longer covered on our policy. Actually I didn't know whether she was or not, but Mark and I had decided that the insurance company had paid enough. After Margey turned eighteen, both Mark and I felt as if it was time for the larger society to help take care of her.

"Then, that's just too bad. There's nothing I can do about it. They brought me in here and did that operation, didn't ask me or nothing. Twelve weeks, that's pretty much."

I counted backwards. Margey must have thrown away her birth control pills the minute she left Magnolia Ridge. She'd gotten pregnant the second month out of the hospital, with the first guy she met. I knew better, but I asked her why she hadn't taken the birth-control pills.

"Look, Mom, I knew you'd say something about that kind of shit. You always have to, don't you? I do not feel anywhere near well enough to discuss such things at this time. Even if I felt great, I probably wouldn't want to discuss anything of that nature with you."

Becky winked at me in sympathy.

I had to get out of there or lose control. I told Margey I'd send her flowers, bring over some food. What was the address of their trailer?

"You can send whatever you want right here to the hospital. I'm going home this afternoon, but Ed can pick anything up for me. Or send his mother. She's been up here twice already. Brought me this flower. Pretty, ain't it? Looks better than real, and I can keep it."

I said maybe it would be better if her dad and I sent flowers to the trailer since she was leaving the hospital so soon. What was the address to give to the florist?

Ed recited a long string of numbers—

"No way, Ed, do *not* give her my address. I don't believe I want her to have that information at this time. If I want her to know anything about my life, I'll tell her myself."

How could I be so furious with Margey after all the pain she'd gone through? So angry with someone lying helpless in a hospital bed? I was shaking with rage.

At the nurses' station, I asked for Margey's address. The head nurse, severe and stern, graying at the temples, said she could not give out confidential information unless Margey granted permission.

I complained. Wasn't that a little silly, I asked, here I am, her mother, visiting, notified at four in the morning by the police that she wanted to see me, yet no one would give me her address?

She said she knew how I felt. She had a girl exactly like Margey. Maybe even worse. Already'd had two babies, no husband, living on AFDC. What to do?

"Good question."

Becky had gotten the address of the trailer park from Ed and suggested that we stop by there on the way home. She stayed in the car and I went into the manager's trailer. Mrs. Moore was more than eager to talk about those two young couples, or whatever they were, living in the park. Nasty, they were, nasty. Everyday she carted off the empty liquor bottles they threw out the door. The one couple was behind on their rent—she was evicting them that very day. Whatever she had to do, call the police, anything, she was getting rid of them. They hadn't had any electricity for a month. She didn't know how they lived, no telling. People like that, you never know, and you don't want to ask. All's you'll ever get is big lies if you do.

Don't think they didn't find the money for liquor and who knows what else. She'd smelled some mighty strange smells. The one girl pregnant out to here. She was going to make it her business to tell somebody that girl didn't have any business keeping that baby.

I asked if Margey and Ed were behind on their rent.

"No. That one, Ed, he just paid. He pays by the week. That one works, I'm sure of that. None of them others, far as I can tell. The three of them sit around and drink and smoke and watch TV the whole day. Good for nothing. How are you connected up with them anyhow?"

"Margey is my daughter."

"I got one just like that," she said. "Always telling me he's quit drinking, going to work, got some new, fancy job that's going to make him a million dollars. Used to be I believed him. Used to be. Not no more. You have to put them out, you do. After they leave, I'm going to have to go in there and clean up that trailer, just you watch and see. My boy, he's the same. I don't know what's going to happen to them."

On the way home, Becky tried to help me figure out something to do. Mostly I was so angry I didn't even want to consider being helpful. Becky was worried that Margey would get pregnant and miscarry again. Better than for her to have a baby, I said. Becky didn't seem to think that a young woman would be able to carry a child if she was drinking so much and eating so little. I wasn't so sure about that—seems like women who did all sorts of things had babies all the time. I was inconsolable. Margey's future stretched in front of me, an endless nightmare of violence and misery. During this episode, and over and over again through the years of crises with Margey and Dawn, my friends Dorothy and Linn, Gail and Penny, Becky and Julie listened, consoled, advised, improvised innumerable solutions. I always hoped they realized how much their support meant in those dark hours.

A few days later, Margey called to thank me for the flowers and to say she was doing fine. I asked if she'd gotten my letter. She said she had.

The letter was a detailed itemization of the damage smoking and drinking do to a fetus. I begged Margey to think about her past experiences with her biological mother and to try not to repeat that pattern. I asked Ed to consider their financial situation and his responsibility for conceiving a child and taking care of Margey and the fetus as it was growing. One page was filled with passionate pleas for Margey and Ed to use birth control. I offered to take Margey to a doctor to talk about alternatives as soon as she was ready.

To my astonishment, Margey said she wanted me to take her to the doctor. No, she wasn't ever going to do that again. She wouldn't go through that much pain for nothing.

Good, I thought. Whatever it takes.

The doctor who had attended Margey during the miscarriage was worried. He didn't understand why she hadn't come in for any follow-up treatment. I explained Margey's diagnosis and asked him what method of birth control he would recommend. He'd had some experience with borderlines and didn't think she would take the pill; the best bet would be the IUD. But, he said, he didn't have any on hand; in fact, he'd quit prescribing the IUD because of its potential side effects. He said that Margey was a poor risk for an IUD because she hadn't had a baby, she wasn't likely to return for periodic checks, and she would be at greater risk of infection and venereal diseases, especially if she had multiple sexual partners. I'd have a hard time, he said, finding anyone willing to give Margey anything but birth-control pills, which, no doubt, she wouldn't take.

I called Planned Parenthood. The receptionist said, no problem, the doctor would prescribe an IUD; they had plenty on hand. Did I know the cost would be $175? I was shocked at the figure; that was a month's rent for a poor woman. I was grateful not to have to worry about the cost.

When I tried to make an appointment the next day, however, the nurse said there was no way they'd give someone like Margey an IUD. She repeated all the Lakeville doctor's hesitations and added the risk to Planned Parenthood of a lawsuit.

I contacted the Omni Women's Health Center and went through the same routine. They recommended three local doctors who might help. Among them was a personal friend, Dr. Doris, who had seen Margey several times before.

I called Dr. Doris and tried to explain the situation and history and the parts of Margey's diagnosis relevant to the choice of birth-control methods: the absence of cause and effect reasoning, the lack of impulse control, and the way Margey lived entirely in the present. Dr. Doris said, yes, she did prescribe the IUD and agreed to see Margey.

At her office, Dr. Doris and Margey talked for about an hour. They agreed that Margey and Ed would return the following week and that she would then prescribe birth-control pills for Margey. The risks of the IUD were too great; the pill was the best alternative. I was devastated. Hadn't Dr. Doris heard what I'd told her? Did it always have to be this way? That no one believed a word a mother said? It felt as if I was back talking with the Happy Day staff about Dawn's eating problem, meeting glazed eyes and plugged ears.

Margey didn't keep the appointment. Of course not; she would have had to get to Dr. Doris's on her own, which was exactly what Dr. Doris wanted her to do and exactly what I'd known she would not do. We had just that one chance, Dr. Doris and me, that one day Margey had agreed to see the doctor.

Dr. Doris heard of my distress from a mutual friend and wrote a note.

March 20, 1989

Dear Ann,

Sabrina has mentioned twice that you are quite angry with the way I dealt with Margey.

If this is true, please let me know. I did not discuss the situation with you fully before as I was trying to deal with Margey's growing independence.

However, she indicated that I could talk with you, if you should so wish.

If there are any problems that we did not clear up in that evening phone call, please let me know.

Sincerely yours, Doris

I wrote back to Dr. Doris, trying to explain the frustration of always knowing what disaster was likely to happen, but never being able to prevent it. I apologized for taking advantage of the friendship and asking for a favor I knew would go against her best medical judgment. I tried to explain that although I knew my request went against customary medical practice, I really believed that, given Margey's present lifestyle, the risks of her getting pregnant were much greater than the risks of the IUD. Nevertheless, Dr. Doris, from her perspective, had given us her best advice and help and I thanked her.

Margey finally called and said she had not kept her appointment with Dr. Doris. No gas, bad muffler, she couldn't find the card and the phone number to cancel the appointment, she knew I would have taken her if she'd asked, but, you know how it is, she didn't want to bother me.

I asked her what she and Ed were using for birth control.

Well, she really didn't want to get pregnant after all she had gone through. And Ed really didn't want her to get pregnant either. So whenever they got ready, they went out and bought a condom. Everything was fine.

Who did she think she was fooling? She had learned one thing from all the counseling: to say what she thought would shut up her interrogators. She had no idea how unconvincing her words were. My heart sank. One or two cycles more and Margey was sure to be pregnant again.

Margey went on with her news. They'd gotten out of that sucky trailer and moved into Ed's parents' apartment. It was teeny-weeny, but they were in town now so she could get out and hang around with her friends, and she was having a whole lot more fun. Thanks, anyhow, for all my help.

More bullshit. What help? Any that mattered? Margey and I were a bad balancing act: she felt as if I was never able to help her when she wanted something from me; I felt as if I was never able to help her when I wanted to do something for her.

My sister sent me a sign for the refrigerator—It Coulda Been Worse. She was always trying to get me to consider how much worse off the girls would have been if we hadn't adopted them. My sister's point was that a lot of bad things had not happened, even if a fair share had. Margey might have just had a miscarriage, and, sure, she was not going to use any birth control, but she had made it all the way to eighteen without getting pregnant. She'd be at least nineteen by the time she had a baby.

And Dawn had made it all the way to seventeen without achieving her dream of getting pregnant. Then along came Charles Hutchison, the cowboy-booted, cowboy-hatted eighteen-year-old from South Dakota. Dawn finally found a young man who welcomed her advances and doubled her ante. Charles had come from Aberdeen to live with his dad and stepmother. He and Dawn fell in together as soon as he got into town. They had so much in common—and most important was that both had parents who were impossible to get along with. Charles's parents were religious, devout member of the Church of Christ. After getting put out of his mother's house, Charles didn't seem too anxious to push his father to his limit.

Ed, Margey's friend, and Charles actually looked as if they could have been brothers. They were two of the skinniest young men around, and both had their hair cut short at the sides and left long and curly in back. They both loved basketball and fought to the finish with their fathers for a win. They were good with machines and loved to "break down" their cars and put them back together. Both also loved to drive fast on city streets. Both were fair and blue-eyed, made tons of grammar errors, and spent a lot of time listening to Dawn and Margey talk.

Dawn started telling stories about fights between Charles and his dad—fist fights and wrestling matches. Charles was slight and his dad a great deal thicker. Mr. Hutchison seemed invested in being able to handle his son physically, and perhaps Charles was a little frightened of overcoming his father. Anyhow, Mr. Hutchison delivered the most damage. Charles grew more bruised and subdued physically, more rebellious emotionally.

One day, Mr. Hutchison called Mark and said he wanted to come over; the two of them had something important to discuss. When Mr. Hutchison was seated in the living room, he pulled out a condom and handed Mark a note from Dawn to Charles describing how sore she was, but how happy she was to be so sore. Those two incriminating bits of evidence had been found in Charles's jeans pocket.

Mark and I had known what was brewing; such moves were all too public with Dawn. Endless whispering on the phone with Angie; notes about sex. Lists of names for their children. Reasons why they both wanted a girl first. So Mark wasn't surprised. He was more relieved by the condom than horrified by the note.

Mr. Hutchison went on to explain that Charles was choosing Dawn over God and thus risking the eternal damnation of his immortal soul. He'd even tried to get out of church on Wednesday night—choosing fornication over bowing before the Lord.

Mark tried to say something about our friend Mother Nature and suggested that sex was a fairly natural activity. Mr. Hutchison would have none of it. These two young people simply were not going to have a sexual relationship, not while Charles was living under his roof.

Mark said he agreed that these two kids had no business having sex—they were much too young and immature, but he wasn't so sure they could be stopped. He was a great deal more interested in preventing Dawn's getting pregnant.

"Yes, indeed, they can be stopped," Mr. Hutchison said. "Indeed they will be stopped. Or Charles will be out on the street. Are you with me, Mr. Kimble, or are you against me?"

"Well, I suppose I'm with you in spirit, but I'm not going to put my daughter out on the street for having sex with your son, if that's what you're asking me to do. There'd be more folks living in the streets than in houses if parents acted like that."

Mr. Hutchison then asked Mark if he was feeling like he wanted to hit somebody—in place of Charles. He knew how Mark must be feeling, that something valuable had been lost, his daughter had been spoiled. Mark had a right to some kind of revenge. Mr. Hutchison volunteered to walk out behind the garage. He wouldn't even hit Mark back.

Mark wasn't feeling anything of the sort: he'd never had a fight; didn't care a thing about a free swing at either Charles or his dad. He was worried about the neighbors' calling the police, he said, when he told the story. Maybe, Sam speculated, we needed a new sexual morality because we didn't still have barns out back.

Kate insisted that I take Dawn to get birth-control pills right away. I couldn't. At some level, Mr. Hutchison and I were allies. There was no way that Dawn was ready to have sex or a child; no way. Every month she left her soiled sanitary materials somewhere; every month the dog shredded them on the hall landing.

My first and only attempt at talking with any of the children about sex had been in a group, when Kate was six, Sam was four and a half, and Jack was three. They asked every last question and of course responded, "Oh, gross." Since then I had always discussed relevant sexual matters in my literature classes and hoped that other teachers and parents would educate my children if I did theirs. So Dawn and I had no history of talking about sexual matters. Kate had helped her get oriented to menstruation. "If only you were here to help her," I told Kate, who was in Mexico for the year, volunteering in an orphanage in Tiajuana. "You can do these things so much better than I can."

"Don't talk like that"—Kate was clear and curt. "This is something you have to do. And now."

I still couldn't, but I asked Dawn to choose someone to take her to get the pill, Becky or me, or Sabrina, a good friend. She said Sabrina, definitely. Sabrina took her to Planned Parenthood, as calmly as you please, and the matter was settled. "You're just so lucky nothing happened while you were being neurotic," Kate shook her finger, "so lucky. You would never have forgiven yourself. And all of us would have had to work endlessly to get you over the guilt, which this time you would have richly deserved."

I was justly chastised, the pill duly purchased. Still none of us had much confidence that Dawn had the slightest interest in not getting pregnant. Quite the contrary.

Dawn and Charles figured out how to have sex in spite of Mr. Hutchison's best efforts. They cut school and went over to friends' houses when their parents were working. Charles's parents found out about the truancies and put an end to that routine. Mrs. Hutchison and I both called the school daily for attendance records and threatened the earth if we found one cut.

Mark was on sabbatical that year and worked at home, so our house was fairly closely supervised. Charles's stepmother worked at home, so there wasn't much opportunity there, either. One day, when Mark came in from soccer practice and I came in from school, we discovered Dawn's underpants on the dining room chair. Charles and Dawn had figured out the one two-hour period in the week when no one would be home.

Charles graduated in June and headed back to Aberdeen to live with his mother. His father had had a god's plenty, he said. That'll be the end of that, don't worry, he said, when he heard that the two had sworn to get together as soon as Dawn turned eighteen. That boy can't stick with anything, he never even remembers his own father's birthday.

Dawn decided to get off the birth-control pills for the summer. She had been accepted to return to Camp Minnehaha as a junior counselor. Although she was disappointed that she hadn't been chosen for the senior staff, Mark and I were relieved that the camp had made an exception and had taken a junior counselor who was seventeen rather than the usual fifteen and sixteen. Dawn struggled, as it was, to keep up with the craft room; she tried but hadn't passed the tests to supervise other activities. Working with young children was perfect for Dawn. She was a child herself.

It makes perfect sense that so many adopted children yearn to procreate and are often successful in their teens. These young people know nothing of their own roots; naturally, they want to create blood kin and a history of their own. Children who were rejected as babies understandably dream of repairing their mothers' and fathers' records and getting it all right with their own babies.

It is also perfectly understandable when their adoptive parents are stricken with fear at the prospect of these babies having babies—often at the height of their adolescent rebellion. There is no better way for the adopted child to get exactly what she thinks she wants than by having a baby. There are few things she can do that terrify her parents more.

What method of birth control was available to keep Dawn from realizing her sentimental fantasies of having a child? What method of birth control was available to protect Margey from the consequences of her thoughtless sexuality?

None. Nothing. Nada.

To object "But why couldn't they use the pill?" entirely misses the point. They couldn't or they wouldn't. End of story. A prescription of the pill as a means of birth control simply meant pregnancy. The IUD was not a realistic possibility; given her lifestyle, an IUD would have put Margey at risk of pelvic inflammatory infections. No responsible doctor would take the risk. We desperately needed a long-term form of birth control, one that would protect a young woman who was unreliable or irregular in her habits as well as an immature woman who yearned to escape all her troubles through pregnancy. To rely on the pill in either of these situations was foolhardy.

Both Margey and Dawn were opposed to abortion—Dawn vehemently and from moral high ground, Margey because she just didn't like the idea. Too messy; too creepy.

We can put a man on the moon, I raged to everyone who would listen, but we haven't yet figured enough ways to stop a sperm from penetrating an egg. What risks we take with the next generation. All in the name of what often seems to me to be the single most significant and abused inalienable right—the right to create a child.

Indiana Street

A month after going to live with them, Margey moved out of Ed's parents' house and in with another young man, named Tony, who was then living in Lakeville. Tony got Margey's attention—at least partially—by being responsive to her curiosity about her biological mother.

Tony knew a lot of the appropriate initiatives in adoption searches. He took Margey to the county hospital, where they asked for the record of births on July 21, 1970, Margey's birthday. A secretary told them the office did not keep records longer than ten years. They filed a request to locate the information in storage, but never returned to pick it up.

Tony also took Margey to the Department of Public Welfare, where she discussed with a social worker her desire to locate her mother. The social worker suggested that Margey could obtain all the information she wanted and eventually meet her mother, if both she and her mother were under the supervision of a therapist at the mental health center. Margey gave up on that idea, too. She seemed to have reservations about the whole search. "I don't know, Mom, how I feel about it. I wish I had a Mom and all, a real relationship with a Mom, you know how that is. I really do. But her, I just don't know about her. Seems like it's just too late. She ain't the one."

The one. An interesting phrase. Did Mom and child need to be matched like lovers? Maybe so. These poor girls had, after all, missed two tries for a good match.

I was willing to help the girls locate their records and parents, although I did not have warm feelings toward their mother. Margey was curious, but she was also frightened of what she might find. Eventually she told Tony, "Quit bugging me, you son of a bitch. How come you want to dig in all this dirt? I don't. And it's my concern. Butt off."

Before long, Tony ran out of work and money in Lakeville, and he and Margey moved in with one of Tony's former girlfriends, Polly, in

Minneapolis. Late one night in March, Tony knocked at our door, introduced himself, and said he'd come with Margey to pick up her trunk; she was out in the car finishing up something. Tony and Mark hauled out the trunk that a friend and I had refinished for Margey's Christmas present.

Tony frightened us: dark hair, dark eyes, dark hair all over his body, black jeans and tee shirt, scuffed black cowboy boots. Mark and I wondered if he meant to scare people.

As soon as the trunk was loaded into the rear of a long, low-slung, black machine, Tony gunned the motor and they disappeared, tires screeching through the neighborhood. Mark came back in the house. "What in God's name was that? He almost slammed my arm in the trunk. Looks to me like Margey's done it this time. Couldn't she even come in?"

"Did you really want her to?"

"Hell, no!"

"Well, maybe she sensed that. Did you see her?"

"Yeah, she was hunched up in the front seat—looked like she'd just had a bad scare. She was drinking out of a bottle in a paper sack."

"Maybe she wanted to introduce the family to her new boyfriend."

"God, why does she do stuff like that?"

Two months later, Margey called and invited me to come visit her at Polly's; she said her friends were all really curious to meet me, what with hearing her story and all. Would I mind coming over to Indiana Street? She said she didn't exactly want to come home; Mark and the other kids made her feel messy inside.

When I drove up, Margey was waiting on the porch. She gave me an excited little hug and grabbed my hand. "Come on in, Mom. I knew you'd come. I told them you would. Tony told me you'd never make it all the way over here. I told him you would, too, if you said you would."

The living room and connected dining room were bare, except for three large, worn couches and big piles of clothes in the dining room. The carpeting and furniture were clean. But it was clear why someone suggested that I might not show up in this neighborhood: it wasn't exactly frightening, but it certainly wasn't familiar.

Margey was wired. "Yeah, man, I really want that job I told you about at Dunkin' Donuts, I really do. They had a sign up on the door for part-time. The hours are perfect—six o'clock 'til midnight. I can get me a tan. Look at me, I'd be white as a ghost without this makeup.

Terrible. I can lay out and clean up the house, all that, before I have to get to work. Make friends with all them cops that hang around drinking coffee and eating doughnuts. Quit taking so many drugs. I know that's bad. Hasn't been a day I haven't done drugs. Anything I can get. When I don't have something, I get a headache and start to feeling bitchy. So I do some more."

I tried to change the subject. "You look great, Margey, I'm so glad to see you. It's been too long, but I didn't know where to look."

She seemed not to hear me. "This guy Eric, he got so messed up the other day—acid you know—he'd been tripping like crazy for four days. He wouldn't a made it if we hadn't taken him into the hospital right when we did. Now he's all against any kinda' drug. You ask him does he want some, he says, 'Hey man, what you talkin 'bout?'"

A group of five or six kids came through the living room and headed for the kitchen. "See that redhead—that one's Polly's. He's checking you out. Being cool. Idn't he cute?" He was. All the children were.

"You got a cold or something?" I said.

"Nuh-huh, my voice always sounds like this. Sexy, ain't it? I did just have me this terrible cold. Snotting all over everywhere. Laying around trying to find some peace in this nutso house. Finally I got some penicillin and that took care of it right away. First I drank some whisky for the cough. I quit coughing, too, and slept a long-ass time."

"I'm glad you got to a doctor."

"Shit, man, I didn't go to no doctor. Where you think I'd get the money for that? I found the pills in the kitchen cabinet. Three different kinds."

"Good God, Margey, how did you know they were penicillin? Honey, would you just call me and I'll take you to Dr. Doris."

"Who cares what they were, they worked. Polly, she said they belonged to the people who lived here before. She said they looked like penicillin, I might as well try them. Them pills made me sleep good. I liked being sick when I was a kid. I mean it. You remember how we used to curl up under the dining-room table with a pillow and a blanket? Make a tent over top? All that attention you gave us then—I really did like being sick."

"All five of you remember that same thing."

A cat was eyeing us from the windowsill. "You just missed the kittens. At first Polly was all mad about them, but then they were so cute. Six of them. We just took them to the pet store yesterday. The mother cat had worms, ringworms, all that shit. This one caramel kitten had, you know, this sore butt, so it musta' had worms, so they had to put that one to sleep. They said the mother musta' had worms, we needed to have her checked, but we said, 'Fuck that shit.' That's the mother over there, ain't she pretty? She's getting real old now. You wanta hold her?"

"No thanks, you know how I feel about cats. Is that your dog out back?"

"Yeah, God, this neighborhood is really wild. That's why we got a dog. But I kinda' like it. Something going on all the time, I mean *all* the time. Cops always around here.

"The other day the cops came chasing these two dudes running this direction from Michigan Avenue. One of them got away, ran over to the house across the street where they mugged that old lady. The cops set the dog on him, the dog caught up with him, too, and grabbed ahold of his leg. Then the cops couldn't get the dog to let go. The guy, he was hollering, 'Woah, you motherfuckers, you get this ass-fucking animal offa' me.' The cops couldn't pull their dog off, either—it chewed up and down the guy's leg. Blood ran down off the porch onto the steps. You can probably still see where it was."

For Margey, there was probably enough excitement. For a middle-class stick-in-the-mud like me, these images were overwhelming.

"The other day, let me tell you, the guys here taped me up with that silver tape and threw me out in front of the house. It hurt, too; that tape is strong, I couldn't get loose. Rambo, across the street, he called the cops. Three cars pulled right up. They go up and down this street all the time, every ten minutes."

What a job to patrol this street. Margey couldn't slow down.

"I was in this accident. Car rolled all the way over. Brand-new car totaled. I didn't even care, you know that? Everybody asked me, how'd you feel when the car rolled over, weren't you scared? I didn't care, didn't hardly notice that something bad was going down. I was high and all. If we'd a' hit this big tree we missed by about a foot, that'd been it. What do I care? I've done about everything I want to do by now. I'm serious, what else is there to do? Not that I'm suicidal or nothing like that. I was calm. Actually I was having fun watching everything. Trying to see everything when it was all going by so fast. Only got this little cut on my lip. The others, they got hurt. I couldn't hardly climb out of the car, the top was so crushed in."

By the rest of our standards, Margey had indeed done plenty. But there was undoubtedly much more to come, which I did and did not want to know about. She hardly caught her breath between stories.

"Eric stole an old army Hummer that was sitting out front of Applebaum's, keys right in the ignition. You believe that! He ran it out in the country—all through the cornfields. The cops chased after him the whole day. He'd just shoot out over a field, they'd have to go all the way round. When they finally caught up with him, they took his license right outta' his back pocket."

Listening to Margey was like watching a terrible night on the news—one ghastly story after another. And she was enjoying it all.

"See this window? That cardboard—that's where someone tried to break in—right before we moved in. They took the guns that belonged to the people who used to live here. This is a really nice house, huh? We got to put up all that stuff over there, fix it up good, put up pictures. Polly, she keeps it real nice, don't she?"

"She does. Where is she?"

"Working. She's fixing to get her ass fired. She don't hardly ever get to work less than an hour late."

Poor Polly, I thought; probably the only one in the house with a job.

"You know Dawn is fucking up bad. She's cutting school all the time to mess around with that Charles guy. I told her, too; told her there was plenty of time for all that shit. She's got it good and she don't even know it. That day I picked her and Charles up after school—all they did was suck face, they didn't talk to me or nothing."

"I didn't know you'd picked her up from school."

"Yeah, me and Tony picked them up. She didn't tell you? I'm not surprised. Did you know she's planning on moving out to South Dakota and living with Charles's family as soon as she turns eighteen? She told me she'd talked to his mother and everything."

"That's what she's telling everyone, but I can't quite believe Charles's mom is going to fall for it, can you? Anyhow, there's a lot of time between now and September tenth. Maybe Dawn'll meet someone at Camp Minnehaha who'll distract her."

Loud laughter came from the men on the porch. Margey watched them over her shoulder. "I went to Chicago a while ago. With Bill. He wanted me to see some of his family there. He's really messing up. Left his wife and everything. She's about to pop a baby, too. First time I met him, he didn't look nothing like he looks now." She motioned toward the group. "He was all suited up then. Now look at him. That's him on the porch rail." She pointed out the window to one of the three guys holding cans of Miller's.

"I got real mad at him—he had this motel room. I got so pissed off I slept out in the car. You wouldn't believe the money we spent. He had this check for fourteen hundred dollars when we started out. We spent a thousand dollars, he said. I can't tell you what on—except a hundred and ninety-five bucks for dope. He's not my boyfriend or nothing, don't get that idea. He's the one wanted me to call you. So he's proba-bly waiting to meet you. You want me to call him in?"

"Sure."

A middle-sized, middle-aged, plain-faced guy came in from the porch and shook my hand.

"I told him you were all down to earth and everything. He was cu-rious about you guys, after hearing my life and everything."

Bill and I passed a few pleasantries. I thanked him for getting me an invitation. He pulled on his beer—it was eleven o'clock on a Tues-day morning. Margey clearly didn't want him to stay. She had the floor.

As soon as he went back out on the porch, Margey leaned over to me and said, "I'm not with anyone. I'm going to be real picky this time. Take my time. I feel kinda' bad about Ed. I was just waiting for him to start yelling at me and then I'd be outta' there. He started yelling all right, so I left. He's an alchy. Bad, I mean bad. You know when I can say that, it's *bad*. When he got the DUI—did I tell you about that? Anyhow, they put him in jail—I had to run all over town to get him bond. More than a thousand dollars—I had to borrow money from anyone who ever heard of Ed."

I was confused about who was who. "What happened to Tony?" I said.

"Tony has these heart attacks. He goes funny, twists himself all up. He fakes 'em, fakes fits and everything. The other night we called the rescue squad again. He was shaking and shouting, his back curled all up. The fireman came running in. Tony started fucking around with them. They finally got him up in that bedroom up there, put him on a cot, and strapped him down—so he couldn't pull nothing. That's where he belongs, you ask me."

Margey's life sounded like a jumble of soap-opera plots.

"I'm still trying to find my mother. You know, I almost asked at the welfare if they had a picture of her. If I could just see what she looked like, I think I'd be satisfied."

"Really? I've always wondered what she looked like, too. I used to stare at women in KMart or in the grocery and wonder if one of them was her."

"I don't know if I want to sit next to her or nothing like that. I might want to know what her voice is like. But I don't know if I'd like to hear her say something to me."

"Dawn's been talking a lot with her counselor about finding your mother. Did she tell you about that?"

"Naw, she didn't. She probably don't think she's my mother too. Just hers. But that's OK. I don't think I want her to be mine, anyhow. She's not really my mother. She's some stranger I'd meet, that's all."

Then Margey careened off in another direction.

"How do you like my hair? I got to get this back part cut off some. You like it? See, all this is from that iron I told you about. A crimper. All these little wrinkles. Takes about an hour to do the front alone. I got to get some money, treat myself to a haircut."

Margey needed a haircut—and some clothes. She had on shorts that must have belonged to Polly or someone much larger, and a man's large T-shirt. Everything seemed to hang off her: hair, shorts, T-shirt, cigarette.

"You want to go out to lunch, get a haircut while we're out?" I asked her. "Come on, let's go."

"That'd be nice. But naw, I can't leave right now. Bill's waiting out there. Him and me and them other guys, we're going to go downtown in a while. I'll give you a call tomorrow or the next day," she said.

Maybe the guys out front worked the night shift. Probably they didn't. I wondered if they all lived in that house.

Of course, that visit to Indiana Street was disturbing. Mark and I went round and round about whether to rent an apartment for Margey. I checked the ads and called around. There was a small place, for only $350 a month. A good price. But then less happy additions began to pile up. A year's lease. Last month's rent and security deposit of one month's rent up front. Utilities and a phone. Moving in would cost close to a thousand dollars. I called Melanie Ross to see what she thought. No go, Melanie said. You can't do it for her; there's no telling what she'd do to that place. Mark agreed. What was the likelihood that Margey would stay put for more than a month, he kept saying. She'd do lots of partying; the neighbors would get involved—the police. We'd be receiving calls from her landlord. No telling how she'd leave the place when she moved on; we'd have to cover the damages. Melanie and Mark were right: the worst thing for Margey was for us to push her to live our way.

There didn't seem to be any sensible way to help Margey. Not that she was asking; that wasn't the point of her stories. She wanted complete freedom—with all its bugs. If anything, she let us know that the consequences were worth it to her.

A friend with a severely retarded child once described a support session she had attended where all the parents were instructed to stand up in front of the group and introduce themselves as, "I am Vittoria Fava and my daughter Laura is retarded." It was enormously difficult, she said, for many in the group to say those words out loud; some had never done so before.

In our family, we were constantly saying words that gave a similar discomfort. At some point, an incredulous person asked each of us, "Is Margey your daughter?"—"Is Dawn your sister?". . . Of course, we all answered, "Yes, Margey is my daughter," or "Yes, Dawn is my sister." Still, we were usually hasty to add, "but she's adopted." Like so much stereotypical thinking, *but she's adopted* was a profound denial.

I never heard Margey and Dawn respond with "I'm adopted" when some thoughtless or bemused person asked them whether they belonged to the Kimble family. They were more likely to go stone silent, glare at the questioner, or become aggressive, "That's none of your business." The difference was sad: apparently Margey and Dawn, at some level, yearned to be like the original Kimbles, but the original Kimbles never came to think of Margey and Dawn as blood kin.

Margey's and Dawn's curiosity about their mother sparked my imagination. What would the two of us have to say to one another if we met? Like Margey, I remained angry with the mother. I felt as if she'd set up both the girls and me for so many of the difficulties between us. Because she'd been able to give the girls so little, they always seemed to want more than I could give. Because she had cared so little for their feelings, they had difficulty considering the feelings of others.

On the other hand, I wondered about what Margey's and Dawn's life had been like before they were taken away from their mother—

what they did all day, how they played, what they'd eaten, how they looked as babies. How all those milestones were celebrated. Walking. Toilet training. Talking. . . .

Basically, I sympathized with Margey's and Dawn's mother in her struggle to love her children. No doubt she tried hard and felt miserable when she failed. We'd be able to talk about that, I thought, if we ever had the chance.

Independence
Day

When she next called, Margey was still on Indiana Street with Tony and Polly, hanging on by a thread. She wanted me to visit: she had lots and lots to tell me.

Again Margey was waiting out on the front steps when I drove up. She grabbed me by the hand. We passed through the living room, where Polly with sitting on Tony's lap dressed in a T-shirt and underpants.

"I gotta get outta' this place, Mom, I mean it. I hate it here. Get me an efficiency, start over. That Tony, he drives me nuts. Now me and Polly, we get along fine. See how she cut my hair? Even though I look like shit, I know it."

It was true, she did not look great. She had on a stained pair of her own shorts, a T-shirt with cigarettes rolled up in the sleeve, no makeup and long, dangling, orange earrings. Her yellow hair had dark roots and split ends.

"All my clothes are ruined, what's left of them. Tony, he picked up a box of my stuff and threw it down the basement stairs. Everything got covered up with sewer water down there. Smelled like shit. Before that he threw all my sweaters in the washing machine. Wool sweaters. You know that blue snowflake one you and Dad gave me for Christmas, Mom, it's as big as this. Oh, yeah, I'm pregnant again. I never got to wear it once."

She'd dropped that phrase about pregnancy as if it were of no special interest.

"When I first met him, he used to walk in the door and lay out all these drugs in front of my face. Everything you ever saw spread in a big fan across the table. He never knew me when I wadn't all fucked up. Yeah, sure, he liked that a lot. Now he says I'm all different, he can't stand to be around me. He asks me every few minutes how come I don't find me a place where I can be mean as hell and not bother anybody?"

I was back at square one processing that other matter of interest. "So it's his baby?"

"Yeah, sure as fuck is. You should see how he's acting. You know he's fucking around with Polly again? Trying to get her pregnant. Then there'd be the two of us. She's thirty-one—think about that. Raised Russell all by herself. And that ain't been easy, I'm telling you. Don't ask me why Polly wants him. She has to have a younger guy."

"How old is he? Does she want to get pregnant?"

"Shit, no. She can't hardly raise Russell decent around here. He's twenty or twenty-one. Polly and him was together a long-ass time— more than a year. He moved out on her. Then we moved back in. She knew he was with me. She didn't even care, she told me. He does stuff like that all the time. One day this smooth red Mustang drove right up in front of the house and sat there 'bout an hour—Tony and this girl in the front seat all over each other. He's a motherfucker. I hate his guts. I get so mad at him I feel like I'm coming apart all inside my chest. I've walked so many miles in these Reeboks you gave me, they got big holes in the soles. My feet are all messed up from so much walking.

"Tony comes after me—pinching me, you know, his hands all over me, every time there's a group of people in the living room to watch his show. All over me. I push him away, and holler, but he keeps on after me, grabbing my tits, like that. He says I'm not nothing like he thought I was. To get my ass outta' town. I hate his goddamn guts."

As usual with Margey, the reality was even worse than what I had dreaded. And it was futile to try to help. "Margey, let's go down to the Y and see if we can get you a room there. I talked with this other mother who has an adopted daughter. Her daughter lived at the Y for almost a year. She liked it fine. Had her own room. They got it all fixed up really nice. You could have a place for all your stuff."

"I can't be having this baby. All the shit I've done. No way. I'm not having it. Not just pot and tons a' alcohol like last time. This time I've done everything, I mean everything. That and not eating. There's a lot of times when I don't get anything to eat the whole day."

"How 'bout we go out to the grocery. Get you a bunch of stuff that'll keep. Do you have any place to store stuff? Oatmeal would be good—remember how much you used to like that? A pile of macaroni and cheese. Margey, you know I'll help you with an abortion anytime."

"Afterwards I'm going to get that IUD. I'm not doing this again. I can't stand it."

"You been to the doctor or anything?"

"Not yet, but I know, like with Ed. By the way, he came round here looking for me. Him and two guys from here, they went to All Hours—that's a liquor store up on University. There wasn't anybody inside but a bunch a' niggers. Ed started up on them, calling them niggers to their face. Coming from Lakeville, he's never been around them. He don't know how to act. One of them pulled a gun on Ed. Little short motherfucker. Took forty dollars. Then they brought him back here, and he got so fucked up he didn't know nothing."

I tried again with the idea of moving to the Y. Margey couldn't hear anything. She was talking.

"I can't ever go out at night. This one time I was up on the corner of Michigan about nine o'clock and this black dude drove up beside me. I was so scared I started running. He pulled up beside me again, then followed me down the street. I went up to this house, acted like I lived there. He knew I didn't. He waited until I came off the porch steps and then pulled up beside me again. Hollered at me to come on and get in, he'd give me a ride. I ran all the way home. I didn't know I could run so far without my lungs falling out. When I got home I had like asthma— hacking and coughing, choking and throwing up. I'm going to get me a gun. I have to have one. I mean it. First time I get my hands on some money."

The idea of Margey with a gun—terrifying. "Do many of the guys around here have guns?"

"Shit, Mom, look around you. Hell, yes, they got guns. You gotta have a gun in this neighborhood. Polly won't let none of them in her house, though. She's afraid about Russell. But she don't know half the shit that goes down round here. The other day I thought I was going to die—I'm serious. I hadn't eaten, it musta' been three days. And it was so hot. I got out of here first thing in the morning and walked around all day. I sat down on the curb in front a' Dunkin' Donuts, smelled all them good smells, and thought, 'This is it, I'm going to die right now.' I didn't care either. Still don't, if you want to know the truth. I've done everything I ever wanted to do. You don't believe me, do you? I have."

Alas, I believed her. She fit my grandmother's description, the tail end of a misspent life. I nodded.

"Holidays are the worst, you know that? Everyone's around their families, you can't go nowhere. There ain't no free lunches at the grade school. Fourth of July was rough, let me tell you. No free lunches for four or five days in a row. Me and Steve. We take three or four of Alma's kids. She's got five kids—'bout every year she has another one.

Her husband treats her like dirt. Beats on her. Hollers at her. And at them kids. We take them over to the grade school for the lunches. But those free lunches taste like jail food. They do, really. Pretty bad, ain't it? I told you. Eating the kids' free lunches. Don't you dare tell nobody any of this shit. I'll be embarrassed for them to know how bad it's been. I told you, anything bad that coulda' happened, happened, you believe me now, right? All in two weeks, too. In the kid lunches they give you two pieces of bread and baloney. A big glob of mayonnaise not even spread around. A carton of milk, an apple, and a cookie. But we have to give the cookie to the kids or they won't go with us."

I thought of Karen at Clayton Home and wondered if Margey was saying she'd hit bottom.

"I found this place where I can sell hot stereos. They don't ask questions. Some way I've got to get me some money. I sold my stereo. You remember the one Jamie gave me when she left the hospital? Her parents got her a complete new unit, cost over a thousand dollars. So she didn't want to pack up her old one and lug it all the way home. I don't have any jewelry. Nothing. I don't have nothing. I hocked everything. These are Polly's—aren't they pretty?" She held out an orange earring.

"Yeah, let me see them up close. What are they made out of?"

"Hell, I don't know, some shit. Yeah, here I am knocked up again. Something, ain't it?"

"You must feel terrible. Especially with Tony acting like this. You want me to make you an appointment with Dr. Doris, come and get you?" Margey so clearly didn't want to take anything from me. She wanted to be free, no strings to Mom.

"How long's it been since my miscarriage anyhow, you remember?"

"Well, I think that was late January, early February. This is July. Must be five or six months."

"Shit man, that ain't no time. I called all over to find out what to do about it. There's one place in the state that will do it. The Women's Pavement, something like that."

"The Women's Pavilion?"

"Woman's something or other. Look at these legs. I got up this morning, didn't take a shower or nothing. It's too hot to go upstairs now—way hotter up there than down here. I haven't shaved my legs in no telling how long." Margey spoke carefully to emphasize the words: "I just do not have any time to shave my legs." Then she ran on, "Don't fix my hair; don't hardly put on any makeup. Well, sometimes. Besides, Tony threw away all my makeup. A brand new blush I just bought. All those condoms—all that foam stuff you sent me—those sponge thing-ies. Told me I didn't need none a' that shit, he'd take care a' things. Be-sides, who'd want me, that's what he said."

"Margey, why don't you let me help you get out of here. We can pack up your stuff right now and head out to the Y. If they don't have room for you yet, you can stay somewhere else until they do."

"I don't know where everything is—all over the place. Lately I've been getting all upset over the littlest things. Going to pieces over noth-ing. All emotional and that. Everything makes me sick. The last time I wadn't sick or nothing. Now I'm sick all the time. You have to watch out. If you don't eat for three days, then when you eat something, you throw it up. This one day I drank a whole cup of coffee to have the taste of something different. You get tired of drinking nothing but wa-ter so you won't feel so hungry. That coffee made me sick to my stom-ach. I threw it up."

She didn't seem to want anything from me. Just wanted me to lis-ten and know. She whirred on like a sewing machine eating up cloth.

"All my friends, they sound just like me. They all grew up with some kinda' messes in their families. Now they're into drugs, all messed up. Every one of them's been in some kind of institution—like me. This one friend, her Daddy brought her this junker, cost about a hundred dollars. A Duster. She took it to the shop and got this guy she knows to cut the top off. We ride around in that all the time. As cool as you please.

"I got to get me some identification. I couldn't work at Arby's no more after two weeks because I didn't have my birth certificate or nothing. I don't have any money to get that shit, neither. I don't have nothing. I got one check from Arby's and gave it to Polly so she could cash it for me. She kept the whole thing, I owed that much for rent—and more. I've got to get me a job. I ain't going to have this kid, either. Not after all the drugs I've done. Plus I do not want a kid. Not and do the same thing to it they done to me. No way. Hell, I don't want noth-ing like that around me all the time."

"You want to go over to the driver's license bureau in South Saint Paul and get some identification? Sam said they make an identification card just like a driver's license. Employers accept that, he said."

"Yeah, we could do that. Polly, she don't believe in that shit. She thinks you can't go and get rid of a kid. That's why she had hers and got into all that trouble. Me, I gotta get out of here. Find me a place of my own. At least I have somewhere to sleep and take a shower. Me and

Polly get on good. We talk about all kinds of really deep things. I mean really emotional stuff. You know? She don't do drugs or no shit like that. I don't like to ask her for nothing. Polly, her and her husband, they go out. She won't let him have no divorce. He picks her up after work and takes her out to eat. Tony he eats no telling. So there won't be nothing around here and I get so hungry."

Good God, couldn't her mother at least make sure this child had something to eat?

"Should I have another one of these cigarettes? I want another one. But then they'll be gone too fast. Then we'll have to gather up these butts from the ashtrays and roll them in cigarette papers. Nasty—that tastes nasty. But we do it. What'd I tell you about everything happening that coulda' happened to a person? You believe me now?"

I wanted one of her last cigarettes, too. "Come on, Margey, let's at least go get some cigarettes. We can get you some groceries. You aren't doing anything, let's go."

"Look at me, Mom. I can't go out looking like this. I'll call you tomorrow. We'll go out. I called you this time, didn't I? Don't worry."

I went straight from Polly's house to the grocery and bought twenty pounds of potatoes and a large box of oatmeal. Then I didn't know what to do with them. The idea of showing up unannounced at that house scared me. They didn't have a phone. I thought maybe Sam or Jack would go with me and we could drop the bag off at the door with a note to Margey. But they thought the idea was stupid. Who was I kidding? What difference would a bag of potatoes make?

All was quiet at Camp Minnehaha. Thank goodness. Dawn came home for the Fourth of July weekend and spent a lot of time on the phone; it was a month before the bill arrived with more than a hundred dollars worth of calls to Aberdeen. Kate and I drove up one weekend; Mark another. That camp always seemed like the best place in the world for Dawn. If only they operated year round, Mark and I wished.

Though Margey was the greatest threat that summer, Sam and Jack managed to get themselves into trouble as well. Both of them were let go from their summer jobs at St. Thomas. As Mark had helped them land those jobs, he was anything but pleased. He and I decided to take away all spending money, all gas money, all fast-food money. It appeared that the boys had lost motivation to work, and we wanted them to find some—immediately.

They were so privileged, I kept concluding when I thought of Margey. They were jerks to blow it. She had nothing, would take nothing. They had so much and expected still more. Infuriating. Both boys soon buckled down, however, and found jobs, much more demanding jobs than their work at the college. Still they had the gall to be resentful of Mark and me for our rigidity. They couldn't, however, have been any more resentful of us than we were of them.

Though the whole scene was ugly, the boys in the end did what they were told, unlike Margey and Dawn, whose wills were as thick as the walls of Italian castles. Why couldn't they obey? They piled up the consequences. Now a baby.

Knocked
Up Again

Three more weeks of Margey's pregnancy passed before she called again. Margey and Tony had fought to the finish; she had moved out and was living a couple of blocks away with a family of seven and the wife's retarded brother.

The house was one of those that makes you ask as you pass by, "I wonder what that place is like inside?" Completely bare of vegetation, the front yard was riddled with hills and holes of various sizes. Two boys digging in the yard and a little girl sitting on a broken tricycle stared at me when I drove up. They said, "Yeah, Margey's inside."

Every square inch of the sinking front porch was packed with machine parts—motorcycles and motorcycle pieces, bicycles and bicycle pieces, televisions and television pieces. You had to squeeze through an aisle in the parts to reach the front door.

I had asked my friend Julie to come along. What was I getting her into? I looked back at her as we passed through the aisle, but she didn't flinch.

The screens on the front porch were pushed out; the front door stood open. Large black flies buzzed and lit and zipped out of reach.

The living room was tidy enough, but it smelled as if it had been closed up on itself for years. Cockroaches walked across the walls and ceiling. Margey and the retarded man slept on two couches pushed against opposite walls in the living room. Margey's trunk was beside her couch: clothes spilled out of it and from a pile of cardboard boxes. A little girl with a big strawberry on her dress stood on an easy chair opposite Margey and me and stared; she scarcely moved.

"You know what Tony's going around telling everyone? He knew I didn't want to get pregnant. He was supposed to be pulling it out, withdrawing, you know about that? Nuh-huh—he didn't, either. He's been telling everyone he shot it up me on purpose when I was too fucked up at the time to know the difference.

"Sex with him was horrible. No foreplay, nothing like that. He'd come in me all dry, like that, shove himself up me. Like a great big two-by-four. Really. I'm serious. I hated it. He knew it, too. That's how come he got so mad at me. I had him pussy-whipped for a while, I did. He followed me around like a little puppy. I ordered him around like a queen.

"I didn't believe anyone would do something like that to me, on purpose, too. Nuh-huh. Then after two weeks and my period didn't come, I figured I better go down and check it out. The woman at the office—you know that women's center on Selby?—she was so nice. She knew I didn't want it. She said, uh-oh, it isn't good when it gets pink so fast. Sure enough, in just a few minutes it was red. I was so pissed off. She said, 'You don't want it, do you?'

"I said, 'Hell, no, I don't want it? What the fuck am I going to do now?'"

Neither Julie nor I dared bring up the word *abortion*. Margey knew already that an abortion would be my recommendation and that I'd be more than willing to help her. But the word and the idea troubled her: she didn't want to get rid of a fetus or suffer any pain.

"You know Tony don't think I dare get rid of it. He acts like there was this great big thing between me and him. Like I wouldn't do nothing 'bout no kid a' his. When I said I was going to do it, he just stared at me."

Did she love that guy? Did she want there to be something big between them? Probably so. Margey, apparently the meanest, toughest woman around, was deep down the most romantic. She wanted the perfect love—someone absolutely devoted to her, someone to worship her. She found plenty who did—for a time. She was lovely to look at and fun to be with, but she always tired of them or they of her. And then she wanted to begin all over again. She loved erasing the chalkboard and beginning with a clean slate. Pregnancy was anything but a clean slate.

Julie asked her if she had thought about other possibilities. Good and vague. But there was no uptake: Margey acted as if she hadn't heard the question.

"So . . . well, what else? I told you how I promised to take Joey to get his hair cut, didn't I? He's the biggest one of Sherry's out there in the yard—has on that yellow T-shirt. I took him all right. That beautician embarrassed me the fuck outta' me. She shouldna' acted that way, neither. She got him in the chair, pulled up his hair, then she hollered so loud everyone in the whole place could hear, 'I ain't 'bout to be cutting this child's hair. He got lice all over his head. Look at them black spots—ain't them ticks? Get this boy outta' here this minute.' Now wasn't that awful?"

"Sounds mean, especially to a kid . . . but lice are contagious." I identified with the beautician and felt sorry for Joey at the same time.

"Yeah, I know. I been worrying I'd get 'em myself. I keep scratching my head all the time. I don't have 'em though. Sherry told me it was because I wash every day even though the water ain't hot. And all that junk I use to color my hair, they don't like that. Ha, I'm glad!

"You should see the way Dave treats them boys. Dave, he's Sherry's husband. He don't care nothing 'bout them. They aren't his. They're Sherry's from this other guy who had to be committed for something. Dave, he gives those three a' his everything. Like all the affection they want. Right in front of the others. He don't give them other two nothing. Sends them up to their room for the slightest thing. They're scared a' him. Soon as he comes into the room, they sit right down in front of the TV. Don't move hardly the whole time he's home. Joey's messed up, too. Y'can tell. He won't go to school any more, no matter what they do to him. He's got one pair of pants and they're floods. Pat, he's just the same, ain't got nothing—one pair of pants, shoes from Salvation Army that used to be Joey's. Them other three kids of Dave's, their grandmother sews. She makes them something new every time she comes over.

"Sherry, she can't do nothing about Dave and the boys. The other day Dave went after Joey. Picked him up by his neck and dropped him off the steps. Sherry told Dave that was the end of his butt—her children came before any son of a bitch she was married to. But she didn't do nothing except holler. Someone should call the welfare—I mean it. I'd like to call them on Dave."

"Do these kids remind you of Dawn and you?" Julie asked.

"Nuh-huh. Well . . . maybe. But I don't remember nothing. I do remember feeling like that, though. A lot. Yeah . . . a whole lot."

"Sherry ain't so good herself. Her brother Bobby told me how she treated Joey when he was a baby. She was real young, left him upstairs in his bed and locked the door—for whole days while she ran around. After a while, Joey didn't even cry much. Joey ain't right—he's always bug-eyed, looking at you, seeing can he get something outta' you."

I thought of Dawn hanging around the kitchen, watching the food.

"But it ain't Joey's fault. Like Sherry and Dave been promising him a new pair of tennis shoes every day since school started. Every day they say for sure they'll take him to the store the next day. Now you know that ain't good for a kid."

I asked if we should take those boys to the store and get some tennis shoes. After all, Margey was living there—no doubt rent free; she clearly wasn't working.

"I don't think so," Margey said. "You can't really do nothing about it. Sherry wouldn't like it—make her feel like we don't think she takes care of them. She's always talking about welfare coming in here and taking them away. Which if you ask me is exactly what oughta happen.

"I've been thinking about it seriously, I mean it. I've had enough. I don't want to stick around anymore. But I don't know how to get outta' here. If I did, I'd snap my fingers and disappear. I'd kill myself if I could, I'm serious, anything to get out."

Julie patted Margey's arm. The little girl with the strawberry on her dress walked over to me and patted my arm, too.

"You know, I'm going to go back after that job dancing at Ramona's. She told me I could have it after the abortion, soon as I feel better. I tell you, I don't care how I make money. Money's money. I do want a nice haircut."

"How 'bout you come with us and go to the beauty parlor right now?" I asked.

"Nuh-huh, I can't be leaving them kids. Nobody's home now but me."

Julie and I both wanted to say something about the abortion, to try to help her make a decision. Time was passing—at least three months already. It bothered me, though, to say I'd pay for an abortion when there were so many other things she needed that I wouldn't offer to pay for. Feeling like the eugenics squad, I didn't say anything.

"Do you want to talk about alternatives to having a baby?" Julie asked. Thank goodness for her nerve.

"I was all dressed and ready to go to Ramona's last night. But I didn't have any sheer hose. Mine had these seams around the crotch. They got to be sheer all the way. Ramona says all I have to do is walk around the dance floor. Kinda' be there. Turn 'em on, you know. Laugh a lot. Talk to them. Get 'em to buy drinks.

"I mean it about the money. Four hundred dollars a week—that's a lot of money. I was scrounging at that restaurant, wearing myself out—couldn't hardly move when I got home—all for a lousy hundred dollars a week. Having to split tips three ways. I wouldn't have to take off my clothes. One thing, I don't know if I can dance."

From what I'd seen of Margey waiting tables at the Fast Stop, she stood around with the dishrag and wiped and rewiped the counter. It didn't look as if she had any idea what she was supposed to do. She loved the immediate gratification of the tips, flirting, being stared at, but the work apparently required more self-confidence than she had.

"This girl who works there. Ruth, now—she can dance. You should see the men coming after her. She hates 'em though. Says she takes 'em for what she can get. I don't blame her. I'm starting to feel the same way. All they want is to do you. I'm serious, you might as well take 'em for all you can get. Hey, you guys want to go over to Ramona's with me some night?"

"Sure," Julie said. "I've always wondered about that place. You sure you don't end up doing stuff beside dancing?"

"Yeah, I know you have to turn tricks if you dance there. But let me tell you, money's money. I don't give a damn how I get it. I want some nice things—some real nice clothes—I look sharp today, don't I? I mean I want some really nice clothes. And drugs whenever I want. I don't care how I get the money. I don't."

"You look really nice, honey," I said. "You always do. You always fix yourself up, as my great aunt used to say."

"Money's the only thing I really care about. Don't look at me like that. I do too mean it. You guys don't know what it's like."

She was right. No question, we did not. Nor could I imagine another direction for Margey's life. To tell the truth, I wondered if prostitution might not be better than dependence on the likes of Tony.

As we were getting ready to leave, I asked Margey about bringing some money to the family. "Nuh-huh, they're getting plenty from me. Don't you worry about it. I'm working my butt off taking care of these kids."

I asked the little girl beside me if Margey was nice to her. "Uh-huh, uh-huh. Gum-m-m."

"Yeah, I always give her gum, she's after me now for some more."

"Gum-m-m, gum-m-m"—she held out her hand.

"I'm sorry, I don't have any. I'll bring you some the next time I come."

"She's so spoiled. She does that to everybody," Margey said.

Back in the car, Julie tried to console me. "She's really doing well. Look how she was taking care of those kids. She was really interested in them."

"Yes, in somebody beside herself. That was good. But, my God, what a place to live! She'll be outta' there and on the street in no time. Then what?"

"I'm not sure you need to worry about that so much as what's she's going to do about the baby. She won't deal with it, will she?"

"That's a tough one," I said. "Think how hard it must be for an adopted kid to get an abortion. How can they resist creating someone to love them?"

"Where'd she put the kid, in a box beside her couch? What a mess."

"There's really no telling what she'll decide—it depends so much on what the people around her say. They get to say all they want and we don't dare open our mouths."

"Is she going to end up a prostitute?" Julie asked.

"What choice does she have? And think of how much worse that'll be if she has this baby."

No life should be so predictable, so inevitable.

"This Is the Pits"

Three or four weeks more went by before Margey called and agreed to see Dr. Doris. Their meeting was fruitful. Margey got the whole picture, but still she couldn't make up her mind. Tony wanted her to have the child; that meant she was inclined to get an abortion. Dave thought she ought to abort; she then thought about having it. The argument that carried the most weight was from Bobby, Sherry's mentally retarded brother, who asked Margey would she take one of Sherry's kids and pour whisky down its throat. When she answered of course not, Bobby told her she'd done far worse to the baby inside her.

"That's it," she said on the phone days later. "I am going to get an abortion. I made up my mind. Dr. Doris said I got to decide, I'm pretty far along—sixteen weeks at least, she said, maybe more. Call that clinic in River Falls."

The nurse who answered the phone was matter-of-fact: "So, how far along is your daughter? We perform no procedures after twenty weeks. You'd have to go to Milwaukee to get help between twenty and twenty-four weeks. After that nobody's going to help you. The procedure will cost between two hundred and fifty and three hundred and fifty dollars, depending upon the number of weeks the pregnancy has advanced. We only accept cash. Bring in the total amount since you are not sure about the date of the last period. Three hundred and fifty dollars—cash."

Dr. Doris had said she wasn't sure how far along Margey was or what procedure they used after fourteen weeks; she said to check in the latest edition of *Our Bodies, Ourselves*. There was a relatively comfortable procedure and an enormously painful procedure, the book said, and described both; it often depended upon the attitude of the clinic which of the two was chosen. According to the book *Our Bodies, Ourselves*, clinics sometimes did not use the more humane technique—one

152

that required two visits instead of one—perhaps because of time constraints, perhaps for punitive reasons.

I was troubled by everything that was happening. Although I was unequivocally pro choice, I had never wanted to get directly involved, especially with aborting a fetus already the size of Margey's palm. No matter how I tried to shut them down, thoughts of my own pregnancies and the way I felt about those fetuses at three and four and five months kept pushing themselves into my mind and shoving out any other thoughts.

Everything seemed too uncertain the morning I picked Margey up and we headed toward Wisconsin. Was she too far along even to get an abortion? What then? Would the clinic use the more painful method? The less painful method? I did not think that the decision to abort the fetus was wrong, but still. . . . The whole business was problematic. Would Margey need to come home until she felt better? How would we all handle that?

The receptionist was as sympathetic in person as she had seemed distant on the phone. She handed Margey a stack of forms to fill out. "Damn, Mom! Look at all this junk they want to know. How come it's any of their business . . . ? Last pregnancy? Damn! Six months ago, isn't that right?"

"Let me think," I said. "This is July—"

"How last pregnancy terminated? They want to know some stuff, don't they? Miscarriage . . . end of January, maybe February, that's close enough. You know, Mom, it wasn't a miscarriage. I did things to get it out."

"Like what?"

"I didn't drink, I poured it down. And I didn't eat nothing—not for days at a time. Look at this. They want to know what form of birth control I intend to use in the future. I'm going to tell the doctor I want my tubes tied. I'm serious. How do you spell that?"

I spelled it out: "*T-u-b-a-l l-i-g-a-t-i-o-n*, I think."

"Look at all I've gone through so far this year. First that miscarriage, which was terrible. And now this. I thought I'd miscarry again—I was waiting. I did enough to make it happen."

The nurse called out her name, "Margey K," and they disappeared. All the chairs but hers and mine were filled by couples—men sitting next to women, alternately, some very young. The men offered a great deal of physical and emotional comfort to the women they were accompanying. That surprised and touched me.

Margey reappeared after about half an hour, sat down, and grabbed my arm. "Goddamn, Mom! He told me it's going to take two days. We gotta come back here tomorrow. Is that alright with you? Can you come? They did a' ultrasound—it's about eighteen weeks. They'll do it, but it will cost more money—three hundred and twenty-five dollars. The first day they have to put in a bunch of little sticks to stretch me out. Those have to stay in overnight so they get a chance to swell up. Then tomorrow they can get it out and it won't hurt so much. Otherwise the pain would kill, he said."

"That sounds like a good idea, honey. Why don't you come home until you're feeling better?" Margey was describing the less painful of the two procedures. I thought she needed help, and I was a bit worried that she night disappear between days one and two.

"Hey, Mom, you want to know what they have on the ceiling above the table you're laying on? A great big poster that says, 'This is the pits.' *That's* the truth. 'This is the pits.' Don't you agree?"

"Entirely."

"The doctor got all pissed off when he read what I wrote, about all the alcohol and drugs. I told him I wadn't about to be lying to him. What was the use? I told him I really wanted my tubes tied.

"He said I was only nineteen years old. What if I changed my mind?

"I told him I knew how old I was. But I've lived a lot in a short time. He said, anyhow, he wouldn't do it. He didn't think I could find a doctor anywhere who would. I begged him, but he said, 'No way, not at your age, not before you're twenty-three—even older.'

"That ain't right, I told him. It wasn't his decision. He wasn't gonna be raising this baby. So then I asked him for an IUD. He didn't want to give me one of them, either. There were too many risks, he said. Since I haven't had any children, it might not stay up there. I could get a bad infection. Plus, he said, IUDs can mess up your insides. He wanted to know how come I wouldn't take the pill.

"I told him I couldn't be promising to do nothing the same time every day. There are whole days—sometimes a lot more than one—when I stay fucked up. Hell, if I can help it, I never do anything the same two days in a row.

"Lookee here, I told him, I'm pregnant right now and only a little while ago I had that terrible miscarriage. Plus an operation. I told him to listen to me and asked him didn't he think I ought to do something safer than a pill I'd never remember? He said he could see where I was coming from—to come back in a week and he'd fix me up with an IUD."

"Thank heavens. What a huge relief. You did great."

Margey looked subdued when she returned sometime later from the doctor's room. "Damn, Mom! That hurt. Let's get out of here. I want me a cigarette."

What a great idea, I thought.

"We gotta be back here at eight tomorrow morning. I'll tell you about it in the car. That nurse was really nice, a lot nicer than the doctor. She asked me if this was my first time. She said she knew how I felt. They tell you all about their personal lives back there.

"Can I use your mirror just a sec? God, I look rough, don't I? Soon as we get home, I'll fix my hair and put on some more makeup. Didn't I look nice this morning? I got all dressed up to cheer myself up. I always do that.

"Look at my stomach. You can tell it, can't you? Them kids at the house, they been asking me how come I'm sick all the time, always laying around on the couch. Joey knows. I'm sure of it. He's always looking at my stomach—he musta' heard somebody talking about it. Think of trying to explain all this to a little kid."

"I can't think of what you'd say."

"Look at my stomach. I can't hardly fit into anything but this one pair of jeans. They're so tight I can hardly breathe. I don't like to wear my clothes this tight."

As we drove back to Saint Paul, I realized that Margey hadn't been home for months, not since the previous Thanksgiving. The house was empty when we got there, and Margey enjoyed being pampered. "God Mom, this soup is great. It was really nice of you to make it for me. Don't throw away this last bit in my bowl. I can't eat any more now, but I'll want it later. I feel kinda' like I'm floating. And my stomach isn't settling down too good. They told me I'd be cramping off and on. I've got to go to bed and take a nap. Where do you want me to go?"

I didn't know where to send her. There wasn't a bed for her in the house anymore.

"Go to my room."

The next morning we arrived at the clinic an hour early, making sure we wouldn't be late. Even so, every chair was taken, and we had to stand. "Hey, Mom, you're the only mother in this waiting room. Did you notice? Isn't that funny? They all got their guys. That Tony—hell, I'd like to stick him up on that table in there, pull his guts out. This is making me nervous. I wish they'd call me in—get it over with."

Margey disappeared behind the nurse. It didn't seem to be an option for me to go with her. As soon as she left, I realized how silly my concerns about the procedure had been. Where had they all come from? I wondered, feeling myself grow angry. And angrier. I was angry with my own experiences, which were nothing like Margey's; angry at my Roman Catholic upbringing; angry remembering far too many "academic" discussions about the morality of abortion. I went out on the front porch to wait in the fresh air. What connection was there between abstract moral principles condemning abortion and the extremely moral decision Margey had just made? She should not be feeling guilty and ashamed; she should be proud of herself. And she was. Margey, the kid without a conscience, had a thing or two to teach some other folks about judging and blaming.

"Oh, good, here you are," Margey said. "Mom, it took longer than they said, didn't it? Do you have to be somewhere?"

"I have to teach at noon, and I want to get you settled down with some lunch before I leave."

"What time is it?"

"Almost ten."

"How long was I in there?"

"Must have been almost an hour."

"You been waiting a long-ass time, haven't you? They made me wait an extra thirty minutes because I started to throw up. They didn't want nothing to happen. They're real careful.

"Now that really hurt. I am not going to go through with that again. I - am - not. When they pulled out those sticks, it hurt something awful. Then that vacuum thingie. Oh my god! That liketa' killed me. My guts pulled up tight, like when I had that miscarriage. But after that it was pretty much okay, except for throwing up. I kept my eyes on the ceiling the whole time. I wish I had one of them posters. 'This is the pits.' That's funny, don't you think?"

"Yeah." Laughing at a mistake was a sign of humility. So many people I knew would find both the mistake and the humor disgusting.

"Look at my stomach. It looks better already, don't it? The nurse said it would be just as flat in a day or two. You know, Mom, I gotta tell you how much I appreciate all you've done for me. I don't know what woulda' happened if you hadn't helped me. I don't. I probably woulda' done something really terrible to that kid. Not just before it got born either.

"You really stood by me. I told everybody. They couldn't believe it. None of them get along with their parents. Polly said her mom liked to' killed her when she got pregnant. Slapped her all around and almost threw her down the stairs. You didn't even act shocked."

"You're welcome, honey, you know that."

"Yeah, I feel pretty good now. I'm hungry. Man, Mom! I'm starved. I can eat more of that chicken soup when we get home. Is there any left? That stuff was so good."

I was surprised that Dawn had so little to do with Margey while she was home. Dawn spoke formally and then was off to Angie's— deliberately it seemed. Mark was awkward with Margey. They also spoke carefully, and then Mark retired to watch TV. Margey didn't seem to notice particularly, though she did comment on how much Dawn was away. Margey provided her own entertainment, and mine. After she rested a while the second day, she wanted to return to Sherry's and Dave's. Enough chicken soup and peace.

Dawn couldn't have been less interested in returning to school that fall. She was biding her time until her birthday, September 10. She and Charles wrote and called one another regularly. Charles promised to send her a ticket to Aberdeen for her birthday. Mark and I tried to convince her to stay and finish school, but that was the last thing she wanted to hear. Mark and I were both torn by opposite and very strong emotions. We were exhausted and wanted desperately to be done with it all. And we didn't think anything good was happening at home with Dawn. But we also thought Dawn should remain at home: she was too young and unequipped to manage alone. Although she was almost eighteen years old, she was only beginning her junior year and was mentally and emotionally no more than age eight or nine.

Then again, perhaps another environment would help. Maybe it was time for someone else to try to motivate Dawn. Maybe Charles's mother was the woman for the job. His stepfather seemed sweet and patient. They both had a great deal of experience with children— eleven between them and a series of foster children. If they could do the job, it would be much better for Dawn.

After escapist fantasies like those, though, Mark and I would be stricken with guilt over abdicating our responsibility.

Before the plane ticket arrived from Charles, I insisted that his mother and I at least talk. That conversation was not pleasant. Charles's mother said she was inviting Dawn to visit, just as she might invite any of Charles's friends. When I asked how she planned to deal with their sexual relationship, she insisted that no such relationship existed. When I asked her as the only responsible female around to help Dawn with her birth-control pills, she assured me that that would not be necessary. Dawn was going to finish school like her other children. She fully expected that Dawn would find another boyfriend in no time. Through the years, she and her husband had taken in fourteen foster teenagers and had never had a serious problem. All Dawn needed was discipline and a loving family, which they were willing and able to provide.

The day before her eighteenth birthday, Dawn left to live with Charles and his family in Aberdeen, South Dakota. I was frankly more relieved than guilty, but Mark was the opposite.

This period in our lives was extremely difficult for Mark. He was deeply hurt and troubled by his inability to convince Dawn to remain at home and finish school. He was quiet on the surface, but he felt rejected—a failure. From our different responses, it was clear how much more Mark was invested in Dawn than I was.

Margey's choice to have an abortion was also easier for me to deal with than for Mark. The only person in the house who would enter into a discussion with him about the morality of abortion was Dawn. Her position was simple: abortion was always terrible; there should never be any such thing. All the abortion houses should be closed and turned into nursery schools. She'd never have an abortion herself; she'd just have the baby and go on welfare and they would all live happily.

Mark's position was much more complicated, of course, but, I felt, equally separated from the real decisions ordinary women have to make. While Margey gained the respect of the rest of the household, Mark and Dawn were both horrified by her decision. But then, Mark did not for one second think that Margey should have had the baby. He was caught between knowing what was best for his child and his more abstract principles. I was not helpful; debating such an obvious decision seemed a waste of time.

At about this time, Mark articulated his theory that the adoption had made me a cynic and him a recluse. He wasn't able to talk with anyone about what was going on in our lives and as a result didn't talk with anyone about anything. Only parents who thought of themselves as close to perfect would have undertaken what we did, he concluded. We had changed a lot from those two idealistic young people, looking through the adoption books, no question. But I wasn't comfortable concluding that Mark was a recluse, nor that I was a cynic.

About the time the kids hit adolescence, Mark had taken on the job of dean of the college—certainly not a reclusive job during working hours, but definitely a job that put distance between old colleagues and the new administrator. Through all these difficult years, Mark also coached the select travel soccer team—a social exchange of some magnitude, both with the boys he coached and their parents, and with soccer aficionados throughout the state. Midway in his coaching career, he was selected as the best soccer coach in the state. His teams regularly won state and regional championships.

Had I become a cynic, as Mark claimed? Well, partly as a result of aging and meeting innumerable chasms I couldn't cross, I had become much more conscious of the limits of my powers of persuasion and will—much less idealistic and optimistic. Perhaps from growing up in a racist society in Mississippi and in a troubled family, I had always had a tendency to overrespond and exaggerate. I had always been delighted to ride out against the evils of the world on my high-stepping white horse—much too delighted. Lately, though, I had grown more reluctant to saddle up.

My efforts with Margey and Dawn had left me with an understanding of how successfully I could scapegoat—how thoroughly I could rationalize. Once when he was angry with me, Jack called me La Perfecta, indicating how well he understood the gap between my actions and my explanations. Every time I saw signs of the biological children's lack of confidence in themselves, or anger with me, I wondered how much my behavior toward Margey and Dawn affected Kate, Sam, and Jack. Did they live in fear that I would treat them as I treated Margey and Dawn?

Margey's abortion brought to the surface the differences that had always existed in Mark's and my positions on abortion, and for that matter on birth control, sexuality, and religion. At some level, Mark didn't think that I should have helped Margey get an abortion, that I should have spent "our" money on an immoral act. It seemed to me, however, that Margey and I had suffered far more than he had, and we wanted to put the experience behind us and move on. We were both much more focused on finding an effective form of birth control than we were on second thoughts about the decision to get an abortion.

Homeless

About two weeks after the abortion, Margey got into a fight with Dave, and he insisted that she leave his house immediately—at ten o'clock at night. Bobby, the man who shared the living-room couches with her, brought Margey over to our house. She asked me to let her stay, just overnight, until she could get herself together and figure out somewhere to go.

"Let's see what we can find for you first," I said. "Neither one of us thinks it's a good idea for you to land here every time you're desperate."

"It wasn't my fault. Mom. Dave's a total asshole. He threw me out for nothing, absolutely nothing."

"Never mind that, let's think about where you can go."

"I promise you, Mom, I didn't do nothing tonight. He's been drinking steady for no telling how many days. I muttered something under my breath—I promise you he didn't hear it. He got all red in the face. I was scared he'd hit me."

I had been afraid the rules would have to be laid down again after Margey spent the night at the house during the abortion. But actually, she seemed to understand: she might even have been relieved when I called the YWCA to see if they had room. The woman on the phone said they had one bed left; to come as soon as possible. Bobby agreed to take her down on his way home, and they left less than an hour after they'd blown in.

The next day, when we met for breakfast, Margey was perky and cheerful: she'd slept fine; she was hungry. When we went back to the YWCA to ask if she could rent a room there on a more permanent basis, the admission counselor insisted that Margey submit to drug testing. Margey was furious, but had no alternative. The results of the testing and interview suggested that she was borderline chemically dependent, an optimistic reading, I thought. The counselor agreed to accept Margey conditionally and spelled out the rules, one by one. Margey grumbled, but signed on the dotted line.

She and I drove over to Sherry's and Dave's to pick up her stuff and take it to the YWCA. My stomach rolled as we unloaded the mildewed cardboard boxes and plastic bags. When I pointed out that she needed to go through her things and throw out the moldy and rotten, Margey told me I'd better tend to my own business. I felt the old rage returning and left immediately.

Mark and I would have been comfortable paying Margey's rent at the YWCA and I volunteered, but her counselor encouraged us to let Margey work within the system. She explained to Margey the procedures for collecting her rent money from the housing-allowance office, and Margey dutifully picked up the first check and paid her bill. After the first month, though, she either didn't make it to the housing office or refused to wait in line. Eventually, more than three months in arrears on her rent, Margey was evicted from the Y.

Equally distressing was Margey's lack of interest in finding a job. Her counselor at the Y said they'd spoken repeatedly about work, and Margey always assured her that she had an interview or a job all lined up—something perfect for her; something she'd always wanted to do. Nothing ever came of all the big promises.

I blamed myself for not driving her to the housing-allowance office to pick up her check every other week. That would have been a small inconvenience—especially in comparison with Mark's and my paying her rent. Somewhere in there I got stubborn: the least she could do to maintain free rent was to stop by and pick up a free check, which she assured me she was doing. If she didn't, she could take the consequences. I should have known better than to insist that Margey could do anything, or to believe her when she promised she had.

Making sure the rent was paid would probably not have made any difference, though. Margey was sick of the YWCA. She hated all their stupid rules, she said.

Besides, she already had her next landing figured out: Margey and a boyfriend were going to stay in an apartment his dad had paid rent on through December. They were going to fix it up nice . . . she was all ready to buy the paint . . . she'd picked out white like in our house. Then she was going to get a couch; she'd found a classy black one at Scan's, and then she was going to buy. . . .

For weeks I didn't hear anything more. Then three days before Christmas, Margey called to chat. She was full of herself, maybe going to get a job at Culligan, no . . . yeah, probably at Ramona's. She wasn't too sure how long she'd be living where she was at now . . . no, not the same place as before, somewhere new. She and that boyfriend had had a fight; she'd moved in with this other guy, then she'd gotten in trouble with his mother who was the biggest bitch on—

Margey went on and on. I was worried about the weather. It was bitterly cold and I was afraid she'd gotten kicked out of her house again. She didn't ask outright for a place to stay, but she did seem to sense that she was at a transition point. The next day, December 23, Mark, Sam, Jack, Dawn, and I were planning to fly out of Minneapolis to spend the Christmas holidays with Kate and her boyfriend in sunny Mexico City.

The contrast between Margey's destitution and the rest of the family's luxury made me sick to my stomach. Every time I thought of not offering to help her more, of not being home in case she got desperate, I began to cry. The differences in our lives were so unfair.

Neither she nor I ever found the courage to spell out what happened after that phone call, but I think Margey spent Christmas at the homeless shelter.

Soon after returning from Mexico, I met Margey at the Cornucopia for lunch. Ever adaptable, she was cheerful and clean, her hair curled, her skin clear. She seemed more beautiful than ever—in a delicate, almost transparent way.

"You're not going to believe it, Mom, but I really like it at the homeless. I do. I don't have to pretend. Everybody there is who they are. No fakes. They all know everything about me; they accept me. Everybody's the same there. At the bottom.

"I want to write about how it is down there. You know, anybody can end up there. Some of them at one time had a lot of money, fancy houses, big businesses. I always ask them, 'How'd you get here?' I ask them lots of questions and listen to their stories. This one guy, he said he went to sleep in Kentucky, he woke up at the shelter. He didn't have any idea what happened in between.

"Nobody can believe I belong. At first they think I'm staff. As soon as they figure out I'm not, they look at me real hard and say, 'How'd you get here?' They say I'm too pretty to be living like them. This one guy, he's so nice. A great sense of humor. He sees somebody hitting on me, he gets them outta' there. But the truth is, he is so ugly. He's got this huge nose from getting it bashed so many times. He's little and kinda' scrunched up.

"He told me I didn't know nothing about living through hard times. He said I'd have to lose my beauty to understand what it is to be on the bottom. I'd have to burn my face, scar it somehow, go through the windshield, get a hundred stitches, bust up a bunch of bones. He said until I get ugly, I'll never have any trouble with money. He's right—I borrow money all the time. I ask for drugs, nobody ever tells me no."

"Do they have drugs in the shelter?"

"Oh my god, yeah! There's every kind of stuff going down. Tons of winos, drinking Wild Irish Rose. Cocaine—all kinds a' drugs. Crack. People shooting up—everything."

"But how do they get the money to buy all that?"

"No problem getting money—they steal, nab stuff outta' stores. Hell, they'll sell you anything. Leather coats for twenty dollars. This guy the other day was trying to sell me the cutest leather miniskirt, but I didn't have no money. He let me try it on—kind of turquoise blue and so soft. He told me he'd love to give it to me, but he had to have a few bucks.

"There's a new person every day. They try and buy friends as soon as they move in. So we take everything offa' them while they're still giving. I went through one hundred and thirty dollars the first day I arrived."

Where had she gotten that much money, I wondered, but didn't dare ask.

"My trunk—did I tell you Tony finally handed it over? He wasn't going to. I told the staff they better not let nothing happen to my trunk. I told them that's all I got, to take good care of it. They watch it for me, don't let nobody go in it. I'll lock this stuff up in my trunk." She was going through her gifts from Mexico.

"Thanks a lot, Mom, these are real pretty. They'd like to steal these bracelets. People sell stuff like this all the time. This pen, too, sell it right away. It's cute, ain't it, does it write? Let me see. Every staff that comes in asks me can they buy my trunk. I say, 'Nuh-huh, no way, José. My mom fixed that trunk up for me—for a Christmas present. That's all I got.'"

It was impossible not to think of her trunk as a symbol of her connection with the past. "Where do you keep it?"

"It's upstairs in this storage room. Lots of them folks got everything they own up there."

As usual, Margey skipped from topic to topic so fast it was hard to keep pace. "I don't know about Rich. That's the guy I'm with. The way it's going, we'll probably end up friends. It ain't like we ever have sex.

We done it three times. In—what's it now?—about a month. He's had it rough. His sister died when he was young—messed him up good. His parents are divorced. He lives with his mother. I couldn't live there.

"You know, Mom, I don't think I can live with a guy. I get real mean when I get fucked up. Mess with them bad. I hit Rich, won't let him get near me. He isn't violent or nothing like that. But I can't live with him, you know what I mean? I go out with him every night. But we don't ever do nothing, except get fucked up."

What a pity, I thought. She must not get much pleasure from sex. I wondered how often we got it wrong when we assumed that women like Margey, whose whole persona was sexual, enjoyed their bodies. Actually, I'd always doubted that sex would work well for Margey. Although she loved to be looked at, she never liked being touched.

"Rich, he didn't believe I was coming down to meet you: he thought I was after somebody else. I asked him why else would I be going to the Cornucopia. They don't allow no homeless in here. We go around other places and drink coffee, hang around, because they put us out of the center at seven A.M.. Won't let us back in until two.

"Rich, he thinks I got something going with one of the guys at the homeless. He won't even come into the place, you understand. I told him, if he'd come in, he'd understand. Some of them don't even got legs. None of them can talk good. Some don't take baths. Lots a them been in jail three or four times. Mental institutions—tons a them been put out of mental institutions.

"This one guy came in, he looked so terrible. As yellow as this salt-shaker. You know that means you got hepatitis. And that's real contagious. When I was in boarding school, they sent one girl home on the airplane when she had hepatitis. You know you ain't supposed to fly if you got that.

"They let this guy into the shelter, though. Didn't ask him one word about how come he was so yellow. His face was all the way out to here. His belly all over his belt—probably he didn't have no belt. He didn't say he felt bad or nothing. I went up to him, told him he was sick, he had to make them get him some help. He still didn't ask for nothing.

"Then three days later the ambulance pulled up in front of the shelter. They bring that guy down on a stretcher. He's bleeding these big clots of blood out' his nose and his mouth. Great big clots. And still as yellow. They said he was dead before he got to the hospital. All because he didn't ask for help."

We were both grateful knowing that Margey would always take care of herself better than that.

"This one old guy here, he's forty-six years old, he claims he's my dad. I call him Father all the time. He makes me so mad though. Watches me all the time. Gets all pissed off if I get high without him. He used to be somebody, too. Used to have a business—you can tell stuff like that about people. Says he was planning to be a priest, a rabbi—yeah, he's Jewish, can you believe that?

"He tells me what to do all the time, in a voice like this: 'You know what Margey, you know why you've ended up here? Because nobody can tell you one thing. You had it good at home, how come you can't go back there now? How come you can't live with your mother? I'll tell you why. You won't let her tell you nothing. You don't let nobody tell you nothing.'

"He's right, though, you know. That's what gets me so pissed off. I call him Father. He's done me many a favor, too. Whenever some guy is pressing me, he comes up and says, 'What you think you're doing, big fellow? Leave her alone, right now.'

"The guys, they'll say, 'Who the hell you think you are?'

"He says, 'I'm her father.'"

"Do you ever wonder if he could be your father?" I asked. "He's about the right age, sounds like. That's a creepy thought, isn't it?"

"Goddamn, you know, Mom, come to think of it, he could be my father. Good god, I gotta tell him that. Now him, he'll love that. He'll go off on that the whole rest of his life. Sometimes he does really weird stuff. He was telling one of the guys about his mother, how he used to love her, how she was the greatest woman in the world, how he used to fuck her every afternoon at four o'clock before she got up to fix supper."

Margey ate as fast as she talked.

"You wouldn't believe how they treat the people who live there. I got to write it down. Everyone says, 'You're smart, do something with yourself. Tell everybody how it is in this shelter. Let the whole world know. All those fat-ass rich guys acting like they're doing so much good. Tell them what it's really like. You can read and write good, you tell 'em.' I'm going to, Mom. I'm going to write it down."

"You really could write all this down, Margey, you really should. Send it to the *Star* or the *Pioneer Press*. What if I brought you the tape recorder so you can record their stories? Then it's lots easier to write them down."

"Yeah, yeah, that'd be good. This friend of mine, she came knocking for them to let her in at four-thirty in the morning. They wouldn't unlock the door, even though they were standing on the other side of the glass looking her straight in the face. She hollered at them, 'You better open the door, it's way below freezing out here. You'll be guilty of murder if you don't open this door.'

"They told her no one was admitted after eleven, she knew the rules. She told them she didn't have nowhere to go.

"They said they couldn't help that. So she went out and got a crowbar and busted out all them front windows. She was so wild they didn't dare touch her until she had every one a' them busted to pieces. Thirteen thousand dollars worth of damage, can you believe that? That's how come all the windows got boards on them."

"What happened to her? Did they arrest her?"

"Oh yeah, she's in jail."

"At least she got out of freezing to death."

"She works off twenty dollars every day she's in the county. How many years is it going to take her to work off thirteen thousand dollars?

"They don't believe me when I tell them about you and Dad. How you're both college teachers. They say I'm making it up. I go and get them the phone book, point out your name, where you live on Carroll Avenue. All they have to do is look there in the book, they can see for themselves. They still don't believe me. They keep on asking how come I'm in here, then.

"Anyhow, I'm living right next to this prostitute. She's kinda' mean, too. But she's real nice to me. She hates men. Really hates them. Uses them. Fakes everything. Everything is fake. She don't like sex or men either, that's how come she's down there.

"This other friend—no, she's an acquaintance really—she got barred. She and her boyfriend got into this big fight. Staff was trying to separate them and she slapped the lady in charge, right in the face. So now she's barred. Her name's Amy and she's a prostitute too. She was married . . . for exactly twenty-six days. That's where I go and stay over when I gotta get outta' here.

"I gotta get back there in time for the clinic, get me some pills. Listen to this, I got bronchitis, can you hear it? They told me to quit smoking. You think my voice is getting lower?"

"Yes, and your cough sounds terrible. Are you sure it's bronchitis and not pneumonia?"

"Nuh-huh, don't worry about it, they'll check it out. Did I tell you I went to church? I couldn't find a Catholic church, it was too far away. So I went to the one across the street—Pentecostal or something. This old woman was standing up in front, moaning and groaning, she had to have some money. She went on like that. No prayers, no reading, no nothing. Steady moaning. I finally got up and said real loud, 'This is another Tammy Bakker, let me outta' here.'

"Then I went to the Catholic church—all the way to Saint Mark's, you know where that's at? It wasn't time for mass or nothing, so I went in and smelled the air, you know what I'm talking about?—"

"Incense—"

"Incense, yeah. I'm going to start going to church every week. Next Saturday I'm going to confession. I read it on the board, they got confession on Saturday afternoon, so I'm going. Then I'm going to the detox center. I'm bad and I know it. That's how come I can't keep none of them jobs. Because I'm always getting fucked up. You can't be working when you're like that.

"I'm gonna get back a bunch a' money on income tax. All them jobs. Arby's, the Twenty-Four Hour, Holiday Inn, Culligan, that factory in Lakeville, they take out taxes like there's no tomorrow at them factories. I wanna get me a haircut. Then get me one of those one-room places, they got a bathroom and a kitchen you can use. They're cheap—sixty dollars a week, and you don't have to pay nothing else. It ain't far—I'll show it to you. Lots of people from the shelter live there. Lot of prostitutes. They don't want to be friends with me. I try and talk to them, but they won't say nothing."

As usual, I wondered about helping Margey get a place to stay. But where could she live and remain completely unfettered? As much as she liked to fantasize about decorating, she didn't like anything safe or permanent.

"Guys pull up all the time beside me out on the street and holler out, 'A hundred bucks, how about it, baby?' A hundred bucks just to pull a trick. Treating me like I'm a prostitute. Them guys at the shelter, they're my friends, they pull them suckers offa' me.

"Rich and me, we go out and get fucked up. But you know whenever I'm out with him, I wanna be back at the shelter. He don't like that, either. He gets all mad and shit. Asks what's wrong with me, how come I can stand that place. We'll be out to a bar on the other side of town, over at his house—anywhere—and I'll get him to bring me back. 'Cuz I miss my friends. I like it there. I lecture people all the time. Tell them to get on birth control. They don't want to be having any children and bringing them around all these weirdos. I tell them, 'You got nothing. Nothing. You got no business having a child.'

"But you know, Mom, some of them got it so hard. This one woman, she's pregnant. Off a rape. She got beat up. Her face was all smashed. Now she's pregnant off it. Don't you think that's horrible?"

"I certainly do. Couldn't she get an abortion?"

"She didn't have no money, I don't think. Abortions cost a fuckload a' money, think about it. Maybe she waited too long—didn't know she was pregnant or nothing. But now she's having this baby in a month and she hates it already—before it's even born."

As she often did, Margey suddenly turned everything negative upside down.

"It's good there, really, I'm happy. Here I am. And I know I got myself to blame. I know that perfectly well. I had everything, but it was never enough. I always wanted more. I lecture to them, tell them all about it. They listen, too. They respect me.

"Now I'm on the bottom, I can do whatever I want to with myself."

Work for Margey was less successful than she described. Her version sounded as if she'd made a thousand dollars or so over the year. According to her W2 form for 1989, her earnings totaled $78.00. What happened to people who couldn't work? If she went through counseling at the mental health center, she would be eligible for disability—so one of Margey's therapists had told her. But how likely was she to go steadily for counseling? Besides, would Margey want to be declared mentally disabled, even if that meant a marginal free ride for the rest of her life?

Communication was sparse between Saint Paul and Aberdeen after Dawn left to join Charles. We sent presents for her birthday and Christmas, and Dawn sent thankyou cards back. During phone calls, we got just enough information to keep us unsettled. Dawn and Cathy, Charles's mother, butted heads early on; school was way too hard. The directions for the birth-control pills were too difficult to follow; she'd quit taking them. But Charles liked his job and Dawn was in a work-study program that sounded much better than anything available at our local high school. Mark and I crossed our fingers.

Then in the middle of January, Dawn called Mark in a panic. She said things were terrible with her: she was pregnant; Charles wasn't standing by her; Charles's mother had put her out of the house weeks ago; she had to get an abortion; she didn't have any money. Charles's mother insisted that they had to get married; that was the only way. But Dawn knew she wasn't ready. She wanted them to have the baby first and be sure about things before they made that big a decision. She wanted me to call her as soon as possible. For three days, I dialed the number she'd left, but she was never there. Mark worried and worried.

"Hello, honey, how ya doing? Your dad says you want to talk with me."

"Well, things were pretty terrible that night I called Dad. I spent that whole night crying, all night long. Nobody could make me stop. I didn't mean to get Dad all upset. I shouldn't have called when I was feeling like that. Everything's fine now. I'm feeling real good today."

"Really? What's happened?"

"Me and Charles had a long talk that night after I called Dad. He called Dad, too, you know. He told Dad things weren't as bad as they sounded. He was planning on moving out with me as soon as he got his transmission paid for. In a month or so, he says, we'll get married."

"Really? It sounds like Charles wanted a baby too."

"Yeah."

"You want to tell me how you're doing?"

"Well, like I told Dad, me and Charles's parents, we were fighting pretty much all the time. I didn't clean up my room or nothing and Cathy kept getting all bad on me. I don't get along good with her at all. She was upset because I was missing school. She told me I had to leave her house if I wasn't going to be in school. Howard, that's Charles's stepdad, he got Cathy to agree to let me stay if I promised not to miss one more day of school. So I promised. Then Cathy came home one morning and I was in bed and she told me to pack up right that minute. That was a couple of weeks before Christmas. So I came over to Barbara's. Plus I'm six weeks pregnant."

"And you've been living with your friend all this time? Over a month now? How is that with her family?"

"They're real nice people."

"I'm sure they're really nice people, but that doesn't mean they have money or room for another child."

"Yeah, well, it's kinda' crowded and they ain't got nothing, that's true. I'm going to get an apartment next week—I had to promise them that. I started working at Hardy's today with Barbara. She's been working there a while. I'm not going back to Subway. I'm such a chicken I couldn't tell them I had to quit. Everyone was telling me I should quit, that they weren't being fair—making me work all those late hours all alone—but I'm such a coward about stuff like that."

"Anyhow, you must have some money if they were making you work so many hours?"

"Not exactly. Maybe five dollars. No, maybe one. I guess maybe I've been spending my checks on foolish things."

"Does Charles have any money?"

"Nuh-huh, and he's gotta get his car fixed before anything else. He hasn't had a car for two weeks. You know for getting to work and like that."

"Do you think you and Charles are in any position to get married?"

"Look, Mom, we made a mistake. But that doesn't make it right for us to take it out on the baby."

Clearly a well-rehearsed line. I followed with the same. "You think you won't be taking it out on the baby if you have a child to raise when neither of its parents has any money?"

"I'll start saving my money."

"Why did you want an abortion three nights ago?"

"I don't want an abortion. I like babies. I could have been aborted myself. I almost was. I have it all planned out. I'll go to school, then to work, and then I'll be with the baby. Charles can take care of it when he's not at work. Other times it can go to a day-care center."

"You could wait until you're done with school and have a little money saved, wait until both of you have steady jobs that you like and are good at. That's a much better environment for a baby. Wait until you're married and used to it. Then have a baby."

"I'm just not strong enough. I can't do things like that."

"You're right, it's a really tough time. I'll come and help you. Come and stay with you. Or we'll send Kate if you'd like that better. You could come back home, too, if you'd rather we take care of you here."

"I'm not strong enough. I couldn't even tell my boss at Subway not to treat me the way they did—they took advantage of me and I couldn't say nothing. For over a month now I've been trying to say something to them, but I couldn't."

"You are not so weak, Dawn. You moved out of our house. You got kicked out of Charles's house. Do those sound like the actions of a weak person?"

"Well . . . I don't know . . ."

"What about your grades, what are those going to be like?"

"I'm not failing anything. Oh, yeah, I'm failing that one subject I was always failing. History. Otherwise I'm not failing anything. Well . . . yeah, since I quit at Subway, that course's gonna be bad, too."

"How come Cathy was so worried about your not going to school? How could you cut all those classes and pass?"

"I wasn't cutting."

"You missed how many days?"

"Eight . . . yeah . . . I think about twelve."

"Is that what they'd tell me if I called the attendance office?"

"About twelve, something like that . . . maybe a little more . . . something like twelve or thirteen."

"You cut twelve days and you're passing all your classes?"

"I wasn't cutting."

"I'm sorry, you skipped twelve days."

"I wasn't skipping."

"What were you doing?"

"I was sick."

"Oh, you were sick for twelve days in one marking period?"

"Yeah."

"What was the matter?"

"Two days I had asthma, the other days I was sick."

"Dawn, do you think it's going to work a miracle on all these problems if you get married? What will be different? Right now you don't have a place to live, you're almost kicked out of school, you just started a new job today, you're only eighteen, and you're six weeks pregnant. How is marriage going to help all of those problems?"

"I'm passing all my courses. I wanted to quit my job, but I kept on going so I could pass that course."

"Do you want to answer me? How is marriage going to help you now? How is marriage going to help you and Charles take care of the baby when you are living with a friend, and he's living with his mother?"

"If we're married, Charles will have to pay for the baby."

"But if he doesn't have enough money to get his car fixed, where will he get enough money to support two other people?"

"He's going to save his money as soon as he gets his car fixed, then we're going to get an apartment and start saving for the baby."

That's what she wanted. An apartment of her own. Well, it might work—no school, no adults. She was eighteen, old enough to vote and marry; maybe all she really needed was to take charge of her own life and get away from critical and bossy adults. One part of me was hopeful, the other, frantic.

"Do you believe that story yourself, Dawn? Is Charles ready to get married?"

"Well, he's gotta fix his car, then he is."

"So you're trying to talk him into getting married and taking care of you and the baby."

"I take good care of myself. But if he leaves he'll have to pay for the baby."

"Seventy-five dollars a week."

"That's pretty good."

"It's not enough to live on. And ninety percent of fathers don't pay one thing after the first year."

"I've found a place that might probably pay for the baby. It's called Healthy Children or Smart Babies, something like that. All I have to pay for is the ultimate sound."

"That's really good. I'm glad you've been looking around for help."

"I can't decide to get an abortion. There's too much going down already."

"Dawn, if you wait until you can't get an abortion, that is a decision."

"Somebody told me you can't even get an abortion around here."

"Dawn, you can still get an abortion in every state in the nation. Nobody thinks abortion is a good idea. Margey suffered over having to make this decision. Every woman who gets an abortion suffers while she's making up her mind. But is not being able to take good care of a baby better than an abortion?"

"What if I couldn't have a baby afterwards?"

"Dawn, where do you hear this kind of stuff? An abortion is one of the safest things the medical profession knows how to do. Lots of women go back to work right afterwards. Margey said her abortion wasn't anything like as bad as she'd expected."

"Margey and me are not the same."

"No, you and Margey are not the same. She knew she couldn't take care of the baby. So she made a decision for the baby's sake."

"Margey's just selfish. Besides she'd been doing all kinds of drugs and she didn't even know who the father was."

"She had been doing all kinds of drugs, but she did know who the father was. She didn't want to hurt anyone else."

"Mom, I like babies. I know how to take care of them. I took care of Galien all those times. Think how much he misses me."

"Honey, you are good with babies. And with young children. You were a great counselor at Camp Minnehaha. But remember how tired you used to get of Galien's following you around all the time, how sick you got of the kids asking you to do stuff for them in the craft shop at camp."

"I really do like kids. I do. And they like me. They do."

"Listen, I have to tell you the truth. I think you just plain want a baby. So you got pregnant. Now you're trying your best to get Charles to take care of you and the baby. And you may luck out and he may do it. I hope so, honey, or else we're all going to be in big trouble. What are you going to do about school now? Will they let you continue while you're pregnant?"

"I'm not exactly in school now. I guess I missed too many days or something."

"Dawn, I can't tell what is going on from this distance and you know that. How about if I answer your questions from three nights ago, just in case. Yes, I will pay for an abortion as you asked. If you need for me or Kate to come out and help you, either of us will be happy to. Or we'll bring you home and help you all we can. If you want to stay in Aberdeen and get the abortion there, you'll need to get the name of the clinic so I can send money directly to them. Let me know what you decide and if you want me to do anything. Good luck, honey. I love you, but I think you're messing up your life—and somebody else's—real bad right now."

"'Bye."

A quarrel over Dawn's getting an abortion, all of five months after Margey's, was about all Mark and I needed. He wanted Dawn to give the baby up for adoption. The literature about adoption I'd been reading said that many adopted children put their first baby and even a second baby up for adoption, repeating the very act that had caused them so much pain. How ironic—and human—that those who wanted in the worst way to correct their parents' mistakes ended up repeating them.

I didn't think Dawn would give up her baby for adoption, not in a million years. And I doubted that an abortion would really help either.

She would probably end up pregnant again in a short time. All she could think to do with her life was to have a baby. After all, what else was there for her? As with Margey, it was easy to criticize but impossible to come up with a workable alternative.

Even in a family with as many resources as ours, we were unable to come between Dawn and her dream to have a child. We were unable to provide her with any other source of pleasure and self-confidence. So many teenagers are like Dawn: they just can't think of anything, not anything, to do with themselves but have a baby. Our schools fail them completely—they hate worksheets; we provide them no alternatives to the nonchoice of school. Unless we can discover ways of motivating these aimless adolescents, of providing them with real opportunities and futures, they will continue having babies while they are still babies. It's their babies who will take the consequences.

All of Jack's sympathies went to Charles when he heard the story. He felt as if Charles were being trapped by Dawn.

But surely Charles knew when she'd quit taking the birth-control pills, and it was his business to use a condom, I told Jack. I wasn't being fair, he said; guys hated condoms; the pill was so much easier. No doubt, but, I asked him, when a woman isn't taking the pill, and there are lots of reasons why women don't, doesn't the guy have to think about the possibilities of pregnancy? Lots don't, Jack said.

Let's just hope Charles isn't like that, I said. You certainly aren't. Jack agreed, but he felt sorry for Charles—Dawn was one, heavy, weight. I guess we all felt sorry for Charles. And for Dawn, too.

Tough Love

Margey and I met at the Cornucopia for breakfast one more time at the end of January. She had moved in with her friend Amy and was enjoying herself. She had plenty of money and wanted to treat me. I wouldn't believe how she had figured out how to make money, she said, not with any of those sorry-ass jobs that paid minimum wage. Nuh-huh, she was talking about a lot a money and not a lot a work. She was going out for lunch and having long, long chats with various men she met, guys who were just lonesome; older men, men like her dad. All they wanted to do was to talk, that's all. And they gave her so much money. For nothing, too. There was one who wanted to get her set up at the Wooden Indian Motel, come to see her whenever he had time. She was thinking about getting some really expensive clothes and hanging out at the Saint Paul Hotel downtown. She'd meet some nice men there.

I asked her to come over to the house, see her dad; she hadn't seen him in months. She said she would. She added that she was sorry for meeting me all fucked up. "Can you tell?"

"Yes." I asked her not to come home like that. We set a date for the following weekend. The day before she called to say she couldn't make it—she was looking into this telephone job at Culligan.

Weeks went by and Margey didn't call. I figured she was embarrassed because she had taken the final step into prostitution. February, March, April, May—still no word from her. That wasn't like her.

June—five months had passed. If she hadn't called by her birthday, I promised myself, I'd go to the places she'd last mentioned and ask if anyone knew where she was. Then to the police.

When I set out to inquire in mid-July, no one at any of her haunts had seen her—not in months. The woman who answered the door at Margey's last address said to check the Lamppost Inn, next to the homeless shelter, and the Steamboat Inn, and Shirley's—Margey always hung out at those bars. But no one at the bars had seen her either.

When I went to the police, Officer Borkowsky was assigned to the case. He pressed me to tell him everything I knew about Amy's house. Finally, he asked if I knew that was a flophouse. I told him, yes. He wanted to know had Margey been all dirty when I last saw her. I said, no, she was always careful about her appearance.

He said the last time he'd been in that house, a couple of months earlier, the police had been called because there was a fight that ran out onto the street; he'd seen these two women in the kitchen. They were nasty-dirty, he said; one of them was curled up under the kitchen table in a blanket. Drugs and all, he supposed. "So what does your daughter look like?" he asked.

"She's about five-five, blue to violet eyes, blonde hair. She's really pretty, though she's awfully thin."

"You got a picture?"

"I'll bring you one. Tell me, would they have found her, I mean . . . her body . . . I mean, if something had happened to her?"

"Do we have her fingerprints on record? Has she ever been arrested?"

"Not in Saint Paul. She has a record in South Saint Paul."

"I'll check over there; they'll have her prints. How about her dental records? Who's her dentist?"

"Dr. Alexander, his office is off University."

"Well, I'll tell you, I don't want to be gruesome or nothing like that, but sometimes we pick up a body alongside the road. And it'll be partially decomposed. It can be hard to identify. That's why I need the prints."

"If anything has happened to her, would you have found the body? Likely?"

"Now, that I can't really say. Do you have any reason to believe she left the area?"

"I've been wondering about that. Somehow I don't think she has the resources. But she's never waited so long to call; being out of town might explain that. It's also true, she's so impetuous, she'd hop in a car with anyone who was heading to Florida that minute."

"I'll put her name on the wire service today. That way they'll call us if she gets arrested anywhere in the country. But I'll tell you, Mrs. Kimble, it doesn't look too good. It can be mighty hard to find them when they don't want to be found. Especially when we're looking at this kind of history."

"So what are our chances, do you think?"

"I couldn't tell you, but not that great."

Anything could have happened to Margey. I wanted to know and hoped never to find out.

Turning the pages of the family album trying to find a photo for Officer Borkowsky, I began to cry. There were so few pictures of Margey after she'd gotten older, not even awkward school pictures. I couldn't bear to part with any of the shots of a younger and happier Margey; those would not have helped the police anyhow—she looked completely different.

Those photograph albums grew heavy in my hands. They had their own story: After the first album or two detailing Kate's and Sam's entrance into the world, and—typically with the third child—slivers of Jack's activities, pictures of the family had pretty much piled up in a desk drawer, unsorted, undisplayed. One day, I had realized I didn't know where that pile of pictures was anymore. A friend—herself an adoptive mother—told me that her daughter had destroyed their family pictures, and I assumed Margey must have gotten rid of ours, too, in one of her rages. I had copies made from what negatives there were, and, as a Christmas present, my sister gave me duplicates of everything she had taken. For a long time, those spotty albums were all we had. Then a couple of years ago, Kate and I were cleaning out the attic and we dragged down that beat-up old desk of Mark's to give to Saint Vincent de Paul. There in the drawer, in all their chaos, were the photos. I was delighted to discover them, felt terrible for having blamed Margey, bought five matching photo albums, and sorted through the years.

Probably the more complicated the family, the more complicated its photo story. As I sat there, I remembered the last time we showed home movies. After a particularly charming stretch of Kate, aged six, Sam, four and a half, and Jack, three, running in and out of waves, Dawn asked, "Where were we?" For once, the Kimbles were speechless.

One Christmas when the children were all growing quickly I got a camera to preserve their growth spurts. When the first sets of pictures came back from the developer, I found myself counting frames—the way Margey and Dawn used to measure the size of everyone's food serving—making sure I had taken an equal number of pictures of each child. Alas, I had not. The next time I got out the camera, I self-consciously tried to even out the count. But before long the camera had mercy on me and broke, and I never had it repaired and never took another picture.

Mark and I assumed that Dawn had decided not to get an abortion when we didn't hear from her again until she wrote Mark asking for her income tax forms. Her note also said that she was terribly in debt: she and Charles had bought furniture on an installment plan; she'd had an asthma attack and had been taken to the emergency room in an ambulance; Charles's radiator had blown up all over him and he'd had to go to the emergency room for the burns on his face and head. Finally she accused Mark of forgetting all about her as soon as she moved out of the house. Mark was offended and wrote a stern letter in response:

Dear Dawn,

I got your letter yesterday after I had already put together all of the tax material, but before we talked on the phone. I was sorry to hear about all of your financial difficulties but I did not like the tone of your letter.

I do not have to say that we have not rejected you, nor that we are concerned about your welfare. Nevertheless, I have to put down my views about your present difficulties. I can understand and respect your views about abortion. I might even share them. But the fact that you are having the baby does not mean that you should keep the baby. Indeed it seems obvious to me that the right thing to do here is to give the baby up for adoption.

You say that having an abortion wouldn't be fair to the baby, but just because it would be wrong to have an abortion, it does not follow that you should try to raise the baby.

The fact is, you are not ready to raise a baby, and if you're worried about what's fair for the baby, the only fair thing is to give the baby up for adoption.

You have no business trying to raise a baby. You're not mature enough and you don't have the financial resources.

I know you won't listen to me. You never do. Only this time it's not just a matter of screwing up your own life. There's a baby that's going to be born and you don't have a right to screw up that baby's life.

I realize you won't do what we're telling you because having a baby is all part of your soap opera. The letter you wrote had a lot of soap opera, a lot of drama and a lot of hysteria. I know I can't get you not to live a soap opera. But please don't bring a baby into your show.

As I have already said, I know you'll do what you want. There's little I can do about it but hope for the best.

Who would blame Dawn for not responding to Mark's letter? The poor kid, she did run into a barrage of words when she tried to deal with her parents.

In early May, I got calls from both Dawn and Charles the same evening. Dawn said that they were having so much trouble getting along with Cathy, Charles's mother, that they had decided to move back to Saint Paul. Charles called a while later and asked me to send him the want ads from the newspaper so he could get together a resume and apply for jobs in Saint Paul. He was miserable; Dawn and his mother were fighting over him all the time.

The thought of Dawn and Charles returning was most unsettling. I wrote her a letter every bit as stern as Mark's:

Dear Dawn,

Maybe I need to say some things straight out, after your calls.

Yes, your dad and I would be happy to see you. And Charles. And the baby, when it comes. No, we are not rejecting you, never have, never will.

Yes, we are accepting what you are doing. You must understand that there is no other choice for us. That's the way it is with parents as you'll soon find out.

But that doesn't mean that we think it would be a good idea for you to move back to Saint Paul. Charles has a good job in Aberdeen. There aren't many jobs here—we're in a real depression, certainly not jobs as good as his with those wonderful health care benefits. Those benefits are really important now that you'll have medical expenses for both you and the baby.

We may be seeming like the nicer parents, too, Dawn, just because we're not in one another's face. But remember, honey, we didn't get along great while you were living here. Not one bit better, I'm afraid, than you get on with Cathy.

For some reason you think that your dad and I are going to all of a sudden get excited that you are having this baby. You think it's a wonderful thing, which after all you have to, or you'd be doing something different. We do not think it's a wonderful thing, we will not change our minds overnight as you would like. If things work out, you will of course be able to persuade us to a better attitude—over a period of time.

Dawn, I'm sorry to say this, but please do not think that you can run home to us every time you get into trouble. Like you ran to South Dakota when you were in trouble here. Like you got pregnant when you wanted to run away from school.

It would be really nice if you would keep in touch with us a little better. We don't hear much from you until things get really bad. Then we get an emergency signal. Keep us rolling with you by telling us some everyday good stuff along the way.

I am hoping to come see you after the baby is born and you get settled in, if you'd like that. If you decide you want me to come, let me know what dates will work out best for you.

Your pregnancy has made me think a lot about having grandchildren. My grandmother was one of the most important people in my life. I grew up in her house and loved her dearly. We moved out of my grandmother's house when I was five, a block down the street. She and I liked all of the same things—we both thought we could do anything, would try anything. She taught me to sew with "a red-hot needle and a burning thread," that means speedy.

I doubt I'll ever have a relationship with a grandchild like I had with my favorite grandmother. Times are very different. I don't live in a big old house. I work outside the home. My grandchildren probably won't live right down the street. They'll live half-way across the United States. They'll love Ninja Turtles and Nintendo and McDonald's. I never have liked those things—didn't with you kids, won't with the next generation.

Dawn, I'm not going to be into taking care of any grandchildren on a regular basis like my grandmother took care of Ray and me. There are so many things I want to do, things I'm pretty good at—teaching and writing. Probably I'll want to spend some time in the future working in an inner-city school.

Of course I do want to spend lots of vacations with grandchildren. I'll make them babies clothes and tell them lots of stories. And if they're around at Christmas, we'll make a house full of people out of gingerbread. Some summers we'll go camping together. I'll put $50.00 into a savings account every birthday and Christmas so that when they get to eighteen, they can either take a trip outside of the United States or use the money for education.

All those seem like really fun things. I look forward to them a lot.

Best of luck to you, honey. Even though we may not always enjoy it, and you may not appreciate our responses, we still look forward to hearing your news.

Why was I so different with Margey and Dawn, I wondered: silenced by Margey, foaming out words all over Dawn. With Margey there seemed to be a floor of understanding where both of us could stand comfortably. That solid base defined our connections and our limits. Nothing of the sort seemed to exist with Dawn. She and I jerked back and forth between crisis and criticism. There was no solid line of trust between us. Dawn seemed to want something large and vague and undefined that I wasn't able to give—like my approval. I was frankly terrified about what would happen with this child of hers—that in the end I would either have to reject it or raise it. But there was also a chance that Dawn and I might finally find common ground as mothers.

In July, Dawn called to invite the family to her wedding—giving us ten days' notice. When I asked her please to give us another week to make arrangements—either her father or I was going to be out of town until then—she said, "No, I got this really pretty dress on sale. It was only thirty dollars. It fits now, but it might not in two more weeks. Besides Charles's mom has already ordered the cake and planned everything and she wouldn't want to change it all around." I offered to buy her a new dress. She said that she'd rather go on with things the way they were. I can't say Mark and I weren't relieved. Mark got a list of her bills and sent enough money to cover them all for a wedding present.

Dawn complained that only eight people showed up for their wedding; she and Charles used the money Mark sent to buy an entertainment center.

A few weeks later, Dawn sent us a formal portrait and snapshots from the wedding. She looked young and sweet in a lavender prom dress; Charles had on a white shirt and tie. She and Charles were smiling and proud. Cathy had obviously gone to a great deal of trouble: Dawn had a pretty bouquet; the guests brought presents for their house, and there was a wedding cake. If only they'd been heading off to the prom, Mark and I said to one another, those pictures would have been perfect. Both Charles and Dawn looked younger even than eighteen.

Weddings, like baptisms, are about wishing the innocent well. Both families made every good wish for their two children.

Doing background reading for this book, I came upon John Bowlby's three thick volumes, *Attachment and Loss*. Most of us take for granted the normal development of our children's attachment behaviors, and as a result Bowlby's observations are boring, boring—an endless detailing of what has been common sense since the origin of the species. But for those of us who have been intimately connected with children who are not attached, Bowlby's meticulous research and quantity of detail bring innumerable insights into how damage might have been done to our adopted children before our paths crossed. His illustrations of how easily attachment behaviors can become distorted help explain the magnitude of the task we set ourselves in parenting children who have suffered parental deprivation.

Unattached children who "never get enough," who will "go to anyone," who continue to steal through the years, in repeated and continual protest against their early deprivation, Bowlby suggests, present an enormous challenge to the naive and unprepared. As silly as it sounds, their parents' feelings are hurt repeatedly by what they interpret as continuous demands and lack of loyalty. I did not realize when raising biological children how delicate the balance was between enough and too much. With Margey and Dawn that balance would not come, most obviously with Dawn and food but also with Margey's obsessive relationship with physical objects, primarily her own body.

Early difficulties with attachment are also connected with impaired cognitive abilities. Unattached children never gain sufficient confidence to become curious and explore and learn about their surroundings. Doubtless Margey's and Dawn's early experiences left them seriously disadvantaged in dealing with the demands of school. I found all of these details consoling. It was a comfort to find an explanation of why school had been such an impossible hurdle for both girls. What would we have done differently if Mark and I had had this information much earlier?

Venturing to reconstruct their attachment history from the scanty background information available, I hypothesized that Margey had been anxiously attached to her mother, and that Dawn had been negatively attached. Although Margey was abused, she was given attention; Dawn seemed to have been almost completely ignored. Margey's attachment pattern seemed to be based on anger, Dawn's, on despair. Margey created conflict with me; Dawn searched for her ideal mother.

At age four, Margey still showed signs of remembering her mother and their life together, although she never let Mark and me know these details. The other children recalled how Margey used to put a cigarette butt in her mouth and walk around the block, puffing away. Then on one occasion when the children stayed with friends, Margey kept approaching Sam and Jack, our friends thought, in a sexually insinuating manner.

Dawn, on the other hand, seemed not to have recorded a thing from the past. She was the one most intent upon finding her mother, a desire that grew with her own motherhood. She dreamed of finding her long-lost best friend.

What about an unattached child's ability to parent, I wondered, as Dawn prepared for the birth of the baby. There was much to fear: that the baby would become an object for Dawn to cling to; that because Dawn needed the child so much, she would not allow it to separate and become independent. From long observation, Mark and I anticipated that Dawn would alternate between smothering and ignoring the baby, depending on her own needs.

But there was hope, too. Perhaps Dawn would finally find the intimacy with Charles and the baby she had been seeking all her life. She was a positive person; if not a star, she was always a very appreciative audience. Charles was attracted by her admiration and praise. Children can thrive with positive people.

Aberdeen,
South Dakota

As the due date of their baby approached, Dawn and Charles became more and more excited. For Mark and me, this was the first grandchild, and we too, began to look forward to its birth. I fantasized that watching Dawn do well in her new role of caring for her baby would help us grow more comfortable with one another. During the last weeks before the baby was born, I shopped for clothes, toys, and books and made plans to go to Aberdeen.

I got into town the day before Dawn had decided to have the baby induced. According to her calculations, she was two weeks overdue, and she wanted to be sure I was there for the birth.

On the plane to Aberdeen, I read a book on temperaments by Alexander Thomas. How well a child fits within its environment, he says, depends on the match, or mismatch, between a child and "the values and demands of [the] given culture or socioeconomic group" in which the child finds itself. Of course, "goodness of fit" greatly influences healthy development. I thought sadly about what a poor "fit" Dawn and I had always been. Perhaps, our relationship would grow smoother now that school wasn't an issue and we were no longer living together. Perhaps, as the therapist had prophesied with Margey, Dawn would do fine once she got past school and into the big world. She had recently turned nineteen—that wasn't so young to be having a baby—we could have done much worse, as my sister always reminded us.

Dawn's and Charles's apartment was cozy and tidy. There was plenty of room to sit: two couches and a comfortable chair. Directly across from the front door, in the middle of the kitchen, was a baby bed with padding all around the inside. "What a great baby bed," I said. "It looks like you're all ready. Are you getting excited about the baby?"

Dawn had on a red knit maternity dress, still her favorite color. She had gained weight in her face and shoulders, but her belly wasn't protruding all that much. I thought she must be carrying the baby around her middle instead of out front.

"Yeah, only one more day to wait. Charles's real excited. More then me, probably. His sister Lovie Mae has a new baby. He's so cute. He's two months old and weighs almost eighteen pounds. Right now he's sick—has real bad diarrhea. His formula was too rich for him. Lovie Mae had to buy some kind of special water at the drug store to feed him with. It cost over twelve dollars just for one day."

We sat near the door on the couch to talk. The couch was soft and comfortable, a brown and gold tweed. On the entertainment center across from the couch was an eight by ten picture of Dawn in her wedding dress, and an eight by ten picture of Dawn with her bridesmaid Barbara, also in a formal. A lace-and-ribbon box with a snapshot of Dawn and Charles hung on the knickknack shelf beside the front door. The entertainment center contained a television, stereo, and Nintendo equipment. The bedroom down the hall was filled to capacity with a king-size bed and a chest covered with stuffed animals. The apartment was roomy, except for the tiny bedroom, and well arranged.

"Charles's brother Willy, he just got out of the hospital. He shot off the tip of his finger. Him and Charles bought these guns, you know, so they can go hunting and all. I told Charles he better not ever bring a gun in here. So anyhow, Willy and Charles's best friend Thommy, they were playing around with this gun. They didn't think it was loaded or nothing. They were aiming it at each other—straight at their heads. Anyhow, then it went off when Willy was holding it. They cleaned his finger up at the hospital and it may come out all right. They may have to cut off some more of his finger if it gets all infected or anything like that.

"You seen Charles's best friend Thommy in the wedding pictures I sent you. He was the one pointing the gun at Willy's head. He's black—you could tell that. He's adopted, too. From this really messed up family, too. Him and Charles came home thirty minutes late one night. His mother kicked him out just like that—put all his clothes and stuff in big boxes outside the back door."

The phone next to Dawn rang and she chatted away with her sister-in-law. I studied the wedding photos again, trying to pick out Willy and Thommy. "She wanted to know if you got here all right. Her husband's going to be working late again tonight so he won't be helping her none with the baby, again. She was up with him all last night—her husband, he didn't do nothing."

Dawn was apparently comfortable with her new family, completely wrapped up in her new world.

"I'm sick of not working. After the baby's born, I'm going to the shopping center and get me a job. I can work from five to nine every night, or from four to eight, something like that, after Charles gets off work at four. Then I'm going to go to night school and get my diploma. I want to start driving, too. I know I gotta get my permit and all first, but I want to be able to get around, like that. I gained too much weight. I gained way over fifty pounds. But I been walking a lot. Charles and I went over to the shopping center the other night and walked for a whole hour. Nothing happened, though."

The phone rang and Dawn chatted with Charles about where to go for supper.

"Charles said to tell you 'Hi.' He might be going to play basketball after work. We can meet him back here. You want to eat here tonight, or what?"

"Let's go out. You don't want to be cooking the night before you have a baby. Is everything going fine with the baby?"

"Well, I been having these big clots every time after I go to the doctor. They told me if anything like that happened it was real serious and to call them right away. So I called them and they said not to worry about it. When I went to North Dakota last weekend, I had a lot of clots when I was doing so much walking. That scared me, you know, because the doctor told me he didn't think I should go on that trip. So, Mom, what you up to these days?"

"I'm still working on the adoption book."

"Have you found out more about my mother?"

"I found out that you and Margey had different last names."

"So we're not sisters?"

"You're certainly half sisters. Your mother might have married your father between you two kids."

Dawn shrugged, "I don't see why we can't find out who she was."

"Even if she doesn't want you to find her?" I asked.

"It's our right to know where we came from."

"What is it that you want?"

"Well, I want to talk with her, find out what she's like. Maybe get to be friends with her. I don't know."

"Margey really doesn't much want to meet her, sit across a couch from her. She says she only wants to know what she looks like. Margey's much more angry with your mother than you seem to be."

"What all did she do to us? I know she couldn't take care of us. I didn't think she was mean to me. What'd she do to me?"

It was amazing that Dawn didn't seem to remember the story of her malnutrition at three months. That episode was so dramatic and had come up again and again through the years in connection with her eating patterns. "You're going to have a baby tomorrow. It just doesn't seem like today's the right day to talk about all that."

"Nuh-huh. How's Margey doing anyhow?"

"I haven't heard from her again."

"She's still a prostitute. I just can't believe she's a prostitute. That's just so disgusting."

"Well, I don't know about that. What else can she do? She isn't unhappy. In some ways she's pretty independent. She seems to be fairly pleased with herself. She had a really rough time, just like you, and that makes a difference."

"Things weren't bad until Margey got to be a teenager."

"Well, there were lots of rough spots." Could Dawn have forgotten all those confrontations—with her, as well as with Margey? Maybe she didn't think they were unusual.

"Really? I don't remember. I still think it's disgusting."

"You've got to remember that neither you nor Margey was ever attached either to your mother or to me, and that can make a big difference. Margey wants to be completely free of anything that reminds her of a mother or a boss. You are always looking for someone to love you, mother you."

"No, I'm not."

"Well, maybe it was just that I felt like you needed a better mom than I was. Not being attached leaves you wanting what you see so many other people having. You want someone to be with you all the time, to help you out."

"No, I don't, I can make it on my own. I've been real independent out here."

"I don't know, Dawn, most women have to depend on someone to help take care of them and a new baby."

"I'm not dependent. I'm going to get a job, leave the baby with a sitter like Lovie Mae."

"Maybe so; we'll see. Still, it's awfully hard to work when you have a new baby, especially when you weren't working before."

"So what's wrong with that? I was always dependent."

"Yeah, that's true. And probably we put too much emphasis on independence in our family. None of us can ever be really independent when you think about it. We all depend on one another for something; just think about who's growing our food and making our clothes, no matter how much we pretend we're doing it all on our own."

"I been thinking about a whole lot of questions I want to ask you, Mom."

"Go ahead, I'll try and answer them."

"Did you dread coming here?"

"No. I was actually looking forward to seeing how well everything's going for you." That was not the whole truth, but *dread* was an overstatement.

"Are you guys all going to just forget about me now that I'm gone? Just forget that I ever lived there, not come see me or nothing?"

This child pushed my defensive button, and I swung rapidly into a favorite form of denial—a question.

"You're asking that question of the person who is sitting beside you on this couch?"

"How about Dad, Kate and Sam and Jack, all a' them? Is Dad ever going to come see me? Are you all just going to forget about me?"

Kate described Margey as eternally varied in her repertoire—too much so, undoubtedly—and Dawn as continually sounding a single note: poor, rejected Dawn. The repetition can be so wearing.

"Dawn, I know I'm not the person you really want here—you'd prefer your father—and I know you enjoy the drama of being the neglected child, but what makes you think your dad has forgotten about you?"

"He don't write or nothing?"

"Do you write him?"

"Well, not since he wrote me that one letter about putting the baby up for adoption. Is he ever going to come see me or nothing?"

"If you write your dad, he'll write you back."

"Yeah, but he . . . Dad goes to see all the other kids . . ."

"Your dad's never been to see any of the other kids. That isn't the sort of thing your dad likes to do. He's really shy, you know."

"I didn't know he never visited them other guys. I thought he did."

"What really happens is that the other kids still come home . . . well, except Margey. How about you come to Saint Paul for a visit?"

"Yeah, I'm thinking about spring vacation. The question I have is, how come you guys never accepted me? They accept me around here. For what I am. How come you guys never accepted me for what I am?"

Dawn deserved a lot of credit: these were all good questions, pressing steadily closer to the heart of the matter. This one was a zinger. The whole family was guilty as accused, though Dawn completely ignored, or forgot, her role in any scene. Why couldn't I manage to concede her point? Perhaps admitting so much seemed destructive.

"We could accept you and still want you to do some things differently. You remember I promised you over and over we'd get along better if you'd quit doing just three things—lying, stealing, disobeying. I'm not so sure you ever really tried not to do those things."

"Well . . . I did try and clean up the house. I remember trying really hard to get the house clean lots of times and you never even noticed. Like when you had those parties and all."

"Dawn, I told you a thousand times what three things I really cared about."

"Yeah . . . but how come you guys didn't accept me?—that's what I want to know."

I wanted to scream, because Dawn was always this same stubborn, self-pitying, one-dimensional whiner. Instead, I denied and attacked from another direction, "We accepted you, Dawn; that's not true, and we accept you now. But it was pretty hard to be happy with some of your behavior. Remember when you wouldn't stop taking my jewelry and clothes, so I put a lock on my door? Even then you wouldn't stop. What were your dad and I supposed to do when you wouldn't go to school or do what your teachers asked you to do? Accept that? How well did Charles's mom's accept your refusing to go to school after you moved out here?"

"Not too well, but that's all over. Now they accept me. After the wedding and everything. Now they're real excited about the baby and everything. How come you guys aren't excited? This is your first grandchild and all."

"We do accept you and Charles and we'll accept the baby. But I can't say we're as excited or delighted as you want us to be. We just don't believe that all your problems are going to be solved by having a baby. Quite the contrary. But just because we don't agree with all your choices doesn't mean that we don't accept you."

"Charles's parents are all excited. And it isn't even their first grandchild. I just want to forget about everything and start all over."

"You've always wanted us to forget everything and start over brand-new every day. And I sincerely wish we could—your approach is much better. My memory just doesn't work that way. Yours does. That's a big difference between us—we can't do much to change the way we remember."

The phone rang and Dawn reached for it. We were both glad for a break.

After she hung up, Dawn summarized her needs.

"Well . . . I just want you to be really happy about the baby, that's all."

"I am actually surprised at how much I've been looking forward to the baby, Dawn. Everyone has been teasing me—I talk about the baby all the time. It seems a miracle, doesn't it?"

"I know one thing. It was the right thing to leave home when I did. There wadn't nothing good going on at home."

"You're right, Dawn, I think so, too. And that means you're happy with your decision and your life. It looks as if life here is good. You seem really happy. Are you all prepared for the birth tomorrow?"

"Well, when I was about seven months I got a sheet from the doctor about Lamaze classes and all, but we didn't have no ride, so we didn't go."

"So you know what to expect during the delivery?"

"Nuh-huh, not really. This one time when I was in the waiting room, they had on this movie about a birth on the TV. I seen that for a little while."

Dawn's insistence on remaining ignorant surprised me. But of course she wasn't insisting; she was just being herself.

"Are you planning on doing natural childbirth?"

"I don't know. What is it? Lovie Mae had an epidural block. I might have one a' them. It makes it a lot easier when the baby's born— Lovie Mae told me, you don't feel nothing."

"You know, any medication you take goes right straight to the baby and makes it hard for it to start breathing."

"Yeah, I guess it does."

"You checked with an allergist after your asthma attack, didn't you?"

"Well, I made an appointment, but then I didn't have no ride or nothing, so I didn't go."

"Have you found out all about nursing the baby?"

"I read somewhere about you couldn't drink caffeine or eat a whole bunch of foods that make the baby sick, I can't remember—fried foods, acid, hot stuff—all kinds of things."

Dawn's descriptions of the external world often confused me. Was she correct that contemporary materials presented breast feeding as a series of don'ts and can'ts? Or was she interpreting bits and pieces of information negatively? It was impossible to know much except that she wasn't interested in breast-feeding. Which should have been my exit cue.

"I told Cathy I was going to breast-feed the baby because it was best for the baby. She said, 'No, it's not,' but even the formula says it's better—it says it right on the package, 'Next to mother's milk, this is best.' But I don't know anyone else who's breast-feeding a baby. I know lots of people who're having babies, nobody's breast-feeding. You do it for something like ten minutes, like that. But I don't know how you'll tell if he's getting enough, if he's gaining weight like he's supposed to."

"That's the hard part, you're exactly right. But you can feel how large your breasts get when they're full of milk, that they've got three or four ounces of milk in each one. Then you can feel how much smaller they get after the baby's nursed, so you know it pulled out all that milk. Breast-fed babies gain really well, exactly the right amount. They're never too fat or too thin; they're real firm. And they don't usually get diarrhea and even if they do, there isn't any danger they'll get dehydrated like you have to worry about with babies on formula. You always hold your baby close when you breast-feed—you have to—and that's good for the baby."

"Lovie Mae's baby's got this terrible diarrhea. Its little butt was all red and swollen yesterday. The day before, too. Lovie Mae has to change its formula, the doctor said."

"It's the rare baby who has trouble digesting its mother's milk. Plus you really enjoy feeding your baby that way. It reaches up and grabs hold of your hair and twists the strands around its fingers; then it puts its fingers up your nose; next it pokes its fingers into the skin of your breast. It's real busy while it's eating. Sometimes it works so hard sucking out the milk that it breaks out in a sweat. Its little head gets soaking wet, especially right up next to your skin. It's harder work to get milk from out of the breast than from out of a bottle. When it gets full, it dozes off, completely satisfied. Sometimes the last few sips of milk drool out the corner of its mouth if it falls sound asleep before it can swallow."

"Well, maybe I'm going to nurse him. At first, anyhow."

"That's really good. You keep calling the baby 'him.' Do you know for sure it's a boy? Do you want a boy?"

"Naw, I don't really care. I didn't have a' ultrasound or nothing like that. Charles wants a boy. Maybe I want a girl. But Charles really does want a boy. And I don't much care."

"That's good. Are you scared about tomorrow?"

"Yeah."

"You're a big strong girl and you've been getting exercise, you said. You'll be just fine. Before you know it, it'll be all over and you'll have your baby."

"I'm tired of waiting."

"Of course you are."

My mother once told me that you have to be a whole lot smarter to think of something good to say about a person than something bad. I believed her. Tried to act on her advice. Her words even provided me with a whole theory for teaching writing. Students thrive when you emphasize what they have accomplished.

Skipping over the negative and mentioning the positive also worked with friends and colleagues. As a director of a writing program, I help faculty recognize their strengths as writers and teachers of writing. Most of the time I simply point out what's working well. In groups I am often regarded as the person who made others feel good about themselves.

Why then couldn't I bring this simple truth home and make my own daughters feel good about themselves? Why couldn't I make them feel appreciated—"accepted"—as Dawn asked? In the overall scope of things, my criticism and failure to affirm Margey and Dawn did so much more harm to them than similar negativity would have done to students or colleagues. After all, I am their mother. The irony of it all added to my guilt. Dawn was asking for exactly what she deserved—to be accepted.

My abiding sense of having exposed my worst side was common to every member of the original family. All of us had scenes that flashed in our minds of when we acted like Cinderella's stepmother or stepsisters to two children without a fairy godmother in the wings. We all knew the limits of our tolerance, the ends of pity and forgiveness, the vastness of anger.

Vittoria, my friend whose daughter was retarded, says that she has come to believe that a community's treatment of its weakest members is emblematic of that society. In her belief, not accommodating the endless needs of a retarded child signals social and personal evil. Her remarks have helped me understand why everyone in the original family felt as if they had been negligent at one time or another toward Margey and Dawn. Margey's and Dawn's needs, like those of a retarded child, seemed endless, and again and again the members of the original family said "no" to meeting those needs. Sometimes we said "no" because we had to respect our own limits; other "no's" were more clearly selfish, but it was rarely possible in the heat of the moment to be certain which "no" was being said.

"But my situation with a retarded daughter was so different from yours," Vittoria once said. "I was always sure my daughter could not do any better. You were never sure about Margey and Dawn." If we had given up trying to have any effect on the girls, we might have operated more tolerantly. Or if we had had more effect, we might have continued more generously. Living in between—having little or no effect, but thinking the girls were capable of more—left us all unsatisfied and uncertain.

A friend once commented about my feelings of guilt and failure. "By definition it is impossible to fail at something over which you had no control—the early abuse of Margey and Dawn. When it's out of our control, we must be humble enough not to be guilty."

A song my father used to sing comes to mind, "There's no hiding place down here." That's the way it is with families. In a family, we know one another inside and out—the admirable and the despicable. It's in the family that we first learn about the lack of fairness in the world and the inevitability of weaknesses in those we love first. In the family, we learn to forgive ourselves and one another.

Margey and I had forgiven one another; perhaps Dawn and I were getting closer.

Having said all this, I must confess one last bit: if I had to live with Margey and Dawn again, I would probably repeat many of the same mistakes, or a whole new set, and require every ounce of forgiveness all over again. Yes, Dawn can provoke a saint; indeed, she can find fault in a angel. I thank goodness every day for the peace Michael Dorris describes in his book *The Broken Cord*—the peace when his son, suffering from fetal-alcohol syndrome, finally left home; peace like the quiet of a painting or a book.

As ardently as I hope to find forgiveness, I hope never to be tempted again.

First Birth

The next day, Dawn and Charles checked into the hospital early in the morning, and the nurses began a pitocin drip to induce birth. Things moved slowly; from the first, Charles's mother called it "the Dawning-baby—stubborn like its mother."

In the labor room, Dawn dozed between contractions unless something on television caught her attention. The TV above the foot of her bed was tuned to *The Young and the Restless*. On the screen, the doctor told a beautiful young woman, "I know you don't want to hear this, but you're right in your suspicions, my dear, you are indeed pregnant."

"No," the ringleted beauty on the screen gasped, "That cannot be. That cannot be. What am I going to do now? How could this have happened to me?"

Dawn said, "She's got no business being pregnant."

Dawn's friend Barbara asked, "Who's pregnant?"

"Josaline," Dawn said, "offa' Warren."

"Oh, no, I knew that was going to happen," Barbara said, "I gotta go tell Lovie Mae."

"She'll be watching out in the waiting room," Dawn told her, "she was real worried this was going to happen."

After *The Young and the Restless*, Charles switched channels to find Dawn's next soap opera. The pitocin drip had been going for three hours without much effect.

Out in the hall, I spoke with the nurse, "Is it all right if I go out for lunch?"

"Oh, sure. Before too long, we're going to give her something for the pain."

I was astonished. "She's still sleeping between the contractions."

"It's best for them not to be in too much pain."

"Dawn's very allergic. It might not be a good idea to give her any unnecessary medication."

"Is she allergic to any pain medication?"

"Well, not specifically that I know of, but she has a delicate system and this might not be the best time to experiment."

"There's no point in letting them suffer."

"That's true, but anything you give her will go straight to the baby."

"We never give them anything that affects the baby."

I swallowed my next line, "Then you don't give them anything," and left for lunch, where I thought back to three of the most wonderful days in Mark's and my life—the births of Kate, Sam, and Jack. Kate had been born in England and delivered by a midwife who had never delivered a baby before. Right after she was delivered, Kate wasn't breathing, so someone swept her out of the room. Her chart said that respiration had not been established for four-and-a-half minutes, and I worried that the sedative I'd taken in the middle of the night had slowed down her breathing reflex. But Kate, born at 12:20 A.M., was alert and ready to nurse at 1:00 P.M. ending any concern. With Sam, I barely made it to the delivery room; he arrived twenty minutes after Mark and I got to the hospital door. Jack's birth was more difficult. He was twisted, somehow, and I couldn't push him out. So the doctor used forceps to turn him a notch.

Mark and I were vehement supporters of natural childbirth and suspicious of the medical profession's intervention into the birth process. Dawn and Charles were completely trusting. I had wanted to understand and remain in control as much as possible; Dawn seemed to enjoy being taken by surprise.

When I returned from lunch, Charles's mother said they had given Dawn a shot of Demerol and something else—she hadn't caught the word. Dawn's blood pressure had risen and her asthma was kicking up. Between one and five o'clock, the nurse gave Dawn three shots of Demerol, or so Charles and his mother reported; the family seemed to think the more medication, the better the medical care. I disagreed, but knew it was inappropriate and useless to interfere any further than I had done already.

Out in the waiting room, Lovie Mae had brought Dawn's stuffed dog so she could have it when everything was over. "She loves this dog so much," Lovie Mae told me, "Dawn says she used to sneak down into her sister Margey's room and take the dog after Margey had fallen asleep so she could sleep with him herself. She drags that dog everywhere—out to eat, to the K-Mart, grocery shopping—everywhere.

We have to pretend it belongs to Shawn, the little boy I baby-sit for, so everybody won't think she's crazy."

The waiting room was overflowing with the family, complete with two toddlers, Dawn's friend Barbara and her boyfriend, and several of their friends, all of whom had cut school for the event. Mark and I, when we had Kate, had been all alone in a foreign country, and by ourselves through labor and delivery when we had the other two. With Sam and Jack we had had "rooming in," which meant that the baby stayed with me in a private room, and no one could visit except Mark. That way the baby and I could rest and start breast-feeding in peace. How different the scene in Aberdeen!

Time moved slowly and the toddlers in the waiting room got more and more cranky. Hamburgers, french fries, and Cokes appeared and disappeared. At last someone said that Dawn and Charles were headed for the delivery room. It was almost over—Dawn and Charles were doing great. Time slowed yet again, and we all wished for the best.

At 5:15 a nurse called the family to the nursery window to see Dawn's and Charles's newborn baby—Billie Ray. His hands and feet were purple, his arms and legs blue. He was small—six pounds, two ounces; his skin hung in folds from his bones. His eyes were shut tight behind two folds of skin.

Charles's mother said, "I'm not so sure that baby was ready to come out yet."

The doctor had taken Dawn's word for when she missed her last period and had agreed to induce labor without checking further. Charles's mother figured that Billie Ray might be two weeks to a month premature. But there were other variables, she thought, that might explain the near-to-six-pounds birth-weight. Charles had been under six pounds at birth, as had his brother and sister; and maybe it wasn't that Billie Ray was so small but that Lovie Mae's baby, at eight pounds, was so big.

The nurse gave Dawn another shot of Demerol, according to Lovie Mae, and rolled her to her room. In the hall outside the nursery window, the family group was happy and exhausted. Charles's mother kept saying, "Well, I guess we'll keep him. I guess he'll have to do." After a while the Hutchisons left to eat and I stayed with Dawn.

"Mom, did you know babies were so blue when they were born?" she said. "Mine was practically purple."

"They put Billie Ray under a warm light and he turned pink really fast," I reassured her.

"He don't look like either Charles or me."

Dawn was disappointed that the baby looked like a wrinkled old man or a little monkey. No doubt she had dreamed of something much cuter and more responsive. She was cuddling her stuffed dog in bed beside her.

"Babies change so much in just a few days," I said. "He'll be completely different in a week."

"What color are his eyes?"

"You can't tell anything yet. He has them closed tight."

"I don't want him to have my ugly old brown eyes."

"Come on, Dawn, your brown eyes are one of your best features. I'm sure Charles would like for the baby to have your beautiful brown eyes."

The next morning, when I returned, Dawn was sound asleep and Charles was watching TV. He said she'd slept all night and morning. He'd come into the room, he said, to find Dawn sleeping with the baby beside her. Charles may have found that as frightening as I did, because he mentioned it, but his attitude was no harm done, so why worry about it?

"The other day me and this guy from my basketball team was in Family Dollar. They got these crazy striped basketballs in there. I said, 'Oh, my God, ain't that neat, let's get us one a' these. Mess up the other team good watching this thing go round!' Them other guys started teasing me. They said I been living too long with Dawn—I'm liable to get excited 'bout most anything nowadays."

The Hutchisons regularly recounted stories like these about Dawn, completely without malice or condescension. They seemed simply to be amused; to be enjoying the antics of a puppy or of a small child. Dawn was right: the Hutchisons accepted her.

Billie Ray remained sound asleep in his plastic box throughout the afternoon. He'd squeak and wiggle only if he came uncovered. He hadn't opened his eyes at all, and I was beginning to worry about his lack of responsiveness. Was there a simple explanation—such as his being a world-class sleeper like his mother or slow and easy temperamentally like his father. Or was there a more serious cause? Had he been forced into the world too early? Was his nervous system still depressed by medication?

At about 5:30 the nurse came in to tell Dawn that she could nurse the baby again at 6:00. Dawn told her he hadn't really gotten anything from the previous feeding. The baby seemed ready to suck as long as no one expected him to open his eyes; he was tugging steadily on his pacifier. Right then, a group of teenagers arrived and the party got underway, but not the breast-feeding. Dawn and Charles were kids having a kid and celebrating their accomplishment with their friends.

The nurses took Billie Ray into the nursery that night and started him on formula, which Dawn then continued the next day. She said Billie Ray wouldn't take the breast after the nurses had fed him. By the next morning, Billie Ray weighed five pounds, five ounces. Although newborns usually drop weight, thirteen ounces is a lot to lose.

The failure of the breast-feeding venture made me feel, in an exaggerated way, as if I had put Billie Ray's life in jeopardy by not realizing what an impossible assignment breast-feeding would be for Dawn, or how bad it would have been for Billie Ray had his mother been solely responsible for his nourishment.

I found myself tense and worried. Of course it was too early to tell much about Dawn's mothering skills. Clearly she was exhausted; probably she was depressed, too. But. . . . So much was unsettling.

Charles and his family stood out as hopeful spots amid these fears. They knew Dawn and no doubt would step in and care for her and the baby. They seemed completely tolerant and nonjudgmental, enjoying funny story after funny story at Dawn's expense. As Dawn's mother, I found the humor less than infectious. I also wondered about the source and stability of the bond between Dawn and the Hutchisons. Helping Dawn always made me feel separate from her incompetence and dependence—an uncomfortable feeling. Helping Dawn made the Hutchisons feel much better; she seemed to make them—especially Charles—feel effective and competent. That new balance seemed to be working to everyone's advantage.

I hoped Billie Ray would help Dawn to mature. Maybe Charles's mother's favorite vision of the day would work out: the grandparents would build a basketball court in their backyard for Lovie Mae's and Charles's sons to shoot hoops with their dads and granddads. Perhaps Dawn had found the family of her dreams—a family that did everything together, from giving birth to raising the children—a family who all agreed, "That's Dawn" when she carried around her stuffed dog and thought *The Young and the Restless* portrayed the real world. Perhaps Dawn had found a world where she could grow and mature, or where, if she didn't, it would never matter.

But for Dawn that party ended all too quickly. Day-to-day life with

Billie Ray and the Hutchisons proved to be more difficult than she had anticipated. When the baby was about a month old, she wrote to let us know how things were going:

Hi How are you. I hope everything is going well. Lovie Mae and I never talk any more. Their is so much competition w/ Lovie Mae's and my baby with Cathy. I am going nuts. Cathy always threatens me to take Billie Ray away from me. She has come out and said she hopes Charles finds someone new. Before I had the baby we got along great! Now we can't stand each other! Charles and I are going to move to Sioux City (maybe) to get away! so all of us stop fighting! I hope so I'm tired of all the crap! I tell you about my Birth control Rubbers aren't that effective but every time I make an appointment I cant get a ride. Kate said go to an after hour clinic. but I don't want to go to just anyone. And with his Mom mad at me we can't get a ride after hours. I'm not doing all that well. I'm really worn out and life Just doesn't seem to be that fun anymore. It's all work, & Billie Ray, all he does Is cry & eat at this age. It's Nothing like I thought it would Be like I was all excited and now—I don't really know if I can handle it much more. His eyes are blue. He is getting longer. But he doesn't seem to be filling out too well. He is going to be small like Charles. Billie Ray doesn't really know anyone yet except by sent, He get calm w/me real good. But Not With other people except Charles. Cathy's preaty good w/him. But She doesnt spend much time w/him. Im really scared about being with him at first, Im so young. I wish I would of waited. I don't really feel like I'm good enough for Billie Ray, although he seems happy. I dont have time for anything all my Freedoms gone. Its like this. 8a.m.–4.00p.m.. I watch Billie Ray. 5–11.30 I work. Come home watch Billie Ray. Same thing every day. I get Wend. & Sunday off. And usually we go to church so that I watch him all day & night I dont get much from Billie Ray. Not many smiles. or laughs, or anything. He's pretty much dead. Eats, & sleeps, crys. But he is fun. I can't wait until I get some help I watch him all the time! Charles never helps when I need it. You know I wanted help. But I guess I'LL have to go out on my own.

In the video shot when he was two months old, Billie Ray was most unresponsive. He slumped and slept, his little arms drawn up tight against his body or flailing about if he was disturbed. The tape made it clear why Dawn called him "pretty much dead." I worried that Dawn had a brain-injured baby.

Several years later Dawn told me that she had been really depressed before Billie Ray was born—*really* depressed. In fact, one night early in the pregnancy, she had taken all of her asthma medication and had to be rushed to the hospital to have her stomach pumped. Cathy had been furious. *Furious.* Just you wait, she kept telling Dawn, I'll bet you've done something terrible to that baby. We'll have to wait and see. You had no right to act like that.

Mark and I were glad we hadn't known. Glad Aberdeen was so many miles away. We had to give Cathy credit: though she protested, that woman was taking the consequences of her actions.

The night Dawn's baby was born, Margey called home. That seemed more than a coincidence. She left a message for me to get in touch with her at Shirley's Motel as soon as I got back from Aberdeen. When I called the following week, the receptionist assured me that Margey Kimble was no longer checked in at his establishment. And he was quite sure he would never hear from her again. She had stolen a microwave.

Daughters

"Hey, Mom. It's Margey." It had been six months since she had called.

"Oh, thank goodness. I'm so happy to hear your voice. Where are you?"

"I'm in jail. They've been trying to get me—you know what for—but they couldn't, so they got me for public intoxication. I need a hundred dollars bail."

"Why haven't you called? Margey, it's been six months."

"You know how it is, Mom. Can you come and get me?"

"Yes. Where are you?"

"At the county jail."

"Where's that?"

"You don't know where it's at?"

"No."

Kate and I went to pick her up. The drunk-tank was packed with the people they'd locked up after two big raids the night before. An officer dressed in a white T-shirt took what seemed a long time to process Margey. We were lucky they worked that fast, the policeman said. There were sixty people in front of her, and he'd had to run her through the computer.

Several middle-class young men with lots of hair and Maui T-shirts were halfway cleaning up the premises. Kate asked them why they were hanging around. They said they were doing time in front of bars: if they worked from six to eleven on the weekends, they got a day off their jail sentence. What had they done, she asked them. Oh, various things—mostly drunk driving.

Margey appeared—so thin. Her hands and feet and face were bone white, her arms and ankles blotchy bronze. All her features looked oversized: her nose stood out on her face. Her hair was trimmed in the front and on the sides, long in the back, thick and healthy looking, its natural color except for the longer strands.

"Hey, you guys. How you doing? Thanks so much for coming to get me. Let me tell you, it's shi-it in there. They had me locked up with this woman they picked up in the alley. She'd killed another woman. Can you believe that? All these guys I used to party with, they're in for felonies. Fucking up big-time. Shit man, I'm dying to pee, I wouldn't go in there, they got bugs in the toilet. No kidding man, I'd rather have the food in Lakeville jail. They brought in some cold coffee—you couldn't taste nothing except bitter."

"You don't even like coffee," I said.

"Fuck, Mom, when you're dying for something to drink, you take anything. And these donuts. We're talking stale and moldy. I looked down and saw mold mounds all over the bottom. I said, no thank you, Mam. Look, I gotta find a phone right away. There's one at Hardee's. The least I can do is buy you guys some breakfast. I wanta mow some chow."

I asked her why she hadn't called; I'd been so worried, sure she was dead.

"Well, you know, Mom, what I was into. I didn't want to talk about none a' that. I thought a whole bunch of times about all the shit I'd like to buy you, Mom, but then I thought you'd want to know where I got the money. It wasn't the bail I called you for. They told me someone had a missing person out on me. I thought, no fucking shit! I gotta call my mom. I figured you musta' been looking for me."

We walked around the block to Hardee's. Margey went up to the counter, asked us what we wanted, and pulled a roll of bills out of her pocket—a twenty, a ten, and ones.

Kate was warm and curious and full of questions.

"So, Margey, what you been doing?"

"I'm doing great. Just great. Now. It wasn't too good for a while, but now everything's cool. For a while I was out on my own. You know that's fucking dangerous. Anything could happen to you. I was mixing up everything I could get my hands on—mostly crack. For a while there I was spending three hundred dollars a day and just barely getting off. Now I got my shit together. I got my own little chemistry lab. That's for cocaine. Ain't that funny? Me, who didn't ever know nothing. I buy rocks and grind them up and make my own—got me a water pipe and everything."

"So, how'd they get you?" Kate asked.

"They been trying to get me for the other thing, you know, but they couldn't prove nothing. Now I got to go to trial. But they won't be able to prove nothing. Then I'll get my money back."

"Well, where're you living?"

"For a while I was paying nine hundred dollars a month, for nothing. They were ripping my ass off."

"Where was that?"

"Shit, man, some fucking apartment kind of place downtown. Now I'm at the Airport Motel and I'm in deep shit if I don't get out there soon. Got to pay my rent today. I work out of these private hotels, They don't give a damn, 'long as I pay them every day."

"How much do you charge?" Kate asked.

I couldn't believe Kate was coming straight out with these questions. She and Margey acted like schoolgirls chatting at the Rexall soda fountain. I was glad, though, for both of them that Margey felt comfortable enough to open up on a tough subject—not that she customarily held back.

"Depends on what they want. You always got to remember, it's a date. You can't ever relax, but you gotta act like you're relaxed. I had it all wrong for a while. I was thinking like they were my friends or something. Like I could trust them. Kenny, he set me straight, told me I was gonna lose my fucking ass if I trusted anybody.

"Those guys, Kenny and Darla, they look up to me. They can't do all the things I take for granted everyone can do, like read and write. They think I know everything; they listen to me, too. You should hear me getting off. Someday I'm going to write about my life. It's a good-ass story."

I halfway wanted to ask if Kenny was her pimp.

"Who's Kenny, your pimp?" Kate asked.

"No way. He's with Darla. Darla's got five kids. None of them are Kenny's, though. Welfare took them away from her. She's supposed to get off the stuff so she can get them back—get rehabed. Hell, she's in there smoking with me every day."

"Do you work with those guys?" Kate wasn't about to stop asking questions.

"Yeah. The three of us, we pull in a thousand dollars a day. Kenny he sells cocaine and me and Darla, we sell pussy. Let me tell you, we take in some big money."

Kate asked her how many tricks a day she did. I looked away. Kate heard Margey say, "Sometimes eighteen." I heard her say, "Sometimes eight."

"I'm so fucking good at this shit. Good as shit. And I just love money. I make so much money, you wouldn't believe it. All the things I never could do—well, I can do this work. I just love to put all my money in a pile on the bed and run my hands through it. Count it. Pile it up different ways. Throw it up and catch it coming down.

"But a relationship, nuh-huh, no way. I tell you what I do have. Power. I got some kinda' power, you better believe it. Everything I say goes. Them sorry-ass guys come at me, ask me how come a beautiful, intelligent young lady is doing this kinda' work. I want to say to them, 'What exactly do you mean? Ain't you the one married, the one was just now talking about your daughter exactly my age? I ain't got you mixed up with some other dude, have I? You old stink bomb, you're sick, that's what you are.' I don't say it. Talking 'bout me!

"I'm single. I like it. I've always been like that. No—before I wanted a boyfriend. You know why? So I could dominate him. Now I demand what I want. I got the power. I can see through any guy I meet. I can say, 'You god-damn bullshitter. . . .'"

"How long have you three been together?" I asked.

"Oh, I don't know, a month or two. They're real good to me."

"You're careful, aren't you, Margey?" Kate asked her.

"Fucking yes. You gotta be. They'll try and do things to you."

Margey started in on her mushroom-burger and ate a few bites, opened up the bacon-burger and bit into that.

"Now this is some good shit. This one is it."

She ate a few french fries.

"What's with these fries? They're cold as ice. Musta' got them outta' the jail kitchen."

Kate said hers weren't any good either, though she'd eaten half of them.

"Take that shit back up there and make them give us some more. These fries been sitting round here the whole damn night. What the fuck do they think is going down?"

Kate picked up both cartons and headed for the counter.

"Man, it's good to see you, Mom. You're looking great. I been missing you. I'm doing good, I am. Kate looks fucking nice. I don't remember her looking so good."

Kate sat back down and asked Margey where she worked.

"I go anywhere. I meet all kinds of people from Saint Thomas. Yeah, I mean the university. But I get some from the high school, too. I do. I met these guys that know Dad. I'm serious. They do. These old guys. One's married to somebody who knows Dad's secretary. There was this big conference—I worked that. You wouldn't believe how much I work Saint Thomas. It's fun as shit. Them Thommies acting too big to button their own pants. I can take care of them just fine."

Kate asked did guys ever try and mess her up.

"Shit, yes, they fuck with me all the time. I mean, all the time. You always gotta be on the lookout. I wadn't kidding when I said I been near dead, lots more than once. These guys kept me up in the room for five hours. Five hours!"

"What'd they do to you?" Kate asked.

I hoped Margey wouldn't answer. She drew pictures that stayed in your memory.

"They fucked with me."

"How many of them were there?"

"Two. They had me in there for five hours. I was so fucking pissed at Kenny and Darla. I told them they knew fucking well it never took me over thirty minutes. What in the shit were they doing waiting for five goddamn hours? All the time calling and knocking on the door and nobody answering. They had to know something bad was going down. I was starting to think about really fucking some guys up."

"What do you mean—like what, cut them or something?" Kate asked.

Oh, my god, I thought.

"Shit, no, I mean fuck them up for good. I was thinking like something satanic. You know what I mean?"

I didn't, but that was fine.

"We got things straight now. That crack was fucking me up. I used to lay back and my eyes would roll in my head. Couldn't do nothing. Messed up my sleep and everything. Freebasing, it's good—smooth, real smooth. I can take it, once every hour, and go out and do my work. Now I'm down to a hundred dollars a day for drugs. This one woman I know, she's getting some big old ugly features from all she done."

It was disorienting to hear Margey talking about "her work," but she had a point.

"Does cocaine do something to your face?" I asked.

"Shit man, they get these big-ass eyes, bug out like this."

Margey pulled at the sides of her face and stretched her eyes out of their sockets. She was worried about her own features.

"Then this big-ass nose, like to take up their whole face. Big-ass lips. God, I want a cigarette right now."

I did, too. No matter how long I'd been off cigarettes, Margey made me want to smoke.

"I look funny like this, don't I? All uneven like." Margey held up her hands. "This shit don't come off, neither. It's been two weeks.

Her haircut looked great, Kate said, and asked her how come she hadn't put the tanning cream on her face and hands.

"You can't, man, it turns you orange. You know what, time's up, I gotta get back. You guys know where the Airport Motel is? Let's get going. Kenny and Darla, they gonna be wondering. Today we gotta move out and all."

We drove out to the Airport Motel.

"See that Buick, that's Kenny's." It was shiny laurel-green with beige trim.

"Ain't that smooth? Smooth riding, too. They're in one-fourteen. I'm here in one-eleven. You guys want to come in?"

Kate said she had to get to work. I was grateful; she must have known I couldn't deal with much more. Margey jumped out of the car.

"Thanks, you guys. I really appreciate it that you came and got me. I'll give you a call later on tonight, Mom."

She headed to room one-fourteen. "I gotta get me a jolt."

As we drove away, Kate said, "Well, Mom, she's really good. She's so sweet. And happy."

"Yes, she is."

I told her Margey and I hadn't had a harsh word for ages, nothing really serious since Lakeville Jail—how long had that been—more than two years.

"And Mom, she looks really good, except she's so thin."

"I thought she was much worse than last time. She's losing her looks. How long can she live like this? Doesn't she have to keep on do- ing more until her body can't take it and . . ."—the words were so hard to pull out—"she dies."

"She'll get AIDS first."

"She isn't using needles. Mostly prostitutes get AIDS from doing hard drugs, I thought." But I had made it sound like a question.

"Plenty of prostitutes get AIDS from sex."

My throat was pulled up tight. "How long do you think she'll live—five years?"

"I think five years is a lot, Mom."

"Well, I guess the only thing to say is how relieved I am in spite of everything. I really had it in my head that she was dead."

"I know you did. And she's really good, Mom. She really is. So sweet and all. I was glad to see her; it's probably been two years now. I thought she was really sweet to us. She's fun to talk to."

"She is."

That there was so much difference between my daughters hurt terribly. The differences all seemed a matter of luck, outside anyone's control. Pity, though, did not seem much called for with Margey: in her scheme of things she was doing fine.

"Kate, how do you think the adoption affected you, Sam, and Jack?"

"I don't know, Mom, that's hard to say. Sometimes I think it made me meaner. You know I used to beat up on Margey when you guys were gone. Really cream her. I mean it. And I never worried about getting punished."

"Why not?"

"She never told on me, really. But I'm not sure it would have done any good if she had."

"God, that's awful, isn't it? Poor kid, no parents to defend her."

"Sam was just as bad. Worse maybe. Sometimes it seemed like he really hated them, especially Margey. Jack used to try and stop us sometimes, threaten to tell you guys, but it didn't do any good. Then sometimes Jack'd really get into it with Dawn—he'd lose it when she took his gum, remember?"

"I asked Sam how he thought the adoption had affected him: he thought it had made him more of an elitist."

"Maybe . . . probably so. But he was gonna be a stud anyhow, know what I mean?"

"Yeah, he's too smart and handsome for his own good. So are you. So is Jack. That never helped, either, though Margey is gorgeous and Dawn is really cute. Did you get to read those early chapters of the adoption book I gave you?"

"I started. And stopped. Then I started them again. They're just too hard, Mom. I don't really think you ought to be doing this. You know that. You gotta get on with your life, Mom. That stuff is all over and done with—I don't think any of us really want to go backwards to think about any of it."

"Jack said the same thing. And he really hated the part where I described myself as some sort of Betty Homemaker. It's all cut out of my new draft. But that is why I really do need your comments, Kate. Your dad feels left out of what he's read, you know. And he told me you guys feel the same way."

"I don't know about that, Mom. Me, I think I'd rather be left out than in there. To tell the truth, I'd rather the whole thing be left out and you get on with your life."

"Yeah, I know what you mean. But I do think this book is helping me do that. I can't tell you how much better I feel about everything after thinking about it and doing all the reading I've been doing all these months. It does feel as if I'm getting perspective. And I'm not nearly as angry. Remember those days? It used to feel like all I could see was a red blaze—like I couldn't escape how furious I was no matter what I did. It would just flame out."

"Mom, you gotta forget all that. You really do."

"When I asked Jack about the adoption, he said he thought it had been lots more unpredictable and interesting growing up with five children rather than three. You know what else he told me the other day? I was late and brought him a candy bar because he had to wait thirty minutes. Then I said something about feeling bad for all the millions of times I'd been late. He said he'd never minded—he just used to stand there and wonder how I'd make it up to him."

"That's just it, like I tell you, Mom, move on."

On and On
and On

Ten weeks after the birth of the baby, Dawn's husband, Charles, called. We talked about the weather and the baby. Then he said Dawn was at work and he hung up. That seemed a little strange.

An hour later he called back.

"Hey, we're doing Christmas cards and like that, and we wanted Grandma Kimble's address." I read out the address and didn't ask any questions, even though they had sent out birth announcements to both grandparents a month earlier. Then Charles asked if I wanted to speak with Dawn. I said sure.

Dawn got on the phone and said, "Hey, we're doing Christmas cards and like that, and we wanted the Brown's address." Sure, I said, and read out that address, too.

Everything was just fine, Dawn said. She'd lost her job a couple of days earlier, but now she was taking care of three children during the day and she got $35 a week for them. They were so cute and Billie Ray was doing . . . well . . . not too much, but he was trying hard. Then she said, "Charles wants to talk to you."

I was beginning to feel like they were playing hot telephone. Charles got on the line again, "Well . . . you told us it was going to happen and it did." I had been begging Dawn since the birth of Billie Ray to decide on some means of birth control, but she had put me off. "That's really too bad," I said into the phone. "I'm awfully sorry."

"Well," Charles said, "we're wondering if we could borrow the money for an abortion. The doctor says Dawn isn't ready to have another baby. It wouldn't be good for her or nothing."

"That sounds like good advice. Sure. Tell me the name of the clinic so I can call in the credit card number."

Dawn did not come back on the phone. The nurse at the clinic knew the case. She sounded concerned and agreed to pay special attention to Dawn.

Three months to the day after Billie Ray was born, Dawn called. It was 12:30 at night, and she junped right in without beating about the bush. "Why didn't you tell me, Mom? Why didn't you tell me? You knew."

"You didn't talk with me, Dawn."

"You could have told me."

"Well, Dawn, I didn't get a chance."

"Why didn't you tell me, Mom? You knew it was terrible."

"Dawn, this isn't a time to blame everything on me. I did not have one thing to do with this."

"You could have told me. That's all I'm asking. How come you didn't tell me?"

"Dawn, we're getting nowhere here. Let's talk about what happened. Did you have a rough time? Were you really scared?"

"You could have told me, Mom. Why didn't you? The thing is, I am not Margey. Margey doesn't give a fuck about anyone else. I'm not Margey."

"Of course you're not Margey. But I have a whole lot of respect for both Margey's and your decisions."

"Margey's completely selfish. She doesn't even care what she does. I'm not like that."

"No one's saying you're like Margey. But you both got into terrible situations, and you both had sense enough not to make the innocent suffer. I admire you both." How horrible, I thought, for any woman to go through an abortion so soon after a birth.

"You could have told me how much it hurt. Why didn't you?"

"Actually, Dawn, I was out in the waiting room when Margey went in for her abortion. I couldn't have told you how much it hurt, because I don't really know. Margey said it hurt like crazy, but only for a few seconds."

"I just don't see why you didn't tell me."

"Look, Dawn, I'm here now and we can talk about why you're so upset."

"I don't want to talk to you. I don't have one thing to say to you."

Ask a specific question, I thought, but pulled out the wrong one, "So how far along were you, Dawn?"

"I don't want to talk to you. It's none of your business."

"That's very true. Let's talk in a day or two. I'll call back soon."

A few days later, Dawn wrote that she was sorry for what she'd said and grateful for the money. She said they'd been using the condoms and all that stuff I'd sent, but somehow it happened.

Mark didn't want to get involved with any of it. He thought Dawn should have had the abortion, but he didn't want to be the one paying for it. I wrote and called, offering to pay for a Norplant if they wanted to try that.

One night, Dawn and Kate got into a heavy conversation about sex. Dawn said she didn't really want to think about anything concerning sex—she hated it. Charles always wanted it and she didn't; they hadn't had sex since she was five months pregnant, and now Charles was telling her "just spread your legs." He'd whisper in her ear, "Now Dawn, what about that little Jennifer you didn't get the first time." Charles thought marriage was only about sex. She thought marriage was about being close to somebody. It was impossible not to sympathize with both of them.

Dawn wrote that they were fighting all the time—that she and Charles were thinking about going to a marriage counselor. They needed it, she said. But they loved each other and would work it out. She finished the letter with, "About the abortion. I don't agree what I did was right, I will hate myself for it forever, I want to change what I did. I would encourage other people to not have one. Charles told me to have it done that I couldn't phically have the child and that I didn't care about me/& him if I didn't have it done and then he went to work and didn't come with me I was awak I felt everything and I cried through it! I think women should have the choice of not having an abortion."

Some months later, I heard a counselor for an abortion clinic describe the most challenging clients she encountered: the right-to-lifers who themselves had sought an abortion but who hated themselves so much for what they had done that they didn't want it to be legal for anyone else to make the same mistake.

Seesaw,
Marjorie Daw

The phone began to ring Friday evening and voice after voice wanted to speak with Margey Kimble. Mark and I kept asking why they were calling our number; she didn't live with us anymore. Through the night, hour after hour, the phone rang.

Saturday morning, a cheerful older gentleman asked if Margey Kimble was available to clean for him; his wife was recovering from surgery. He gave his name and number—a first—so Margey could return his call. I thought, "Great, maybe she's going legit."

I asked the next caller how he'd gotten the phone number. He'd gone out with Margey a couple of times the previous week, he said. Who was I, he wanted to know. Margey's mother, I told him. "Do you go out," he asked.

"No."

"Why not?"

"Well, I'm married."

"So," he said, "are you as good looking as Margey."

"We look a lot alike, in some ways," I laughed, thinking of my grandmother's saying that Margey looked more like me than any of the other children.

All day Saturday, callers, dozens of them, asked for Margey. Mark and I were mystified. Late in the afternoon, the older gentleman who had requested a housekeeper called back. "I owe you an apology," he said. "I really was looking for someone to clean. These boys at the restaurant where I was eating breakfast, they told me to call this number for a real good cleaner. They asked me when I saw them just now, 'Don't you ever read the newspaper?' It turned out they was funning me."

What was in the newspaper? I wondered. A suggestive line in the personals? Mention of Margey in the call girls' column? I didn't have any idea—nor the heart to scour the paper. The next day, Sunday, a friend called to tell me about the article that had appeared in Friday's paper. Under the headline

"20-year-old arrested on prostitution charge," it read:

> Margey Brown Kimble, 20, of [here the report gave our address] was arrested on charges of prostitution after she attempted to solicit an undercover police officer about midnight Wednesday on Selby Street, city police said. Kimble was released from the county jail after appearing in Superior Court Thursday. Police said Kimble solicited a police officer who was working undercover with the Metro Special Operations of the city police. According to police, the officer was driving on Selby when Kimble allegedly waved him down and offered to perform sexual acts for money.

At least all the phone calls made sense and there was reason to hope we wouldn't need an answering machine after all.

Then Margey called. She was in jail, she said; she'd been arrested again for the same thing; this time she wanted me to come down and get her out. I said no.

"I just can't believe this, I really can't. My own mother won't come down here and get me out of this nasty place. This is what I should have expected. I mean, really, who was I kidding? Every time I ask you for something, and I mean every time, you're not there. You have not ever been there. Not fucking one single time."

"It doesn't feel quite like that to me, Margey. Maybe I haven't ever done what you wanted, but I have been here."

"All right then, when, name just one time? When the fuck have you been there for me? Just name one time."

"I can't say anything when you're feeling like this."

"When the fuck do you ever say anything? Here I am completely on my own, making my own way, working the streets, and that ain't no easy life, let me tell you. All them other kids, they're on easy street. Whatever they want, they just go down and pick it out and you pay the bill. You're so happy with everything they do. Work? Ha! Any one of them ever done a good day's work? Ha, ha. Fat joke."

"You're right that they've been given a whole lot more than you have, Margey. Your father and I do wish we could do more for you."

"Then come down here and get me out. But no, you won't, no— you're just a fat-assed hypocrite."

"You know good and well, honey, I'd much rather see you in jail than out on the streets. I'm not about to help you get out of a place where you're safe."

"One phone call, I get one fucking phone call. So I call my dear old mother. Do you think she'd get off her ass and come help me? Same old bullshit, same old goddamn bullshit."

"Margey, tell me how are you doing otherwise."

"Now, yeah, I get it, now we get to be motherfucking polite. 'And how's the weather in jail, Margey. Weather's lovely, Mom, not so nice outside though, around about twenty degrees last I was out there busting my ass, but it's cozy and warm in this here jail. Smells kinda' like pines, you know, fresh pine trees. Least that's what the deodorant hanging above the piss hole says. A regular old camping trip.'"

"Where are you living now? I couldn't get you the last time I called Shirley's."

"Naw, man. Shit, I been outta' there awhile. I'm not far from home, at the Midway Motel. They treat me real good out there. I gotta get back and take care a' my shit."

"I'll try and visit you tomorrow."

"Yeah, you do that. Come on down and we'll visit, you and me; we'll have us a girley chat, just like the old days. You won't do nothing I fucking ask you to do, but you come on down here anyhow and gawk your eyes out. That's real good, Mom."

"You're going to attack whatever I say, Margey, but I'm really glad to talk with you. It has been so long. I keep telling you, after a while I get really worried. You promised you'd call, no matter what, remember?"

"So now I'm fucking calling. So where does that get me?"

"You think they'll keep you long?"

"Shit, no. They were out after me, didn't give a shit how they got me. That motherfucking policeman, I hate his guts; he was wired. The stupid bastard, he quoted me a price. Now that's funny. He set me up plain as day, they gotta have heard the whole thing down at the station. They knew the whole fucking time they couldn't make nothing stick. I'll be outta' here in a few hours—most, a day. I got a good record for showing up to stand trial. Besides, they ain't got nothing on me."

The public defender got her out of jail the next day, Thursday, Margey said when she called. Stupid motherfuckers, too dumb to wipe their own asses, she said. Why couldn't they have kept her, I wondered. In jail only one night and then out on the streets again. She apologized for being so rude on the phone and promised to call in a few days.

Generally Margey makes her life as a prostitute sound like an exciting game of hide-and-seek, all on the chiller-thriller side. The officer who called later Thursday night gave an entirely different impression. After the preceding week, the article in the newspaper, and all the phone calls, including several from collection agencies wanting money and two from fundamentalist sects, I was pretty worn down.

"This is Officer O'Brien, Mrs. Kimble. Can I speak with you for a few minutes?"

"Yes."

"Margey Kimble is your daughter, is that correct?"

"Yes, she is."

"Margey's having a great deal of trouble these days."

"It sounds as if she is."

"Margey hates my guts. She hates me worse than all the other police on the beat. She thinks I'm after her. I been keeping an eye on her for some time."

"It makes me feel better that you're keeping good track of her."

"I been looking out for her, that's how come she hates me. Now can you tell me, Mrs. Kimble, how come she's like this . . . you know . . . how come she's gotta do this?"

"That's a hard question, officer. She can't seem to keep a job and she has to live somehow. She's had a rough time—taken away from her mother when she was four—supposedly she was abused and neglected."

"Is that right? She never told me that."

"She doesn't usually. She just tells people her parents are both college teachers. She enjoys shocking them."

"Do you think there's anything that can be done? I mean do you got any suggestions, any idea what I might try and do? That kid is headed for serious trouble, you know that, don't you, and I hate to see it. She is a beautiful girl, too, but here lately she's losing her looks. She's lost about fifteen pounds in the last six months. Her features are so prominent now, she's almost unattractive."

"Fifteen pounds . . . that's terrible, the last time I saw her she didn't have a single ounce to lose. I wish I knew what to tell you. She's had a lot of help; she was in mental hospitals for over a year, but she isn't interested in changing. Actually in some ways she's happier now than she's ever been. She loves excitement and danger."

"You got that right. Did you know she's been dancing in the

streets? She's gonna get herself killed. She goes all alone into places on the west side black policemen won't even walk through. All by herself, half the time, dancing right smack-dab in the middle of the street, three . . . four o'clock in the morning."

"She doesn't have exactly what you'd call good sense, does she?"

"What's she on, you know? Drugs, I mean."

"Well, she does a lot of cocaine. Basically, she's an alcoholic—I think, has been for a long time."

"What about crack?"

"She said she'd gotten off that and was doing better on cocaine. But you can't believe anything she says. I don't know for sure."

"She don't know what kinda' folks she's messing with. We're talking big trouble, big trouble. The toughest guys in this town. They don't hesitate, not for a second."

"You know what I think you should do? Go out to that motel room, find the cocaine, and get her sentenced to some kind of rehabilitation program."

"Is she trying to commit suicide or something?"

"Actually she's never tried that directly, but what would you say she's doing with all the alcohol and drugs?"

"Well, I wanted to call you, Mrs. Kimble, because since I'm the cop on that beat—I work from seven til three—I'm the one who has to inform the parents. And I don't want the family to have any surprises. What I'm thinking . . . it has happened a whole lot before in situations like this . . . what I'm thinking is . . . I'm going to find your daughter's head one place and her body another."

Finally everything broke inside me, just the way Margey describes it when talking about her own crises. I couldn't leave the house; I sobbed if I thought about her or talked about her. It was as if the officer had just said my daughter was terminally ill. It did not help one bit that she'd been on the same path for years; it did not help that she wanted it that way and could not do any different.

"Head in one place—" The language, the details: "dancing down the middle of the street," the hopelessness. It was too much to try and hold myself together any more. If I wondered, and at times I had, how much I cared for Margey, I found that one answer. The thought of losing her was agony.

After a week of despair, I gave myself another week to reach a decision: should I intervene one more time, or let go and begin to prepare for Margey's death? It did not feel possible to do both at the same time. My brother Ray explained the procedure for getting someone committed; my brother Jack suggested that I contact Al-Anon.

Somehow Margey always knows exactly what's going on between us—what I'm thinking about doing. Or maybe the policeman warned her that he had called Mark and me. Anyhow, she called.

"I missed your birthday, didn't I Mom? Can't I buy you some rubies? That's both our birthstones and I was looking at them for you. Do you want a spice rack, you know, like the one you had that got broken? Clothes, how 'bout clothes? You don't ever get anything nice for yourself. I got so much money now that I quit. I threw my stuff, you know what I mean, out the window, out the window of the car over in Wisconsin. I did. You know what I thought about getting you? One of those thingies that go in the bathtub. Makes like whirlpools, according to what it says. You want one of them? They're real good for your back and stuff like arthritis.

"I got all the money in the world now that I'm not doing any stuff. How 'bout I stop by school for a visit? Then we go out for lunch? I'll tell you what, I'll call you back Valentine's Day. We'll go out to lunch. To Pepe's, I know you like that. How 'bout that, Mom?"

"I want a picture of you too, and, yes, I definitely want to go to Pepe's."

And I want you to be happy, go to school, ride a bicycle, run down a soccer field, dress for a prom, fall in love, find a job, get a picture taken for the mantle, come over for coffee. . . . I love your laugh and the way you like to be teased, the way you tell stories. How brave you've always been, how you cut to the bone with the truth. I love how you hold my eyes, how sweet you are to me. You made me your mother.

No, I'm not sorry I adopted you. Yes, at times it has felt like that, and you scare the heart out of me, that's often true. But, Margey, Margey, the thought of losing you. . . .

My grandmother, who lost two of her four children, always said parents were not meant to bury their children. Nothing, nothing, on earth, is worse. . . .

Margey did not call on Valentine's Day, or the day after, or . . .

At the end of the week, I called the police and the local mental health center. The police said they would have to wait until they had enough evidence to arrest her. My old friend Melanie Ross at the mental health center said it did not sound as if Margey could be put away for psychiatric reasons; what she was doing was criminal. Besides, there was a six months' waiting period for a permanent bed at the state hospital. She suggested that I call Al-Anon and take care of myself. Kate said to quit waiting for Margey to call or come see me; for me to go see her.

A couple of weeks later, Jack and I stopped by the Midway Motel and asked a matronly looking woman at the front desk if she would let Margey Kimble know we were waiting to see her. The woman asked who we were. Margey kept calling her back, trying to see if something was up. Jack and I wondered what the prim lady knew about Margey—they seemed on cordial terms—and how such a respectable-looking motel dealt with Margey.

Actually I was relieved: the whole arrangement seemed a lot safer for Margey than anything I would have anticipated. Anyone could hear her if she cried for help. After about thirty minutes, Margey told the woman at the desk to send us on to her room.

"So, what the hell are you guys doing?" she was hanging out the door of room 227.

"Well, we just had lunch and we were right here, didn't have much to do, so we decided to come see you. That okay?"

"Yeah, yeah, I had to get me a shower and dress, that's all. Yeah, I went back on the stuff, you know what I'm talking about, Mom? You knew that."

"Yeah. You look great, Margey," I said. She did, too. Jack nodded his head in agreement. Margey had on a apricot blouse with lipstick that matched. Her hair was bright yellow, but nicely cut.

"Do I really? You mean that, Mom?"

"Yeah, you look terrific." Did anything else really matter to Margey, I often wondered.

"See, I gained some weight. Do you really think I look that good?"

"Yes, you look great. But I don't know about gaining weight, you're still awfully thin for my taste."

"I ain't thin, am I Jack?" Margey stood up, turned her back to us, and twisted around to see her buttocks. "Nuh-huh, I ain't thin at all, you shoulda' seen me a while back. I gained a whole bunch a weight since then. I was down to ninety-five pounds—nuh-huh, less than that. You saw me then, Mom, yeah, that's what I weighed this summer."

"Well, you're a little on the thin side, but you do look good," Jack said.

"Do I really? That's fine, ha! I had to get rid of, you know, this guy, he was still around. That's how come it took me a while. I'm going to California next week."

"So, where in California?" Jack asked.

"To Los Angeles. Hang out in a motel. Swim and party all day and night."

"Will you hit the ocean?" Jack asked.

"I got me a bathing suit. Sure. He'll be working, you know what I mean, I can just hang out all day long. He's old, you hear what I'm saying; older than you, Mom. He's married, got a kid my age."

"What's his name?" Jack asked.

"Curtis Bianco."

"Does he have a kid who goes to Penn, plays soccer, James Bianco?"

"Shit, I don't know his kids' names. Pretty weird, huh? He wants to get a divorce, you know what I mean, but she told him she'd take him for all he's worth. Brought out the Bible and swore on it. So what's the point? He's got this other young girl like me, he set her up nice, got her a trailer. She's got these twins. What I need me is a driver's license. Then I can get him to get me a car and I'd be fine."

"You mean this guy will buy you a car?" Jack asked.

"Not brand-new or nothing like that. But sure. He's gonna take me shopping this afternoon, let me get whatever I want. Every time he comes back into town he's got plenty of money and we go straight out shopping. He might be doing some dope runs with his semis—he owns this fleet of semis. When he gets back, he throws money around. I say, hey! Let's play catch.

"Hey, what's up with Dad anyhow? He quit his job or something?" Margey pulled a crumpled newspaper clipping from out of the drawer beside her bed.

As she closed the drawer, I could see a jumble of makeup and fingernail polish and a condom on top.

Jack reached for the clipping, "Hey, let me see that. You seen this, Mom?"

"No," I said, "I saw the story in the school newspaper."

"So what's up, anyhow?" Margey said.

"Not much. He was done with being dean and ready to go back to teaching. He's been in administration eight years. That's tough work; it's someone else's turn."

"Oh yeah? God, check out that picture? Look how old Dad looks. Goddamn, what's happened to him, Mom?"

"He looks regular. Actually I thought that was a pretty good picture," I said, "but there's no question that we're getting older, Margey."

"You guys doing OK, Mom?"

"Not great. Pretty much going our own ways."

"I don't know. He don't look so good to me. But I ain't seen him in a fucking long time."

The phone rang, Margey picked it up and said, "Wrong number." She left the receiver off the hook.

"Too bad you couldn't stay off the stuff, Margey. Didn't you say crack was hard on you?"

"Shit, the other don't hardly last. One, two minutes, then I'd be after some more. Sometimes I'd get a hit every thirty minutes. Now crack, that sticks with you. Sometimes I think, 'You ain't got nothing, but it ain't because you don't make no money. When I think of all the money that comes through here. Shit . . . I mean if I coulda' saved some of that. Too bad you didn't come see this place a while back. I had a microwave and a stereo—a fine stereo. All these excellent tapes."

Jack was turning a tape over in his hands. "You want that?" Margey asked him.

"I think I've got it. Thanks. I like it a lot. So what happened to your stereo?"

"That stereo was cool, but shit, man, they'd come in here and start messing with that thing. Looking through my tapes, asking could they hear something or other, wanting to talk about some dumb-ass singer, that kinda' shit. Like to took them the whole goddamn night. So I got rid a' that thing, you know what I'm saying? That sucker was costing me money.

"Shit, them guys give me stuff all the time, I keep it a day or two, then it goes for drugs. I don't keep nothing til it cools down."

"So you snaked a microwave outta' your last motel?" Jack said.

"You heard about that, did you? Shit, that wadn't none of me. That was Darla and Kenny. They ripped it off for his mother."

"Are you still with them, Margey?" I asked.

"I didn't need none a their shit, you know what I'm saying? Kenny, he's a big-time dealer. Drugs, big-time. See. That's why I can't be hanging out with them, because he would keep me supplied. And even if he didn't, I'd just take it. He'd have these big-assed jars of the shit. I'd just take some out, mix in some plain white powder. Hell, I'd take damn near an eight ball and he'd never know."

"Has Darla gotten her kids back?" I asked.

"What you talking about? She don't even go see them. She used to visit them all the time, buy them stuff. Now she don't do nothing. And fat, she's fatter than . . . hell, I don't know, but she's fat. Darla ain't even pretty no more, she's so fat. You can't tell where one a her features begins and the other ends."

"Are you by yourself, then? Didn't you say that was dangerous?"

"Shit, Mom, I know how to do it. I check 'em out. They got a gun, a knife, I take it offa' them first thing. Make them pay me big bucks, their whole wallet. You can't be taking no chances."

"Honey, this policeman called and said he was worried about you—"

"That son of a bitch, I know who it was. What was his name?"

"I can't remember, honest, but he said you hated his guts."

"That's gotta be Tim O'Brien. All them cops is cool with me. We got an understanding. Except that motherfucking bastard. Something's wrong with him. He's trying to get me, all right. Hoe'in ain't nothing but a misdemeanor, did you know that?"

"Is that right?" Jack asked.

"They can't put you away for hoe'in, so they try and get you for something else. Yeah, see cops are dirty. You know what he's after, Mom? He wants me to turn on them guys. He knows that I know them all. I mean all them black guys way up there with the drugs, you hear what I'm saying? He wants to wire me up, send me into one of them houses. Now that's stupid, Mom. That's how you end up dead. Them guys get out of prison, they come back and kill you. Or they send back word and get someone to kill you. Nuh-huh, that's what that motherfucker wants. Nuh-huh, nuh-huh, you get what I'm saying?"

"He said he was really worried about you, Margey."

"Shit, Mom, listen to what I'm telling you. He wants me to turn them guys in. That's all he wants. He don't care nothing about me, I promise you that."

"He seemed pretty concerned. Margey, what do you think about trying to go to a drug rehabilitation—"

"Mom. You gotta want to do that. Not me, man, not now."

"He said you thought you were mighty smart, too smart to get caught."

"That's what I mean. He just don't know it yet." Margey laughed and settled back against the headboard of her bed.

"Sometimes they ask me to get another girl for them, a third like, all of us together. Why should I care? Hell, I don't even hardly go out on the streets, not unless I want to. I got plenty of business come walking in that door."

"So what's with this guy you're going to California with?" Jack asked.

"That's Curtis. He was in here when ya'll called. He's this really nice old guy."

"Does he do drugs?"

"Oh no. I don't ever do drugs with none a' my dates. Nuh-huh, no way, you hear what I'm saying?"

"So how are you going to make it all week in California without drugs?" Jack bounced up and down on the other bed.

"Shit, man, I been thinking about that. But I don't know what to do. I thought about taking me some in my suitcase. But then, what if I get caught?"

"You better not try; they got dogs," Jack said.

"That's just it. Anyhow, I'd take it all at once soon as he went to work. That's the way I am. So it wouldn't last me anyhow. It ain't no big deal. I'll be fine. I been cutting down since I heard about the trip. It ain't no problem—hanging out by the swimming pool all day. Take me a few days break from work."

"Does this guy drink?" I asked.

"Yeah man, what you think? I coulda' gone to California lots a' times. New York. I coulda' gone to Japan once."

"Why didn't you go?" Jack was trying to get a job teaching English in Japan.

"I get scared, kinda' froze up, you know what I'm saying? Can't go nowhere. Sometimes I can't even move."

"So, you want to go out to lunch sometime next week?" I wanted to keep hold of her.

"Yeah, sure. I gotta leave on Wednesday, at seven thirty in the morning, ain't that a bitch?"

"So, how about Tuesday?"

"Give me a call. You guys gotta go then?"

It seemed ludicrous that I'd been in mourning over this young woman. She was anything but at death's door. Her skin was clear; she was full of herself, an answer for everything, very much alive.

"She looks great, doesn't she?" I asked Jack.

"She is really beautiful. She seems happy, too. Better off than she was in our house."

That thought always made me feel so bad. "Yeah, probably so. This is the life she's always wanted, all right."

"She really gets to you, doesn't she?"

"Well . . . it's like I freeze up until it's over, try not to feel anything. And then it takes a long while to deal with everything she says."

"She's pretty cool."

"Thanks for going with me. It's hard to go alone."

"It's pretty interesting, actually. You shouldn't let it get to you like that, Mom. You should've learned by now."

"Yeah, another whole world. Pretty hard not to."

"Yeah, you think she'll go to California?"

"No telling until Wednesday morning."

When I called on Tuesday, Margey was way, way down.

"You ready for your trip? You need anything?"

"Shit, no. I don't even want to go. It's just something more tiring. Traveling and all is really tiring."

"You want to go to lunch at Pepe's."

"Shit, no. I'm so tired all I want to do is sleep. I don't want to see nobody or do nothing, not for days. I just want to close myself up in this room all by myself. I don't give a fuck about anything. I mean it. You know how old I feel, Mom. So old and tired. Tired. Period."

"Margey, do you want to try and get some help?"

"Nuh-huh, Mom, I'll probably have to overdose before I'll stop. That's just the way I am. That's what I did with sniffing. This one time I did way too much. There I was all pale, perspiring all over and freezing at the same time. Them crazy motherfuckers, they said, 'What's the matter with you, you want another line?'

"Those bastards, I can't tell you how much I hate them. Men. I really do hate men, Mom. And here I am making my living off them, ain't that strange. But the work is great, at that time I am boss-lady. They do exactly what I say. I don't give a fuck about them, not about anything. I don't even look at a guy, don't feel them or nothing. Don't even kiss them. Don't foreplay them, nothing. You get five, ten minutes, I tell 'em, and you're outta' here. Out."

"Are you able to be careful?"

"Hell, I use condoms for a blow job. They don't even get their clothes off before they got on a condom.

"What the hell do I care about them? I can't even get off on sex myself. Sometimes I tell them, 'Take your dirty dick and bury it in the Grand Canyon.' I got plenty business, what do I care? I can get by with being such a bitch because I'm white and young and nice looking. They'll put up with me. Shit, I tell them, you didn't get no guarantee before you come in here. And there ain't no refunds. If I'm tired, that's the way it is.

"I'm looking for somebody to do something to me. Relieve me, you hear? I've had it. I ain't got the guts to do it myself. Oh yeah, I'm doing it myself with the coke, but that's about as far as I can go.

"You know what I think about my mother sometimes. That she lived like me. Only she had kids. I'm wondering if she didn't do this same stuff except she let her tricks mess with Dawn and me? I'd like to knock her down on the sidewalk, jump on top of her and beat her to pieces. You know what I'm saying?"

"I don't feel very good about her either, sometimes, but we can't know what she was up against."

"Like I told you, I went up to the welfare; they told me she was six-teen, seventeen, eighteen years old when she had us."

"Really, you never told me that. I've always wondered how old she was."

"Yeah, she was young, younger'n me. They said I could see her and all if we both went to counseling. Now just think about that. You know what I think, I think they shoulda' told you guys about all that. I do. That adoption was a trick, it really was. A trick adoption, pretty funny, ain't it?

"You know what, I'll bet she's dead. That's what's happened, I'll bet."

"I'd bet so, too. Well, maybe if they'd told us more, we wouldn't have kept on trying to make you into something you couldn't be."

"Shit, I don't know. You know I've always been depressed. Always."

"Yeah, I think you're right. And there hasn't ever been anything that helped—not for long, anyhow."

"Nuh-huh. I'm not ever happy unless I'm high. Out of my mind. Oh yeah, I can make myself go into moods and like that. But I can't ever not be depressed, not really."

Margey always had so much insight, but she never lingered. An-other breath, another topic.

"I took some really cool pictures of myself after you guys left, when was that, yesterday? Sunday? I look really nice. You know, Mom, I'm photogenic, I mean it. Did you know that, Mom?"

"Absolutely. Who's been trying to get a picture of you for months?"

"You'd really like these. I'm smiling in all of them. One's of me and Curtis—you can see what he looks like."

"I'm coming right over and pick them up."

"Are you really? I feel like shit."

"Yeah, I've been bugging you for months, haven't I?"

"That's okay, you can have them."

In my favorite of those pictures, Margey's lips and eyes are pursed exactly like Marilyn Monroe's. Carefully posed and self-conscious, her expression pleads, "Aren't I irresistible? Please, please, want me."

Mark hated the picture; he refused to let me put an enlargement alongside the other children's current pictures in the living room.

Too Nearly Full Circle

Much excitement preceded the first visit to Saint Paul by Dawn, Charles, and Billie Ray. The baby was six months old. Dawn was pleased to be home, and it was good to see them all. Billie Ray seemed tired from the trip—they had driven most of the night: he didn't smile and seemed cranky. All the hair on the back of his head was rubbed off. Mark said Billie Ray had Dawn's genes; when she first came, her hair used to fall out in clumps. Dawn said the baby had gotten his shots before they left Aberdeen and he was teething. Thirty minutes later they left, promising to return for dinner the next day.

When I called Margey the next morning to let her know Dawn was home, she said, "Yeah, I saw her last night."

"You did?"

"Yeah, downtown. She looks good. She's doing great. She really looks good. Which is not what I've been hearing from you guys."

"What do you mean? I haven't said anything to you about Dawn."

"Yeah, she looks great. I saw her and Angie. Angie has a baby, too, huh. How come all I heard was how terrible she was doing?"

"Margey, I haven't said one thing to you about Dawn. Not one thing." Margey had never asked.

"Yeah, she looks fine. I know all you guys think me and Dawn are the assholes of the family, but I think she's doing great. You know it's all your fault that I'm where I'm at."

What had happened to Margey, I wondered. Then it came clear: Dawn's driving up in her big Taurus, married lady with baby. Margey must have felt like a poor show.

"Look, Margey, I haven't said one bad thing to you about Dawn, and I haven't said anything bad to Dawn about you, either."

"Yeah, Kate told me last summer how she'd gained a whole bunch of weight. I think she looks really good. I like the way she's fixing her hair. I don't know how come me and Dawn always gotta be not worth nothing. You made me what I am."

"Let's talk another day, Margey."

"You think I want to talk to you?"

"Okay, Margey, I just wanted you to know Dawn was in town. I'll call you in a while."

"No rush."

When Dawn, Charles, and Billie Ray came for dinner that night, Billie Ray was clean and all dressed up in a clown suit. He was asleep in his car seat.

Dawn told Mark about seeing Margey the night before.

"So me and Angie, we went out to the Randall's Inn to find Margey, but she wasn't there. They told us we might find her at the Kitty Kat Lounge. You know where that is?" Mark said he did. "So we went in there looking for her. You ever been in that place?" Mark said he hadn't.

"Well, it's something. I never been anywhere like that. Those people are weird looking. And they stared at me and Angie so we left. They told us to drive up and down University and we'd find Margey sooner or later. So we did. We found her down around Broadway, you know where that is?" Mark said he did. "Well, you know what I'm talking about then. It was raining so we came up next to her and asked her to get in the car. She got in the back seat. She was really high and acted like she was mad or something." Mark told her I had talked to Margey earlier and that she'd been upset.

"Yeah, she wouldn't stay with us for long. She was all drugged out and crazy and said she had somewhere to go, so we left."

I told Dawn she'd be better off trying to catch Margey in her motel room. Otherwise, please, to leave her alone. My heart ached for Margey. And for Dawn who understandably wanted to see her sister, but who was riding a little too high.

I gave Dawn the memory-book her foster mother had collected for her, and she and Charles looked through the snapshots and occasional cards. Then they looked through the family photograph albums and Dawn told Charles all about camping trips and holiday rituals and commented on her outfits. She kept saying how much she wanted Charles to know something about her family. She was always with his family and knew everything about them there was to know.

Billie Ray slept on. During dinner, Charles said the doctor had told them Billie Ray was about two months behind, underweight, and not developing on schedule. He had suggested that they take the baby to a pediatrician. They hadn't gotten around to it. Dawn said Billie Ray just had his own way of doing things. He would do what he wanted to do when he got ready. Charles said they didn't know what else to do, they were loving him as much as they could.

Both Dawn and Charles were furious with Cathy, Charles's mother. They were positive it was her who had called welfare on them. Someone had reported that the baby was being left alone—that it was crawling around in dog mess. They had gotten a puppy, and they couldn't get it trained, that was true. But the baby wasn't even crawling; he wasn't about to get into any dog poop. When welfare came out and asked a bunch of questions, they found out it was all a big lie. So they left. Served Cathy right; she was nothing but a liar.

"Billie Ray was a month premature and I was two weeks past my due date," Dawn said.

"We got the pregnancy test done at Planned Parenthood in December," Charles said. "They must notta' been too good at it."

Neither Mark nor I wanted to try to unravel that reportage. "Why didn't they do an ultrasound before they induced it?" I tried. "Did they do an ultrasound anywhere along the way?"

"They told us that woulda' cost a hundred dollars. So we decided not to have one," Charles said. What doctor in his right mind, I wondered, would take the word of an eighteen-year-old on the date of her last period?

When Billie Ray woke up after dinner, I held him and tried to feed him his bottle. He didn't seem to have much appetite. He would draw in a mouthful of milk, hold it in his mouth, and then bubble it around before he sort of swallowed. After he took an ounce or so of milk, Billie Ray started to cry, more of a high-pitched whine than a cry. He wouldn't be soothed. He wouldn't lay back in my arms or cuddle while I rocked him. He didn't smile. Charles laid him down on his quilt and he soon fell asleep again.

After they left, Mark and I fretted about why the baby wasn't smiling. We tried to remember when Kate, Sam, and Jack had first smiled, but our memories were vague. Billie Ray seemed like a grim little old man; we found ourselves calling him Sad Sack.

The next night, Mark and I met Dawn, Charles and Billie Ray at a restaurant. The baby was asleep. About halfway through the meal, he woke up and started his cry. Dawn put some formula in his bottle and Charles went to the bathroom to add water. Then Dawn laid the baby on the seat beside her, put the bottle in his mouth, and told him, "Now you hold this. I'm not going to hold it for you." Dawn turned to me and said, "See, he can hold his own bottle." The bottle rolled onto the floor.

I looked at her askance.

She said, "He can, too. He can hold his own bottle. He's six months old now."

I looked dubious.

"He can too hold his bottle, can't he, Charles?"

"Well, sometimes he can," Charles said.

"He can hold his bottle any time he wants to," Dawn said.

I got up, picked up the baby, and tried to feed him the bottle. He didn't seem interested and was restless in my arms. Mark tried, then in few minutes handed the baby back to me. Dawn commented on what a fat little tummy he had. I said babies were shaped like that, but he wasn't at all fat. Billie Ray began to cry steadily. He wasn't interested in anything and soon fell asleep.

It was time for me to leave for class. I was confused and worried; getting through a three-hour class seemed impossible. Dawn's laying the baby down flat on his back and insisting that he hold his bottle upset me. He was so tiny and underweight—so uninterested in anything, even in eating.

I wanted to cry and cry and then scream about what was happening to those young people. How could adults have handed that baby over to two babies? For once, and that was a great relief, I wasn't angry with Dawn and Charles. They were clearly doing the best they could. But that poor baby!

My anger focused on the doctors and the hospital staff. Why hadn't they intervened before they sent that baby home? Hadn't they seen plenty before those kids left the hospital? I cried, angry and bitter.

When I got home after class, I told Mark how worried I was about Billie Ray. I kept saying I wasn't blaming Dawn and Charles, they were doing the best they could, that was clear. But something was going wrong.

Mark said there was nothing wrong with the baby; I was being overly critical. Why couldn't I let the kids have a peaceful visit? Finally he said he thought the baby might be autistic, that was all.

"Do you realize what you're saying?" I yelled.

The next day at school, I talked to my friend Becky, a developmental psychologist. She agreed to meet Dawn, Charles, Billie Ray, and me at the dining hall that afternoon. If she could observe the baby, she could reassure me.

Becky was not reassuring. She thought the baby was seriously underdeveloped. His head was wobbly like a three-month-old's. He wasn't nestling at all; in fact, he kept arching his back when she held him, perhaps as a result of a hypersensitive temperament. She thought Billie Ray might well have been a difficult baby from birth, but that things were also going poorly for him in his environment. He wasn't smiling. And more to the point, he wasn't gazing at anyone who held him. No matter how she tried, Becky said, she couldn't get him to meet her eyes. And he also didn't seem attached to his parents. All the while she was holding him, he hadn't looked around for them or tried to pick up the sounds of their voices.

Babies smiled, Becky said, from six weeks, or even earlier—as soon as they learned how to get attention. When they succeeded in getting someone to look at them, they smiled. It would take Billie Ray a long time to learn to smile, unless his parents looked at him, consistently, and he looked back.

Billie Ray's behavior and development were all too typical of the children of teen parents who were not given the training they needed. It was very important, Becky thought, that I try to get in touch with someone in Aberdeen who could intervene. She would call the University of South Dakota and find out what she could about parent-training programs. Don't give up, Becky told me; so much can be done for babies now—such good programs.

At breakfast the next morning, Dawn and Charles talked about trying to buy a house through HUD. All they had to do was pay up on their bills for a month and then they could get a good credit rating. After that, they would be in the house and they could pay as little as they wanted on those old bills. They were ready to leave and eager to get back to their life in Aberdeen. They gave me a peace plant and wrote a sweet card thanking Mark and me for a happy vacation. I was touched by their thoughtfulness but still profoundly disturbed about the baby.

Then I talked with Charles's stepmother, Jane. Charles and Dawn had stayed at her house. When Dawn complained that she missed having the baby's swing, Jane had borrowed one. Dawn and Charles left the baby in that swing all night long. The first night it happened, Jane said, she told Dawn and Charles she dared them to sit up in a kitchen chair the whole night; they'd see how sorry they felt the next day. What was going to happen to the baby's back? What about the circulation in his legs?

So they didn't put the baby in the swing the next night, Jane said, but the third morning when she got up, she found the baby in the swing. Charles swore to her that he'd only put Billie Ray in the swing at six o'clock in the morning because he was crying.

Jane told the kids the baby needed to be eating something more than formula: he was so small—still in newborn Pampers at six months—and they'd gone out and bought a dozen jars of baby food. Then when Billie Ray cried, Charles laid the baby on his knees and Dawn stood over him and poked food into his mouth, the baby crying at the top of his lungs all the while.

I was relieved that Dawn, Charles, and Billie Ray had not stayed with us. Again and again I saw Billie Ray's serious little face in my dreams, his eyes wandering from side to side, up and down. But was there anything to do other than mourn for him and all babies in similar situations? Meeting his needs seemed beyond the range of his parents, who were perfectly well-intentioned.

What could be done, I wondered, to keep adolescents like Dawn from having babies so young? There had never been anything else Dawn wanted to do. Nothing. Couldn't the adults in charge arrange things so that young people had other goals—goals in addition to having babies? Mark and I had certainly not been successful with Dawn.

Like so many young people, Dawn was desperately seeking affirmation. And she managed to find it through the baby. That baby was undeniable; he dominated the family's consciousness. I kept wondering if it was beneficial for Dawn in the long run that her strategy worked so well.

The issue, in Dawn's case, was certainly not prevention. We were much further down the road than that. Could Mark and I stand by and watch Billie Ray go to foster parents? Or adoptive parents? After my frustrations with his mother, could I think about trying to raise Billie Ray myself, if it came to that? Would it ever be possible to believe that early damage didn't matter all that much, or this time to accept the damage that had been done with more grace? Those questions were too hard. It was much easier to hope for the best.

I wrote Dawn and Charles all the nice things possible about their visit, but also told them how worried I was about the baby, and why. They didn't respond.

A month after their return to Aberdeen, Charles called to ask us to pay for child care. Dawn was working the day shift. Had they made any arrangements to check into how the baby was doing, I asked. The baby was doing just fine. After all, he said, Billie Ray had not come with a set of instructions pinned to his diaper. What did we expect them to do, hold his bottle until he was eighteen? His real problem was that he didn't have any grandparents.

Dawn called a few minutes later and insisted that I had promised to pay for day care. She had a letter from me to prove it. Ordinary day care was a family expense they needed to build into their budget, I told her. If she would find a good child development center for Billie Ray, some place that would provide him with a diagnosis and appropriate stimulation, she could make both of us happy.

I asked if they had made any decisions about birth control and offered to help with that. What was she using?

"Nothing."

"Nothing?"

"Nothing. I really mean *nothing*. No sex. I hate sex, anyhow."

I wrestled with whether to say more. It felt too controlling to offer to pay for an implant. I was uncomfortable insisting, always, that money be spent to my specifications.

Dawn demanded that I tell her who I had sent to check up on the baby. What did I think I was doing anyhow? Why was I always interfering? "Mom, how do you think you know anything? You have hardly ever seen Billie Ray his whole life."

"Dawn, I haven't called anyone or talked to anyone except you—I promise. I wrote you everything I was worried about. And asked you please to take the baby to the pediatrician as your doctor advised. Have you done that yet?"

"There's nothing wrong with Billie Ray. When you saw him he was on the wrong formula, that's what was wrong. What makes you think you know so much about him? You've only seen him once in his whole life."

"Twice. And you are right, that is not very much. But I've raised three babies and my mother had seven children younger than me, remember?"

"So how'd you learn how to take care of a baby?"

"Well, I knew a lot from watching my mom. And I read books on nursing and how to feed a baby."

"You think I'm going to raise Billie Ray out of some stupid ole book? I'm not about to read a book to find out how to take care of my baby. You expect me to hold his bottle for him his whole life so he never becomes independent, don't you?"

"Dawn, babies are not independent, they are entirely, completely dependent. Especially one who is slow developing. I'm not the only one who is telling you Billie Ray needs help—all three mothers you know are telling you exactly the same thing—Cathy, Jane, and me."

"You don't even know them. None of you have hardly seen the baby. You don't know what you're talking about. Cathy says you never cared anything about me and you don't care anything about Billie Ray."

"She may have said so, but that sounds more like you, Dawn, than Cathy."

"You know, Mom, I'm doing exactly what everyone does who has a baby the same age as Billie Ray. What's wrong with Billie Ray anyhow, tell me that?"

"That's just it, Dawn. Billie Ray isn't responding as he should at his age. There might even be something wrong with him biologically that you should check into. Look, Dawn, I wrote you all that, let's not start all over again."

"So you think he's not drinking his bottle good. I'll have you know, Mother, that he's had an ear infection almost the whole time since he's been born."

"I don't know if sore ears would affect his sucking or not. Maybe it does hurt his ears if he sucks hard. Dawn, *I* don't know, either. All I'm saying is that you need to take the baby to someone who *does* know."

"Why don't you go right ahead and call my doctor. His name is Doctor Brinkley. Every time I see him, he tells me how great Billie Ray's doing."

"Fine, Dawn, I'll try and call him."

"I just wanta know how you think you know everything? You haven't seen the baby but once in his whole life."

"We are not going to start again. It's a good idea to call the doctor—maybe he'll ease my mind."

The nurse would not put me through to the doctor without permission from the patient's parents. Dawn would not grant permission, either then or later.

My friend Becky suggested that Dawn could not possibly admit the baby's problems. That would be too hard for someone with as little ego-strength as she had. She was too invested in doing well by her baby. Because she wasn't able to separate Billie Ray's growth from her mothering, Dawn interpreted every question about him as, "What's wrong with me?" or she insisted, "I am, too, being a good mother."

Frustrated and worried, I called the child protective service in Aberdeen to ask about parenting classes. The receptionist referred me to the public health department. The nurse who answered the phone had been assigned to Dawn's case several months earlier. She was glad to hear from me; both she and the social worker had lost track of Dawn and Charles since they had gotten the car. She couldn't catch them at home. She had been wondering how the visit in Saint Paul had gone and how the baby was doing. I told her my concerns. She said she had exactly the same concerns, but she had been hoping things would get better. She would get back with Dawn as soon as possible and check on the baby. Sometimes they had to threaten to take the baby away; parents usually straightened up pretty well once that was done.

Augustine, the early Christian saint, believed that hope is the greatest of virtues. And that hope has two beautiful daughters, anger and courage: anger to insure that the bad things that need to be changed, get changed; courage to insure that good things that need to be done, get done.

Where a baby—a grandchild—is involved, it is impossible not to feel anger, not to need courage, not to keep searching for hope.

The Hallmark Child

The staff at Women, Infants, and Children (WIC) finally insisted that Dawn take the baby to a specialist and made an appointment for her. Dawn called, very upset, after that visit.

"Mom, I took Billie Ray to the specialist today. He's the only one who knows all he knows in this four-state area. He's a specialist in children with different development. Like he's one of the few people in the whole country who knows anything about what Billie Ray's got. He says he's got Williams syndrome. But I don't know whether he does or not. I don't know what to believe."

"What does that mean? What did he say?"

"Well . . . a bunch a stuff. You know how Billie Ray's eyes got that star in them, kinda' a yellow star in the center. Anyhow, that's part of it. And he's not growing. That's it, too. And he doesn't much like to eat. He's probably having difficulty with his food and his digestion. That's why he can't do stuff like the other kids. It might even take him as long as two years before he gets up and walking good. Maybe longer."

"Heavens, Dawn, what a lot for you to hear all at once. How upsetting!"

"There's a bunch more stuff, Mom. I want you to try and find out something else because the doctor was talking real fast, with a lotta' big words, so I couldn't understand nearly all he said. Yeah . . . plus, he showed me some pictures. Billie Ray looks exactly like the kids in the pictures, you can even see the stars in their eyes. You can't when they got blue eyes, but his are brown so it's easy to see after the doctor shows it to you. I never noticed it before."

"I haven't, either. I'd like to see. Give me a few days and I'll talk to a friend in the biology department. He's a geneticist and he'll know where to look up Williams syndrome—that's right, isn't it?"

"Yeah, I don't know why they call it that. You know how Billie Ray don't grab stuff with his fingers? He like smacks the thing he wants to get hold of, shoves it with his fist? That's part of it, too, using his hand like a club."

"I didn't know he did that. That does sound important. My friend Tom Berry will know. He's got an adopted daughter himself. She's got really high cholesterol and has to be on a special diet. I'll call you back as soon as I can talk with him, OK? How are you feeling about all this? Worried? Sick? A little bit relieved?"

"I feel a little better, I was getting so worried. But everybody I know keeps telling me there ain't nothing wrong, so I don't know what to think— Billie Ray is just taking his time; he's just premature and he don't have a fast nature. I think they might be right, too.

"Then there's this other thing . . . I keep remembering stuff that doctor said. Billie Ray puts his tongue up when he's supposed to be putting it down. So he gets his tongue up on top of his food—then he can't swallow good. That's how come he don't eat good."

"Course you don't want anything to be wrong. Neither does anyone else. Can they teach him how to swallow better?"

"You gotta find out all that kinda' stuff, okay Mom?"

My friend Tom Berry was ready with several books for my appointment with him. He was his best teaching self explaining Williams syndrome. No one knew the cause, for sure, he said. Sometimes there were patterns of instances in families; sometimes a case appeared completely out of the blue. The problem seemed to be a deletion in a chromosome that the doctor would be able to detect in a sophisticated blood test.

There were quite a few symptoms, Tom said, involving lack of muscular tone—respiratory and cardiovascular problems. Williams syndrome babies were slow to grow, especially in the first four years; they remained small all their lives. Their joints gave them problems, he said; many had to be replaced as the children grew older, especially their knee joints.

"Is that why the baby has so much trouble walking?"

"Probably so," Tom said, "and when he does walk, he may be stiff-legged. Because of an excess of calcium, their bones grow thicker, too. See this little face"—Tom pointed to a picture—"they call it the elfin face, because the baby looks so puckish—the wide-set eyes, the broad forehead and narrow chin, the stellate iris pattern, the upturned nose and depressed nasal bridge, low ears and long upper lip."

"Hmm, Dawn has that flat bridge; we always thought someone had broken her nose. Isn't it terrible that we were so suspicious? She had such bad sinuses—we thought because her nose was misshapen. Some of these children have really big lips"—I turned the page. "What about intelligence?"

"There's a great deal of variation from individual to individual, but the average given here is an IQ of 51 to 57 or so. Of course, that doesn't necessarily mean anything regarding your grandchild; there's far too much individual variation. In terms of the personality, things are good. Williams syndrome children have what these doctors—listen to their so-called humor—have labeled a 'cocktail party personality.' They're bubbly and outgoing, happy-go-lucky."

"That's good, isn't it, something like a Downs syndrome child?"

"They sound somewhat alike in this description, but the details are spotty. Downs syndrome children are extremely affectionate."

"What about Dawn's having more children?"

"I'll tell you what: I want to see the earliest picture you have of your daughter, to see what she looked like as a child. What I'm wondering is if she might not be a carrier."

"Hmm. She has this nose for sure, and this long upper lip. But we'd always thought that was because she had some fetal-alcohol damage. She's slow, that's true, too."

"Look at these two pictures—see the similarities? In both fetal alcohol syndrome and Williams syndrome children, the features in the middle region of the face—the upper and lower lips, the chin—are ill-defined. You usually don't see, for example, an indention in the upper lip, below the nose, like you and I have. See here?"

"You haven't answered my question about her having other children."

"Well, that's a terrible question. We both know that. And I don't know the answer, so I'm hesitant to say anything that will give the wrong impression. The answer depends on whether the mother is a carrier and there really may not be any way to get definitive information, except perhaps through a chromosome check, and even that might not be a hundred percent. But if your daughter is indeed a carrier, there could be a fifty-fifty chance she would have another Williams syndrome baby. She really should talk with the doctor in Aberdeen about these questions before she decides to have another baby."

I was grateful to my colleague for his gentleness and wisdom. His words spun around in my head. Both Mark and I realized without looking at Dawn's early pictures, which we did immediately, that she had that elfin look. We had always called her a pixie—after her haircut. She had the pug nose, the broad forehead and long upper lip, the pointed chin.

Four years earlier, when I first read about fetal alcohol syndrome in Michael Dorris's book *The Broken Cord,* I had felt enormously relieved. Margey's and Dawn's mother had been an alcoholic. Quite possibly, I reasoned, her mother's drinking had led to a number of Dawn's behavioral patterns that Dorris described as associated with fetal alcohol effect: her difficulties with learning from experience; her frustrations with cause-and-effect reasoning; her inability to understand abstractions; and later, in high school, what was diagnosed as attention deficit disorder.

My fetal alcohol effect "diagnosis" had provided me with a great deal of understanding and sympathy for Dawn. This possibility of Dawn's being a Williams syndrome carrier explained her difficulties even better and also laid them on a much less negative and judgmental foundation: a pregnant woman is negligent if she drinks to excess, but none of us is responsible for the genes we have.

Dawn sent on a pamphlet she had received detailing the symptoms of Williams syndrome. Phrase after phrase made me think back to three-year-old Dawn—to nineteen-year-old Dawn, for that matter: Speaks in clichés, incessant chatter . . . may use long words and sophisticated phrases . . . but often their speech is inappropriate and repetitive . . . asks incessant and irrelevant questions . . . feeding difficulties, including vomiting and refusal to feed.

The list went on and on: Fascinated or obsessed by particular topics or objects . . . overfriendly and overfamiliar with adults . . . no interest in playing and interacting with their peers . . . difficulties in establishing and maintaining friendships with others of their own age . . . anxious and easily upset by criticism and frustration . . . frequently demands attention and seeks reassurance from the people around. . . . I continued reading: Excessive preoccupation with certain objects (such as insects, cars, or electrical gadgets), particular topics (disasters and violence on the news, illness, future events such as birthdays and holidays), or an obsessive interest in certain people (a particular member of the school staff, a classmate or neighbor) . . . concentration difficulties and hyperactivity, sometimes described as impulsive.

Speaks in clichés—the essence of Dawn's language. I had called her my Hallmark card child. I had even developed a theory for why Dawn spoke in clichés: in an effort to construct the identity she did not have, I believed, Dawn strung together sentimental bits and pieces of how she heard the world described—everything's for the best or God's in his heaven and all's right with families, especially mothers and babies.

When Dawn gets rolling on one of her platitudes, I have to pray for patience. "I just got back from the store and I got Billie Ray some of that instant oatmeal. They told me at WIC that would be so good for him in the morning before he goes off on the bus to school. On these cold mornings, that warm oatmeal will feel so good in his tummy. When he chews and swallows, all that warm oatmeal will go all the way down to his tummy and make his little tummy feel so warm and toasty. When I see Billie Ray's teacher I'm going to tell her that he's eating oatmeal before he goes to school in the morning and that his warm breakfast makes him feel so good in his tummy and. . . ."

For weeks, my thoughts swung back and forth between Billie Ray and Dawn, child and grandchild. Then questions about parenting sprang into the mix—Margey's and Dawn's mother and my own memories of mothering Dawn. No wonder it was so difficult to feed Billie Ray; no wonder his poor parents poked food down his mouth when they couldn't figure out how to deal with him. Heavens, what if Dawn had all those feeding problems when she was a baby? Her mother would have had a terrible time getting her to eat. With a social worker checking up on her all the time, how stressful it must have been to have a baby who cried all the time, and didn't eat and gain weight. Only the social worker had it easy: she must have been positive she was seeing a textbook case of "failure to thrive." Did the foster parents have better luck feeding Dawn? I wondered; perhaps not. Maybe that was why the child was constantly being returned to her mother. At six months, Billie Ray had certainly looked like a neglected and unattached baby if ever there was one. If at three months Dawn's appearance had been similar to his at six, no wonder she was hospitalized for malnutrition.

Dawn was certainly obsessed with food when she first came to the house. Was that, too, a Williams syndrome symptom rather than the result of neglect and malnutrition as Mark and I had always concluded? Those two hypotheses were certainly a world apart in terms of the biological mother's responsibility. Perhaps I could have relaxed more with Dawn and food if I hadn't felt so responsible for her compulsiveness.

Overfriendly and overfamiliar with adults. Yes, that was exactly what had disturbed Mark and me about Dawn's behavior when she first came. Dawn said she worried constantly that when Billie Ray learned to walk he would wander off and never return, he was so friendly. She was thinking of putting him on a leash. Perhaps if Mark and I had known about Williams syndrome, we might not have concluded that Dawn's friendliness implied a rejection of us.

Perhaps, too, I was wrong, years later when I was reading the literature on mother-child attachment, in thinking that Dawn's overfriendliness and excessive attachments to objects were signs of her lack of attachment to her mother. How tragic if Dawn's excessive friendliness was a Williams syndrome pattern that got her mother into trouble with the social workers, who may have interpreted excessive friendliness as a sign of attachment problems. Following a flash of insight, I began to worry about how Dawn's mother must have felt when she was blamed for things she kept trying to remedy as best she could—and about how she must have felt when she lost her struggle for custody of her two daughters. The social worker had said she tried and tried—kept on trying, just as Dawn and Charles kept struggling with Billie Ray. Poor woman. Maybe Dawn was right after all: she and her biological mother might well become good friends if they had the opportunity to get to know one another.

Everything I had ever concluded about Dawn and her mother had to be reevaluated. Would I ever understand Dawn? Or would I always be on the lookout for a new and better explanation?

Billie Ray's diagnosis with Williams syndrome shoved Dawn and me right through the bad period we were going through after that visit to Saint Paul. I was so relieved that there was a physical reason for Billie Ray's delayed development; Dawn was relieved to have someone to talk with about the details of the diagnosis. Charles understood and all, but he wanted to talk about other things. Most of the time, Dawn's mother-in-law denied that there was anything wrong with the baby. But the other way Cathy handled the situation was even worse: she continually accused Dawn of damaging the baby the time she took that overdose of asthma medicine early in the pregnancy. Dawn got angry with her mother-in-law and refused to see her for weeks at a time, but then they would make up. Dawn's ability to forgive and begin anew was remarkable.

I would like to add a few points of my own to any list of Williams syndrome characteristics: enduring and persevering, cheerful and eager to laugh, capable of forgiving easily and forgetting completely, fun-loving, playful, fresh and bright every morning, accepting and loyal, optimistic and enthusiastic.

Billie Ray and Dawn share a long list of good traits. And with Billie Ray, Dawn and I began to have much more in common.

Dear Mom

How are you? I Just wanted to say thank-you for all the phone calls and for the Advice you have give me. I think that you have helped me alot lattely You dont know how much I'm sending some wallet size pictures of Billie Ray and I'll send the 5x7 when I get a Bigger Evelepoe. But I wanted you to see how much he has changed and his smile If you look real close you can see his teeth! But its Better in his 5'7. Let me know what you think He was so good at his theropy yesterday that he got a cookie! The theopy Lady likes that I can really talk to you and she really likes Billie Ray. He gets 4 toys this year from "Santa" He only got one last year. I'm glad I can talk to you about Billie Ray. Its hard to talk about him to other people they always say he's not that Bad. For once I just want to Yell it's gonna get worse if he doesn't get help. He's not like the Other Children and I'm tierd of hearing all this crap about all the Other Kids can do this and he cant do it. It drives me Nuts. But I cant tell you how good it feels to have a mother to talk to again. I Love You so much I always have it's Been hard But I want to make a new start with everyone. A lot has changed. With Everything. I gotta go gotta clean up so Billie Ray can destroy the house again. Have a wonderful thanksgiving.

It has helped me to identify with both Dawn and her biological mother in imagining all three of us trying to deal with a Williams syndrome child. Dawn keeps asking me, "How come you understand when I talk with you about Billie Ray, Mom?"

"Because I'm your mother, Dawn."

Crack House

Margey burst into the visiting area of the county jail dressed in tidy blue elastic pants and a matching V-neck shirt. Her bright yellow hair was braided neatly in cornrows. "Look what my roomie done to my hair. Ain't it cool?

"God, Mom, did I ever get busted. Those raids on the crack houses I been telling you about, well, I got caught right in the middle of one. First thing you know, the door crashes open, every window busts out, and there are policemen coming at you from every direction. Everywhere. Like something outta' *Star Wars*. Face masks and space suits— you know, so's they won't get shot. Their guns pointing, ready to blow your guts out. There was a little baby upstairs, too; something terrible coulda' happened to her if she'd cried.

"God, Mom, I was so scared, I 'bout had a heart attack. Those guys with these big guns right up in your face, hollering, "You move, you're dead."

"I'm telling you, Mom, I gotta get straight. I gotta stop before it's too late, I'm serious."

"Are you really?"

"I mean it, Mom, two a' my friends just got killed. And don't think the cops are gonna do one thing about it. They don't even admit they're dead. They're dead all right. Their bodies shoved away somewhere so they'll rot good and nobody'll be able to identify nothing.

"I got cut real bad myself. Real bad, I had to go to the hospital to get stitches 'cause it wouldn't quit bleeding. You know . . . in my privates. You think that's not embarrassing? This son of a bitch had me tied up. Hell, I was so high I didn't know nothing. But then I came round and it hurt like a motherfucker."

"Oh, Margey."

"And it's cold out there, Mom. I wanta take off for Florida. Next year I ain't working no Saint Paul winter. How come you landed me in this town, Mom? Ain't no climate for my kinda' business."

We laughed. "I'm serious, Mom. I gotta get higher and higher to keep warm. I get so hot I rip off all my clothes—run around in this below-zero weather with my bathing-suit top.

"Wanda—you remember Wanda?—she's the one in love with her father. He's been having sex with her since she was a little girl. He's real sweet to her, too. So she hates him some a' the time, but she mostly loves him. I really do think they still do it. She's always trying to get me to go in with them. We're talking free and you know I ain't into that. Anyhow, they nabbed her for shoplifting. Planted something on her. So she's in for a year, maybe six months. I'm next, I know I am. That's the way they work—split us up, get us running scared, then we slip up, and bang!—they smack us in jail. I gotta come clean. I gotta."

"You've never said anything like this before. Never. Are you sure?"

"I ain't never been ready before. The raid on the crack house, that scared me, Mom. You know what happened—I peed all over myself. I ain't never been so scared before."

"Now . . . are you telling me you want me to do something—find a place where they'll help you?"

"Fuck, yeah. I'm gonna party this weekend—I mean party *hard*. Then on Monday I'm gonna call you and we'll see about something to fix me up. I'm dead serious, I'll call you on Monday."

I didn't know what to do. Margey had never even pretended the least interest in getting off drugs. I had to take her seriously because it was a first.

So where could she get help? What about money? Margey didn't have a penny. Mark was teaching in England that semester. With the children all out of college or pretty much on their own, he and I were gradually going our separate ways. We didn't need a big hospital bill from Margey just as we were trying to work out two households. Nor, after our previous experiences, were we convinced that in Margey's case the psychiatric profession offered good value for the money.

I started checking the options: (1) six-month waiting period at the state mental hospital's drug-rehab unit; (2) eight-week waiting period for the YWCA treatment program; (3) a month's treatment at Charter Hospital, with prices starting at $30,000.00; (4) admission into Ramsey County Hospital on Medicaid. Mark and I felt plenty sorry for ourselves, but we agreed that we would pay the $30,000 if that was the only alternative.

Dr. Doris gave us hope that she could get Margey admitted to

Ramsey County Hospital, if that was still what she wanted to do after partying the weekend. Just in case, Dr. Doris made the necessary arrangements.

On Monday at 10: A.M. Margey called. Yes, she was serious; yes, she wanted to get treatment. She had done her partying, serious partying— no question about that. Now she was ready. Margey and I approached the registration desk a little after noon. They were expecting her.

The fifth floor was like old home week for Margey. "How you doing, girl, what you doing up here?"

"Well, look at you. Glad to see you coming in here. You sho' do need it."

"Girl, we got us a good group, uh-huh. We gonna fix this place Up." The three women slapped hands and laughed.

A thick, stolid nurse approached Margey, clipboard in the crook of her arm. "I need some information from you." Margey left her friends and joined the nurse beside her desk. They went through Margey's history. The nurse seemed to get annoyed as she gathered details: occupation, drugs, previous psychiatric help.

Nurse Sachet approached me where I was sitting with Margey's friends. "Well, are you the mother of this young woman?"

"Yes, I am Margey's mother."

"Well, I have a question for you, then, Mrs. Kimble. Where do you want me to send the billing?"

Margey said, "Why are you asking her that question? I already gave you my address."

The nurse looked at me, "The address she gave for the billing is your home address?"

"Yes, that's our address."

"But Margey doesn't live with you, does she?"

"No, she doesn't."

"Then what is going to happen to this bill?"

Margey shrugged.

Ramsey County Hospital was a public facility responsible for caring for all the sick in the area, regardless of their financial situation. Nurse Sachet eyeballed me. "What are you going to do about this bill?"

I looked at Margey. Obviously she had no money. She had told the woman her occupation straight out. What were we supposed to say? I made the mistake of telling the truth. "I'll do what I always do when Margey's bills come to the house, put them in the trash."

"We'll see about that." Nurse Sachet turned and walked past her desk into a room behind the nurses' station. A few minutes later she came back.

"I'm very sorry, we cannot admit your daughter at this time."

"Why not?"

"The doctor called the Salvation Army Treatment Center on Hennipen Avenue, and they have room for another client. We don't take nonpaying patients into the hospital if there is anything else available. Your daughter can dry out over there just as well as she can dry out here. There is a considerable differential in the expense."

"It's because I'm a whore," Margey whispered into my ear.

"May I speak with the doctor—please?"

"I'll see, but I believe that he has already departed the premises."

The nurse returned from the back room shaking her head. "No, I'm sorry, he's out of the office at this point in time."

"Would you please tell him that Dr. Kimble would like to speak with him." I was flaming mad; not once in my life had I ever addressed myself as Doctor.

She peddled off and peddled back, shaking her head. "No, I'm sorry, the doctor's occupied and cannot be disturbed. Do you want me to call the Salvation Army Treatment Center and tell them you're coming? Or not?"

Margey nodded. She said she knew lots of people who'd been to the Salvation. It was a good place. Not to worry, she'd be just fine there. "God, Mom, you're mad, aren't you. I've never seen you this mad." Like hell, she hadn't.

The Salvation Army Treatment Center was in a comfortable, rambling old home. The staff was as kind and welcoming as Nurse Sachet had been chilly and negating. They greeted Margey warmly, congratulating her on coming to them. That was never an easy decision. They would keep Margey until she was dried out. That took three days— roughly seventy-two hours. No visitors, no phone calls.

Then what?

Well, they had a residential facility for men on the premises, but they didn't take women.

What were we supposed to do after seventy-two hours? Margey would really need help then.

The intake counselor shrugged his shoulders. They'd take good care of her, monitor her bodily functions, feed her good while she was drying out. That's what she needed right then.

Dr. Doris said she couldn't understand what had happened, she had made all the arrangements. For two days I tried to speak with the psychiatrist in charge of the drug rehabilitation unit at Ramsey County Hospital. He refused to talk with me or answer my calls. Time was running out.

At the ninth hour, Dr. Doris called to say that Margey could return to the hospital after we checked her out of the Salvation Army center. The doctor had agreed to accept her into their forty-day treatment program.

"What happened?"

"Apparently the doctor heard you say you would throw the bills in the garbage and he lost his temper."

"That's what I was afraid of. I shouldn't have said that. But that nurse just kept on. She knew Margey didn't have any money. Were we supposed to tell her that Margey would take on a couple of extra tricks every night to pay the bill?"

"Well, the Salvation was free and since she agreed to go there, they could tell that Margey was serious." She hesitated. "Maybe."

"Yes, I know not to count on anything. Those people at the Salvation were wonderful; they got her off to a great start. Actually, I prefer that place. It isn't at all fancy like the hospital, but the staff was so kind. And competent."

"I've heard good things about their program. For a while they were working with women, too, but they were having to turn away more men than women. We've got this big war on drugs, but that doesn't include fighting for those who are already addicted."

Monday morning I met Margey at the hospital for a therapy session with Dr. Jarvis. He was a wonderful therapist. Perhaps because he was crippled, he understood Margey's pain. She told him that she was "on top of" guys in her job as a whore. He told her that prostitution was the ultimate in abuse of women.

Dr. Jarvis suggested that Margey and I spend a few moments telling one another exactly when we first realized we loved each other. He wanted us to be as specific as possible. Margey said it was when I was away one summer at a meeting in Colorado. She'd written me, she said, telling me how she felt. I told her that I remembered being panicked once when a sore on her ankle got infected, and a red line began to move up her leg. I was terrified that she'd get lockjaw and die.

On Wednesday night, ten days after she first decided to go straight, I called the hospital to speak with Margey and was told by our favorite nurse that she had left the premises that very evening, not twenty minutes earlier. Apparently she had called one of her boy-friends and asked him to come pick her up. No, she hadn't left a message.

I wandered around the house for a long time, not really expecting a phone call, having no idea where to lay my disappointment. Finally I decided to go through the box of things I'd saved of the children's over the years. I came upon the letter Margey had mentioned, the one she'd written the summer I was away in Colorado.

> TO: Mommy   6-23-81
> When I am writing this letter I let my soup cool off know its cold. OH Well. Every since you left the house its all worked up and loud. Well I hope you come back soon.
> Venus bit Marsey Baby's ear it started bleeding all over the wal and the floor. Yuck! I went nuts.
> I cant stand having nothing to do without you. Sam and Jack are doing nice things for me so one day Jack was gone I hurried up and did his route. I liked doing it. Because I thought they were being nice so why can't I. Things are going fine down here I'm reading this book I checked out from the libary. It's fun reading: I really enjoy my book. I read: Kid Power Pipi goes to South Shore They are so good I could read them over and over. Thank you for this PEN it really is neatO
> O my gosh I got to get you a present. The day's are going by so quickly I forgot.
> The reason why I only wrote you two letters is because I don't have any time to myself.

The letter ended with a verse: "Roses are red, violets are blue. My teacher is nice, And so are you." Margey signed it: "I miss you: Well: By: LOVE MARGEY BROWN KIMBLE. P.S. Thanks for the stamps. Your daughter. I'm ready to cry. I want you back."

Transformations

Dawn—our little Dawn—found her mother all by herself. It was an amazing accomplishment. After Billie Ray was diagnosed with Williams syndrome, Dawn wanted to have the preadoption records opened for medical reasons. Mark and I thought she was justified and we hired a lawyer, but the few details that came of it we already knew. The lawyer's report included the name of the social worker at Catholic Social Services, but she refused to give any more information; those files were legally sealed.

Dawn got on the phone with that social worker and talked her into giving her the names of both her foster parents and her parents. Next she called up the foster mother, and the two of them had a long chat. Mrs. Bowen was delighted to hear from Dawn; she'd always wondered what had happened to the girls.

Feeling mighty pleased with herself, Dawn dialed information and got her biological father's number. She asked him if he recognized the date September 10, 1971. He said he didn't. How about July 21, 1970? That didn't do anything for him either. So Dawn asked if he knew Ginny Mikelsky. Sure, he said, they'd been married for ten years or so and had three daughters between them. Dawn finally introduced herself. Her father was glad to hear from her; he gave her her mother's unlisted telephone number and told her, "Yeah, sure, give her a call. She'll be real happy to hear from you."

So Dawn got her mother on the phone and asked her whether she recognized the date September 10, 1971. Yes, she said, yes. How about July 21, 1970? Yes, she said. And then Ginny wanted to know if someone was kidding her. Was this a prank? No, Dawn told her, this is your daughter.

Ginny and Dawn then had the conversation Dawn had always dreamed of—her mother tender and caring, bemoaning all those lost years, insistent that they get together at the first opportunity. She sent Dawn and Charles the money to visit Saint Paul a couple of weekends later. Mother and daughter drove to visit Albert and Ginny's third

249

child, Paula, who was spending six months in girls' school, just north of Hibbing. Dawn wasn't too impressed with either her sister or her father. Both seemed more like Margey than her.

But when Dawn first found her mother, it was like she had found salvation. Gleefully, she threw off her old parents and took on the new mother. She was rude to Mark and me and told and retold stories about how miserable her life with us had been. I was furious with her, especially for including Mark in her abuse. He didn't deserve it, and his feelings were badly hurt. Even so, we both wished her the best with her long-lost mother. Dawn had been cheated out of her biological mother long enough.

It turned out that no easy substitutes were to be had. Dawn's second visit with Ginny lasted two days, not the planned two weeks. She and her newly found sister Paula had a fist fight in the middle of the kitchen floor, and Ginny took Paula's side. Things hit bottom when Ginny began criticizing Billie Ray's behavior. In her opinion, Dawn needed to discipline him; nothing would help him but a good spanking. Dawn gave the irresistible response: Who do you think you are? Telling *me* how to raise a child! Then she stormed out of the house and caught the first plane home. A few days later, Dawn wrote Mark and me thanking us for all we had done for her over the years, saying there was no telling what would have happened to her if we hadn't adopted her—no telling. She claimed Ginny had been high on marijuana the whole time she was baby-sitting Billy Ray.

The reunion of Ginny and Margey was at the county jail. Margey wasn't very interested in her new-found parent. She thought her mother had let herself go—gotten way too fat. "You could see from across the room that she didn't have any self-confidence," Margey reported. "She's just someone I met. She's not my mom. I'm not about to call her Mom. You'll always be my mom." Margey's loyalty was touching, but then we'd earned it.

Margey met her father Albert a few weeks later in a bar. They got drunk together. "He's a wild one," Margey said. "Him and Dawn look just alike, but he's where I come from. That doesn't mean I like him. Nothing there."

I always ask Dawn how she and her mother are getting along. Fine, all right, she always says, but there are no more rich and full accounts. After the first rush, it has all been anticlimactic. That very ordinary, squatty woman had dominated the girls' fantasies—and mine—for years. What a waste of imagination! There just wasn't much to love or hate. My first impression was the same as Margey's: no self-confidence, maybe depressed or burned out, or on downers—way too much alcohol. Yes, she cared for her daughters still, always had. But not the way I cared for them. Those gaps were way too big to fill.

Ginny and I got together a couple of times and exchanged stories. "What-all did those people at welfare tell you about me?" she asked over and over. Basically, too much alcohol, I summarized in reply. It was too cruel and the past too distant to respond more frankly. Her story was that she had been young and foolishly in love with the girls' father, Albert. She never should have left her family and followed him to Saint Paul, she admitted. She was all alone with the little girls; he was no help whatsoever. No, no, it absolutely was not true that Margey had been sexually abused. And she ought to know.

She insisted that she really had cared about Margey. Ginny had been jailed for trying to run away with Margey (that's why she hated it so when either of her daughters, Margey or Paula, got locked up: she knew what that felt like). But she would have done anything to keep Margey with her. When the police came that last time, she hid with Margey in the garage. It took them four hours, but the policemen finally dragged them out. That was the last time she had seen her baby doll.

Dawn, although the youngest child, was taken first. When Dawn was born, things became just way too hard. There was no way she could handle both little girls. No money. No place to live. But she'd really thought she could keep Margey—she'd tried so hard to do everything welfare asked her to do. It was just too late. They were after her from the start and they were going to get her no matter what. She was also stupid—kept chasing after their dad, thinking he would come back. She was so young and all alone. Then her sister tried to help. She even came down to Saint Paul, got the girls, and tried to keep them herself. But no way she'd let her sister keep her kids. Her sister had her own—three of them.

Ginny showed me a couple of snapshots she had of Margey. She also had a picture of Margey holding Dawn. The shots had been taken from far away, and I couldn't see anything clearly. There was also a larger photo, an eight-by-ten, of Margey in a sweet, flowered dress and that long hair the foster mother had saved, combed carefully over her shoulder. Ginny must have loved Margey's hair. That was all: three snapshots and an eight-by-ten. There were a few other pictures of Paula, who was born five years after Dawn.

Another day Ginny came to our house and looked through the family photo albums. She asked for copies of pictures of Margey and Dawn as they were growing up. She wanted to know all about the years she had missed. I found it hard to describe something so big, or to be entirely positive. Though she must have suffered, I felt as if she had left behind too much damage to smooth over so easily.

Not long ago, Ginny and I met on the back bench of the courtroom where Margey was about to be sentenced. We agreed that Margey needed a whole row of mothers—that we'd better call in reinforcements. Occasionally since then we've passed in the hall, visiting Margey at the county jail.

While I was fretting about whether or not to write this chapter, I had a dream that someone was trying to talk me into taking Dawn. I said, no, I couldn't do it. It just wouldn't work—I'd be terrible at it.

"You've got to," the shadowy person said.

"No, I can't."

"You have to."

We went back and forth. Dawn was lying asleep on a bed, way at the other end of a long, narrow room. As we argued, she began, very gradually, to curl into a fetal position. The covers disappeared and the two of us watched in horror as she began to shrink. Suddenly she was lying between us on the bed, her present-day self, but shrunken to the size of a baby. She was blind, surely, and probably deaf. There was no question of her speaking. She seemed uncomfortable and miserable, like Billie Ray at six months. Everything was silent. She wasn't sleeping, however; her chalky eyes were wide open, and she was staring beyond me, unblinking, at the wall. Then her body began to stiffen.

I cried, "Yes, I'll take her. That's just too awful." I picked her up. She was very heavy for her size, way too heavy to carry. I had to find someplace to put her down . . . and that seemed possible. Not easy, but, yes, possible.

So ends that dramatic story—those years of wondering and yearning for some ghost. The space is clear now for healthier business. At this point Dawn has accumulated a total of three mothers—Ginny, Ann, and mother-in-law Cathy. She makes good distinctions among us, appreciates our very different virtues, and gets a variety of help with mothering her two sons. Nor is Dawn repeating the mistakes made by any of the three of us. She has broken not one but three cycles. No doubt she will make other mistakes, but she has learned from ours.

Neither of the girls has seen their father again. Margey is happy enough that she knows her mother, gets drunk with her on occasion. She was initially fascinated by how alike she and her sister Paula are; they went out soliciting and partying together, until Margey decided Paula was nothing but a taker—gimmie, gimmie all the time.

For me, this chapter illustrates how the finding of biological parents reduces the power these parents hold over the imaginations of everyone concerned. They do not deserve the power they exert. In all probability, they're far less interesting and less threatening when present than they are in their absence. I yearn to reassure adoptive parents how helpful it is to have the biological parents solidly in the background and not wandering through the attic, haunting the inhabitants. It seems especially important with the adoption of older children not to pretend to erase, not to ignore or fear, the child's residual memories.

Both of my daughters now believe—as I do, too—that they were taken away from their biological mother for some pretty good reasons. And although she has turned her life around to a great extent—she now keeps a job and has friends, pays for car and house—she is still the same person. The last time Dawn went to visit, she didn't last one day in Ginny's cigarette-smoke-filled house before having a bad asthma attack. And when Ginny and Paula took Margey to meet Dawn the night she arrived, Margey persuaded Ginny to stop first at the dope house. The police were waiting there and Margey was arrested and taken to jail. Only with a lot of fast talk did Ginny keep them from hauling Paula off to jail, too; they were holding a warrant for her arrest, in addition to the one they had on Margey.

But Ginny is determined to make up for the past this time around. Indeed, she is a proud and thoughtful grandmother. She never forgets a birthday or holiday; she is always wearing her Grandmother sweatshirt with Dawn's, Charles's, and the boys' handprints on the front; one whole wall of her living room is taken up with pictures of Dawn and the boys. In a masterpiece of engineering, she managed to gather Margey, Paula, and herself in Aberdeen last Christmas for the first re-union of the three girls. They all stayed with Dawn and Charles and had a wonderful time making Christmas for one another and for Billie Ray and Dwight Roy.

At this point I believe it's impossible to forget any woman who has mothered us, and equally impossible to have too many mothers.

Predictions
and Retractions

When I first began this book seven years ago, I felt as if I "had" to tell the story. So many things had happened in my family's life as a result of the adoption, and they had never been thought through or articulated. Through reading and thinking and writing, I hoped to dilute my sense of failure and anger. Through honesty and empathy, I hoped to overcome guilt and blame. Above all, I yearned for a better understanding of my two adopted daughters.

Seven years ago I needed to write the story because it was so painful. I felt as if everything was going to end badly, very badly; specifically, with Margey dying and with Dawn's having baby after baby removed from her care. Now I feel different: my daughters have earned respect for their lifestyles and choices.

Margey has not gone through one abusive relationship after another, ending up dead or institutionalized, as was predicted. Far from it; after Tony, her choice of men changed radically. Now she has a knack for finding sweet men who are delighted to take care of her—who yearn to rescue her. She meets older men who live peacefully on the outskirts of town, moves in, and adds zest to their lives. Sometimes they drink together, but not always; several of her male friends have been straight, balding, churchgoing types. John or Curtis or Tom takes Margey to town when she's ready for a wild rumpus and picks her up when she's exhausted. In between, he keeps her in videos and clothes, food and booze. He's always a good cook. She keeps all the money she makes from prostitution to buy drugs. These men don't abuse her; on the contrary, her exes call the house months after Margey has passed through their lives, and we chat about how she's doing. They miss her. When she lands in jail, Rick (or Frank, or Pat) goes to visit and bails her out.

Yes, he's always an enabler of the first order, and if he doesn't set limits on use of his possessions, he gets into serious trouble. Once, for example, Bob let her take his car when he had to be hospitalized with a blood clot. Margey needed transportation, he said, to take care of the kitten he'd gotten her and to come visit him. Margey and car disappeared, for months, until the police found the car, complete with a dead drug dealer—from Detroit, shot in the head. These gentlemen may sin on the side of being too nice for Margey's own good, but they are neither a Tony who would leave her pregnant nor a pimp who would take everything from her. At times such as midwinter and midweek, life is nearly ordinary and platonic for Margey and her friend of the moment.

Margey realizes that if she got pregnant she would damage a fetus interuterine. Or a child, if it was born: motherhood is not for her. Not now. When her IUD had to be removed after she developed a pelvic inflammatory infection, Margey called right away and asked me to take her to Dr. Doris for the Norplant. Margey knows, too, that she cannot yet manage intimate relationships, but she has the self-control to remain courteous and charming with her gentleman friends. She treats them well and they are devoted to her. She knows herself and can control many aspects of her behavior.

In terms of her profession as a prostitute, Margey has lucked upon a match between her talents and tastes and the job requirements. No, Margey wasn't good at school; when she was trying to learn to play the flute and couldn't tell she was off tune, she'd repeat her errors dutifully even after she was corrected. She can't pay bills; she couldn't run a house. But Margey can provide a spectacle. She loves to dress up—the gaudier the better. Minute to minute, she's perfectly aware of what role she's playing: "Mom, this is the way you gotta do it. How do I look? Un-huh—high-hoe style, ain't I fine?" Her life is an adventure, not suited to many tastes certainly, but she wants every day to be different. It's often difficult for me to admit it, but Margey is much happier with her life than she was living with our family, and probably happier now than in any of the scenarios I wanted for her. I no longer hope that someday she will change; instead, I appreciate her humor and her verse:

Prostitute Poem

To make a change I'll have to search deep
For it is my life that I want to keep.
Working the streets is a hard living to do,
Especially the mental destruction you put yourself through.

All the men have to do is stop and pay
And then they can have their own way.

They pick me up to cure their desires
When all I want to do is get higher.
When all my work is finally done
It' time to get high and have some fun.
Most of the men make me want to puke,
But here I am still a prostitute.
Many say my life is sad and that might be true,
But I'm sure you'd rather it be me doing this than you.

With Dawn, I dreaded a series of men who would get fed up and leave her with a new baby each time. That has not been the case at all. She and Charles are still married, and they work hard on their relationship. It did not seem possible in her early interactions with Billie Ray, but Dawn has proved to be an excellent mother. She is unfussy and affectionate, accepting and patient, sensible and devoted to the children. For many of us, the physical conditions of Dawn's life would be overwhelming, but she remains cheerful and happy with her complicated family. Her first child, Billie Ray, has—as I described earlier—Williams syndrome; the second, Dwight Roy, at two years has serious developmental delays. But there's hope his developmental delays are the result of his being premature and that he will grow out of them. Late in her pregnancy, Dawn suddenly developed toxemia. The baby had to be induced six weeks early, and Dwight Roy spent his first three weeks in an incubator.

Money is tight for Dawn and Charles, especially given Dawn's and the boys' medical emergencies. They filed bankruptcy their first year together, but they learned a great deal from that experience. Although so far Dawn has been unable to keep a job, she has managed to get help from the system. She enrolls the family in every program available: WIC, physical therapy, a nursery school for the handicapped, respite child care for parents of handicapped children, a Williams syndrome support group. She has even managed all the complicated paper work and testimonials so that the family receives more than $400 a month in social security for Billie Ray's care. Thus her indirect financial contributions to the family more than make up for the little she would be able to clear from a job. Managing the system so well is a source of pride for Dawn. She even has a therapist coming in to help her train Billie Ray to stop biting his younger brother.

At present, Dawn is vehement that she does not want more children, not even the daughter she yearned for during her second pregnancy. Nor is she all talk on the subject. She asked Mark and me to pay for the insertion of an IUD after the second baby, because her insurance covered only the cost of the device itself. Both Mark and I were delighted. Dawn and Charles seem to have matured in all aspects of their love for one another.

Perhaps as with the match between Margey and prostitution, Dawn is fortunate to have a retarded child. As her friend Sabrina says, "Dawn will always have someone to love her, to need her." Billie Ray will provide her with years of intensive mothering, which so far is Dawn's preferred profession.

Not long ago, a student asked to interview me about the adoption. In her written conclusion to the interview, she commented that the family had finally worked out its communication problems. She's largely right, I think; communication between Margey and Dawn, Mark and me, has become consistently more honest and tolerant since the girls left home. Margey knows that Mark and I will not bail her out of jail, which is where she was at the time of this writing. We are pleased when she's safe behind bars. But she also knows that she can call us for help whenever she needs to see a doctor, when she's down and out, or when she's running a good show she knows we will appreciate. Margey keeps in touch better now than before: she visited my mother over Easter and called for both Mother's Day and my birthday. She even promised delivery of a birthday present as soon as she got through the jail thing.

As for Dawn, since she has had children, communication with her, too, has improved. She and I talk frankly about Billie Ray's progress, and I respect how she has converted this potentially tragic situation into a happy life. Yes, her stories are full of medical and financial disasters: asthma, ear infections and high fevers, pneumonia, car wrecks, lack of transportation and insurance, bills-bills-bills. But that young couple also has all the amenities of modern life: VCR, Nintendo, camcorder, their personal beeper. She and Charles are buying their house and, most of the time, they manage transportation for both of them.

I have to admit that the miles between us contribute toward all these improvements in my relationship with Dawn. I am certain Mark and I could not maintain the same equilibrium if we had to participate in her daily dramas. Neither Mark nor I would ever agree to live with either Margey or Dawn. We learned our limits the hard way.

Afterword:
The Limits of Hope

Beyond a personal need, I wrote this book to set down the internal dialogue that has been going on in my head for the last nineteen years, ever since Mark and I were asked to speak to that group of prospective adoptive parents. During these discussions with myself and with many other adoptive parents, I have been formulating the things I would like to say publicly as an adoptive mother.

First I want to comment on the "advertising" of children available for adoption. Every Sunday, my local newspaper carries a column, "Sunday's Child," that describes the physical and mental qualities and the accomplishments of a local child who is available for adoption. (The paper runs another column on Thursday evenings, "Adopt-A-Pet.") Reporting in a similar mode, an article in *Time* (30 April 1990), "Putting Kids on Display," described a "style show" of children available for adoption arranged by a J.C. Penny store in New Orleans. Children selected by the state's department of social services "who were willing and able to take a gamble . . . were brought to the store, decked out in the latest spring fashions, given tips on modeling and sent onstage. The audience, including an invited group of prospective parents, got a chance to size up the kids and obtain information on the applications and processing." Such presentations make children appear beautiful, pathetic, and irresistible.

Advertising hard-to-place children is an attempt to serve their best interests—in this instance to create a need within adults to help these children. But adoptive parents need as much protection as these children. Adoption is no place for impulse buying, for decisions based primarily on pity. A whole family's well-being is the last place in the world for a hard sell, regardless of how many thousands of children are waiting placement. Impulses fade fast; pity is the least sustainable of emotions. Adoption of at-risk children is much too difficult, far too complicated, to end up in a marketplace so expert at playing upon sentimental motives and encouraging hasty, uninformed decisions. The social system, in focusing so exclusively on the needs and beauty of children, is at odds with the psychiatric profession, which focuses on dynamic interrelationships within the family system.

Some agency policies have changed for the better in the past fifteen years, especially with regard to more commonsense attitudes toward permitting foster parents to adopt. In 1974, when Mark and I adopted Margey and Dawn, the agencies in most states maintained a rigid distinction between foster families and adoptive families. No family who signed on to give foster care could be considered as an adoptive family, no matter how much they loved and wanted the child, and no matter how well family and child matched. More to the point in our history, when a family agreed to adopt hard-to-place children, they immediately undertook a lifetime commitment exactly like that of deciding to conceive a child. At first I didn't give much thought to what seemed like a natural distinction between short-term and long-term parenting. However, not long after Dawn and Margey came, I began to wonder if there could have been another way to handle things, a way our family could have tried out parenting the girls to see if that decision was sound for all of us.

Any form of parenting should require a deliberate decision—a decision often compared in its seriousness with the decision to marry and the commitment to remain married. But this comparison is obviously invalidated when adoptive parents and children have no grounds for exploring and coming to believe in their compatibility before making a commitment.

A family's decision to adopt at-risk children cannot be equated with the decision to have a biological child or to adopt an infant. Adopting hard-to-place children is another whole category of raising children, and I believe we must beware of those who imply that there are no differences or who simplify the complexities. I'm fearful for the thousands of generous families who will try to solve other families' problems by loving enough. I am angry that families fortunate enough to be intact are being asked to solve social problems without the extensive expertise and support such undertakings require.

Rather than arrange a hasty placement, I would recommend that parents prepare themselves carefully for the adoption of an older child— that is, a child aged more than one year—by reading widely on early childhood development, by working directly with troubled children in shelters and homeless centers, in group homes, and mental hospitals, by becoming foster parents, by tutoring children with learning disabilities, and by asking as many questions as possible of social workers, pediatricians, therapists, and adoptive and foster parents, and listening to their responses.

Ways to protect, advise and replenish adoptive parents, I also believe, should be fully in place prior to an adoption: an extended and helpful family, support groups, a circle of friends embarking on the same challenge, highly competent professional help, respite care, diagnostic and therapeutic living situations.

Perhaps many older abused and neglected children should not be "adopted" but should instead become members of surrogate families in which the knots to the family can be tied more loosely. In the present system, we are forcing children with complicated histories into the model of "adopted" infants because we are unwilling or unable to acknowledge exactly how they are different, or because we have not explored alternatives.

It would have been better for our family if a team of case workers had checked in with us at periodic intervals, asked each member how things were going, and offered counsel and options. It would have helped so much if Mark and I had been warned prior to Margey's and Dawn's entering adolescence of the frequent acting out and identity crises in adopted teenagers, and of the associated drive among adopted children to procreate. As it was, our family ended up making decisions alone, in desperation. And because the decisions (for example, to send Margey to boarding school and then to a residential treatment center) were so unprecedented in our experience, to Margey these choices read like desertion. In Dawn's case, we wanted to send her away to a boarding school, realizing how destructive life was among us at home, but no boarding school would accept her. When we were unable to provide her with alternatives, Dawn found her own way to engineer a separation.

In a more flexible system, surrogate families would be expected to encounter periods where it would be advantageous for everyone to consider a period of separation: summer camps for children with similar backgrounds, like those for childhood diabetics; a boarding school perhaps; or a period in a group home or residential treatment center. Unable to find or pay for such alternatives, many families are forced to choose between maintaining control at any cost, permitting a child to act in violent and self-destructive ways, or accepting the anguish and stigma—to family and child alike—of a failed adoption.

Working with agencies that encouraged alternatives, troubled adopted children could move in and out of their surrogate families, depending on their developing needs for autonomy and their abilities to tolerate the expectations of family life. If a wider range of choices were available, these frightened children might then be less likely to provoke irrevocable separations, first with one family, then another.

At present, having to return a child to an adoption agency seems so tragic at least in part because we are located within a system that pays no attention to the memories and emotions of the adopted child. The older child in particular rarely has an unequivocal desire to sever ties with biological and foster families or to become a member of one family to the exclusion of all others. Adoption policies need somehow to reflect these multiple pulls from past and present.

It often seemed that Margey and Dawn needed other possibilities in addition to a family that did not match them too well. If the girls had been the ones making the selection—and they'd had other offers—I wonder would they would have "chosen" us.

I now believe that parents considering adopting should ask immediately whether the prospective adoptee is unattached. My reading on the subject suggests that psychologists who have dealt extensively with negatively or anxiously attached children can make a relatively sound assessment. Finding such a professional will by no means be simple, and it is not an effort an agency is likely to support without being pressured.

If the child is unattached, its adoptive parents will need to ask themselves if they are willing and able to spend years of their lives working directly on attachment issues, aided by experienced professionals, with a child who must begin all over learning to trust others and love itself.

Much of the attachment literature seems quite pessimistic about the reversibility of the damage resulting from early parental rejection. But many other psychologists and sociologists argue that since the human character is constantly evolving and adapting, a child's development cannot be permanently arrested. I would wager that although some professionals have and will set forth simple formulas for curing severely disturbed children, in reality there will never be any guarantees that children who do not trust will change their minds. Thus the label *at risk* means what it says: successful rebonding will not always follow the best of efforts.

A phrase often used in accounts of adoptions of older children is "when love is not enough." A friend once asked me what I thought about those words. I told her I was afraid they did not ring true for me; I am far from satisfied that I have been able to love the girls enough by *any* standard, certainly not by the measure of how much I love the biological children.

When Margey and Dawn came into the family at the ages of three and four, their ability to love was already affected. Trying to describe how they loved initially, I'd choose words like *exacting* and *jealous*. My responses to these distortions was not to return to the girls "unconditional love," though I wanted to, as much as I have ever wanted anything.

Exacting and jealous children may evoke something much more calculating and self-protective in their mothers. My understanding of the dynamic between Margey, Dawn, and myself is not that love was not enough, but rather that there was not enough straightforward love, or trust upon which to build love. We cannot always move from the *desire* for love to being lovable and loving.

I firmly believe that it is necessary to talk about the possibility that children adopted at an older stage can wreak havoc in families—and that the discussion should start from the first consideration of the adoption. Adoptive families, then, would expect to need extensive counseling and extended periods of respite. To counter a rebuttal I sometimes hear, not for a moment do I believe that parents will begin to imagine and create problematic behaviors because they have been told true stories of other struggling families; they will only see themselves as less alone. I had no idea until recently, nor do I think many people do, that, nationwide, nearly 25 percent of at-risk adoptions are terminated, according to statistics compiled by the Child Welfare League of America. From my own and others' experiences, I would wager that an additional sizable percentage of adoptive families seriously question whether theirs is a "successful" adoption.

For years I have been struggling with how hopeful, but naive or uncommunicative, so many of the professionals were about the risks our family undertook in adopting Margey and Dawn. We were all coming out of a behaviorist framework, clearly, and we believed that a new environment would bring about radical changes. But it is also true that many social workers fear that giving parents more information will lead to the adoptive children's lives becoming self-fulfilling prophecies. Everyone dreams that these children can begin anew. Such blind hope is not in the best interest of families who consider adoption.

It is not good for families to be ignorant of what might be in store for them. If the whole society treats adoption of at-risk children as unproblematic, the family is left to shoulder the blame and guilt.

The decision to return an adopted child must be excruciating—a decision parents are driven to only after they have concluded that they and their adopted children are not only mutually incompatible but also mutually destructive. These families made a deliberate decision to try to help children who had been badly hurt; above all, they do not want to fail these children one more time, one last time. To those in this situation, returning an adopted child to an agency does not seem like "tough love"; it seems like despair.

Adoptive families make generous commitments in good faith; they have not been treated with the same generosity and good faith. All too often, they find themselves in positions where they cannot realize and acknowledge their own limits. Families who return their adopted children are likely to judge themselves mercilessly, and to be judged mercilessly by others.

In Western society, we have come over time to concede that in some cases divorce is better than continuing the marriage. I do not believe, however, that we have reached the same consensus regarding adoption—that in some cases it is better to terminate the arrangement. Adoptive parents need to be convinced in advance that there is only so much any parent can accomplish—that at some point the larger society is willing to offer sympathy and accept responsibility.

Finally, I believe that adoptive parents need to speak out—to ask hard questions and demand that the adoptive system serve the whole family better. In my experience, adoptive families have been the best keepers of the secret of the difficulties of adopting unattached children. Adoptive families are the ones who know the whole story; we need their help in collecting information in order to change the system. A willingness to speak out does not come easily. It means putting aside the brave front these families have built for themselves and for their children, as well as challenging the larger society's denial of the difficulties of adoption.

Parents who adopt disturbed children are often praised as modern-day heroes. Everyone admires us. We've done the bravest of all brave deeds. Everyone greets us with, "Isn't that wonderful!" and "Surely God will bless you." Like tragic heroes of old, we fall from great heights if we betray our misgivings. Nobody wants to hear a hero whine.

In conversations with one another, some adoptive parents comment on how often we are our own worst enemies. We deny our pain and dismiss those who would help us. I don't know what it would have taken to open up my hard head to all I needed to learn about the effects of Margey's and Dawn's early history. Early on, one of my colleagues gave me a book on abused and neglected children. I read through the first chapter, describing characteristic behaviors: difficulties with abstract thinking, tendencies to hoard things. I thought, "I'm living this book, I don't need to read any further." Like some cancer victims, I did not want to anticipate. Instead of profiting from the help my friend offered, I closed the book and returned it to my colleague.

Last Christmas, a friend with two troubled adopted daughters—the same ages as Margey and Dawn—sent on to me two Christmas letters from a friend of hers. One was the public Christmas letter to all and sundry—a letter describing the perfect adoptive family: this child was the center halfback on the village soccer team; that child was excelling as a poet; a third child had perfect pitch and a lovely voice. The second letter, addressed only to another adoptive mother, described a private world of doubts and misgivings and told of an angelic-voiced child who was intractable within the family, cruel and abusive with friends, disruptive in school. True, there are always differences between what we care to publicize to the world and the other side of the story, but these two letters suggest that troubled adoptive parents feel free to speak only with other frustrated adoptive parents.

In conclusion, I believe that both families and the adoption establishment need to raise the most controversial question of all: Are families the best environment for seriously troubled children? Many times through the years I have recalled the cryptic words of a family therapist who said she suspected that, for disturbed children, families were too intimate, too intrusive, too demanding.

The phrase *and then she was adopted* often appears as the upbeat finale of a sad story. The message is like a fairy tale's "and then they all lived happily ever after." But *and then she was adopted* can also serve as the first line of a second story—a tale of a long and arduous journey. For me, phrases like "until they are available for adoption" arouse misgivings. Such optimistic use of the word *adoption* illustrates the limits of our thinking on the subject, which runs something like: There can be no better alternative than adoption, the equivalent of being born again.

The author of *Orphans, Real and Imaginary*, Eileen Simpson, herself lived both with a surrogate family and in an institution. She preferred the institution, because she felt that what children suffered most from was unfairness, and that at least institutions were fair. The word *unfairness* in Eileen Simpson's statement rings in my ears because it encompasses so many of my misgivings about raising two very different kinds of children—attached and unattached—within the same family.

I often wonder if Margey and Dawn might have been better off in an optimal group home where the standard of comparison was with others like themselves. If we ask and explore such questions thoroughly, we may conclude that many problem children who enter stable group homes gradually progress toward the mean over time, rather than toward a reactionary extreme, as often happens in family life.

In telling my family's story, I hope to expand our thinking about the placement of neglected and abused children.